Cornwall

timeout.com / cornwall

55

163

83

Contents

98

3

Kynance Cove *see p129*

ABOUT THE GUIDE

This is one of a series of Time Out guidebooks to cities and regions across the globe. Written by local experts, our guides are thoroughly researched and meticulously updated. They aim to be inspiring, irreverent, well-informed and trustworthy.

Hearts

We use hearts ♥ to pick out venues, sights and experiences in Cornwall that we particularly recommend.

Telephone numbers

All phone numbers listed in this guide assume that you are calling from within Britain. If you're calling from elsewhere, dial your international access code, then 44 for the UK; follow that with the phone number, dropping the first zero of the area code.

Opening times

At the time of writing, the country was still under lockdown due to the Covid-19 pandemic. This has been a particularly challenging time for the hospitality industry who have suffered unprecedented restrictions for over 12 months. Opening times may continue to be subject to government measures for some considerable time.

Part of the charm of the countryside is that it's not like the city. But this means you need to be aware of opening times: places shut up shop for the winter months, or only open at weekends, and some shops still shut for lunch. If you're eating out, many places still stop serving lunch at 2pm sharp and dinner at 9pm. If you're making a journey, always phone to check first. This goes for attractions too, especially outside the summer holiday season. While every effort has been made to ensure the accuracy of the information contained in this guide, the publisher cannot accept any responsibility for errors it may contain.

Maps

The map at the start of each chapter is from the 1:250,000 Ordnance Survey OpenData.

Feedback

We hope you enjoy the guide. We always welcome suggestions for places to include in future editions and take note of your criticism of our choices. You can email us at guides@timeout.com.

Introduction

Cornwall offers a huge variety of experiences and terrains: landscapes run from wild moorland to luxuriant wooded valleys; several hundred miles of magnificent coastline include hidden coves, pine-backed bays and sandy surfing beaches. Exploring the towns and villages – lively Falmouth, picture-perfect Mousehole – brings rewards too. There's a vibrant arts scene as well as lots of messing about on boats, from million-pound yachts to small sea kayaks. Attractions range from Tate St Ives and the Eden Project to prehistoric sites on Bodmin Moor. And the region's food and accommodation options are now some of the best in the country, though the delights of cream teas and Cornish pasties are timeless.

Cornwall is one of Time Out's regional guides covering Britain. We've used our local knowledge to reveal the best of the region, and while we've included all the big attractions, we've gone beneath the surface to uncover plenty of small or hidden treasures too.

Festivals and Events

MARCH

St Piran's Day
01872 575254, www.perranporthinfo. co.uk. Date 5 Mar.

Cornwall's patron saint is said to have landed on the beach at Perranporth, after being cast out of Ireland. On St Piran's Day, hundreds of people trek across the sands to visit the oratory he built, and to watch the St Piran play.

Walk Scilly & Isles of Scilly Folk Festival
01720 424043, www.walkscilly.co.uk. Date late Mar-early Apr.

Over 30 guided walks take in some of the Isles of Scilly's most stunning landscapes; the event is organised to tie in with the Isles of Scilly Folk Festival, with walks fitting in with the music schedule.

APRIL

Trevithick Day
https://trevithickday.org.uk. Date late Apr.

Held in Camborne, this free one-day festival celebrates the area's industrial heritage. There are dances through the streets and processions led by miniature steam engines, along with larger displays of steam power.

Porthleven Food Festival
www.porthlevenfoodfestival.com. Date Apr.

A weekend of food-related talks, walks and demonstrations, showcasing the best of the South-West, from organic beers to traditionally reared meat.

MAY

Minack Theatre season opens
01736 810181, www.minack.com. Date mid May.

Cornwall's breathtaking open-air theatre is a great visit out of season but a better one when you can actually catch a performance – an eclectic variety of performances run against its mercurial backdrop from May until the autumn.

World Pilot Gig Championships
0845 710 5555, www.worldgigs.co.uk. Date early May.

See these colourfully painted, traditional Cornish rowing boats take to the water around the Isles of Scilly.

'Obby 'Oss
https://padstowlive.com. Date 1 May.

On 1 May, dancers and musicians weave through Padstow's narrow streets following the two 'Obby 'Osses, in what is thought to be an ancient celebration of fertility and the arrival of spring.

Trevithick Day

'Obby 'Oss

Flora Day

www.helstonfloraday.org.uk.
Date 7 May in 2022; 6 May in 2023 and 8 May 2024.

On 8 May unless it falls on a Sunday or Monday (*see above*), the village of Helston is bedecked with bluebells and gorse, and a series of dances reenacts St Michael slaying the devil and St George dispatching the dragon. Festivities culminate in the 'Furry Dance', with townsfolk dressing up and dancing in and out of the houses.

Fowey Festival of Arts & Literature

01726 879500, www.foweyfestival.com.
Date mid May.

Held at various locations in and around Fowey, this week-long festival features dance and comedy performances, art exhibitions, walks and film screenings.

JUNE

Eden Sessions

01726 811911, www.edensessions.com.
Date June/July.

Every year a delightfully random selection of the world's biggest artists rock up to play a series of outdoor concerts in front of the iconic biomes of the Eden Project.

They return in 2022 after a pandemic-induced hiatus.

Falmouth International Sea Shanty Festival

01326 313553, www.falmouthseashanty. co.uk. Date mid June.

Long before anybody on TikTok had heard of them, sea shanties were massive business in Cornwall. After a digital-only 2021 edition, Europe's biggest festival of nautical song will return in the flesh from 2022.

Polperro Festival

www.polperrofestivalsandlights.co.uk.
Date late June.

Music, art, theatre, parades, children's entertainment and morris dancing feature at this fishing village's community-run festival.

Royal Cornwall Show

01208 812183, www.rcaa.org.uk. Date mid June.

The showground at Wadebridge comes alive for the annual county show. Livestock and horses compete in the judging area, while a flower show, steam fair, sheep dog trials, falconry, crafts and games are among the other highlights.

JULY

Lafrowda Festival
www.lafrowda-festival.co.uk.
Date early-mid July.

Anything goes at St Just's community arts festival, from Cornish songs and ballroom dancing competitions to samba. Visitors can participate in various arty workshops, making sculptures, lanterns and banners for the festival's closing processions on Lafrowda Day.

Charles Causley Festival
01566 708649, www.causleytrust.org.

Named after the late, great Cornish poet, this eclectic festival of poetry, film, music and literature made the successful transition to a digital offering during the pandemic but should hopefully be back IRL from 2021.

St Endellion Summer Festival
www.endellionfestivals.org.uk.
Date late July-early Aug.

This long-running festival boasts a stellar programme of choral, chamber, orchestral and operatic works, with performances taking place in the village's lovely 15th-century church. Check the website for details of the Easter Festival.

AUGUST

Boardmasters
www.boardmasters.com.
Date early Aug.

Five days of surfing, skateboarding, BMXing and partying in Newquay. The world's top professionals show off their skills during the day, and by night some of the biggest acts in the music industry entertain the masses.

Falmouth Week
www.falmouthweek.co.uk.
Date mid Aug.

With a week of racing for keelboats, dinghies and traditional craft around the waters of Falmouth Bay, the Carrick Roads and the harbour, this is the largest sailing regatta in the South-West. A dazzling firework display rounds off proceedings.

Fowey Regatta
01726 832133, www.foweyroyalregatta.
co.uk. Date mid Aug.

As well as boat races and daredevil manoeuvres from the Red Arrows, Fowey's seven-day regatta features the crowning of the carnival queen, daily storytelling sessions, bands on the quayside, and pasty-eating contests.

Bude Jazz Festival
01288 356360, www.visitbude.info. Date late Aug-early Sept.

This week-long jazz fest brings plenty of international musical talent to town, with events in 14 venues: the Stroller ticket buys you entry to every performance. Note that the festival will not be running in 2021, but will return in 2022.

SEPTEMBER

World Belly Boarding Championships
Date early Sept.

Chapel Porth, St Agnes *See p98.*

OCTOBER

Falmouth Oyster Festival
01326 312300, www.falmouthoyster festival.co.uk. Date mid Oct.

Falmouth's four-day festival marks the beginning of oyster-dredging season. There's Cornish produce, crafts, oyster and shellfish bars, oyster-shucking contests and plenty of family-friendly entertainment.

DECEMBER

Mousehole Harbour Lights and Tom Bawcock's Eve
Date from mid-December

The tiny, beautiful village of Mousehole is where it's at in December: its waterside Christmas illuminations are some of the finest in the country, and if you happen to visit on December 23 – aka Tom Bawcock's Eve – you can partake in the esoteric seasonal dish Starry Gazey Pie.

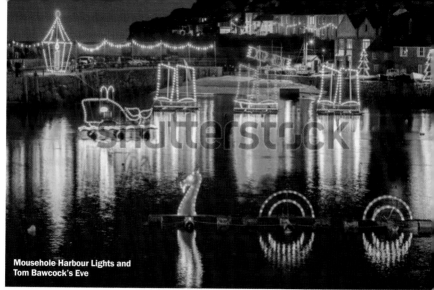

Mousehole Harbour Lights and Tom Bawcock's Eve

World Pilot Gig Championships

Falmouth Oyster Festival

9

Bodmin Moor

Bodmin Moor might be smaller in scale than Dartmoor further east, but there is enough drama and unprocessed beauty within its 80 square miles to stir even the most jaded of travellers: surreal, weather-warped granite tors towering over wild expanses of moorland and vast, treeless downs. Remote as the moor may feel, high on the granite spine of Cornwall, it is actually deceptively well connected, thanks to the A30 main road that slices through its centre, from Launceston in the east to Bodmin in the west. The north and south coasts are both an easy drive away, as are the Eden Project, the gastronomic delights of Padstow and the windswept ruins of Tintagel Castle.

Bodmin & the western moor

The sober, no-frills town of Bodmin is the largest of the settlements around the moor. An important religious centre in the Dark Ages, thanks to the foundation of a priory at St Petroc in the sixth century, the town has an impressive 15th-century granite church dedicated to the saint.

Bodmin was also once the county town of Cornwall before judicial and administrative powers moved to Truro, as evinced by some important-looking public buildings in the centre. Beyond the old-fashioned high street, there is a handful of visitor attractions, including the foreboding **Bodmin Jail** (*see p14*) on the outskirts and the quaint **Bodmin & Wenford Railway** (*see p18*).

One of the most attractive villages on the moor is Blisland, on its western edge. It centres on a pretty green surrounded by granite cottages, a Norman church and the superb **Blisland Inn** (*see p21*). Three miles north-east of Blisland is **Hawk's Tor**; home to a circle of neolithic standing stones known as the **Stripple Stones**, it's a wild and primitive spot.

By car, the narrow and at times very steep country lanes to the west of the moor take in some gorgeous countryside, covered in ancient deciduous woodland. Traditional villages such as **St Mabyn** and **St Tudy** are also worth a look.

The southern moor

South of the A30, Bodmin Moor is characterised by wide open expanses of heath, softened by tracts of thick woodland, deep river valleys and gorges. Viciously prickly, vivid yellow gorse bushes proliferate, competing by midsummer with the subtler purple of moorland heather.

Prehistoric stone circles and burial sites are concentrated on the south-eastern edge of the moor, and are the source of a host of local legends involving piskies and spriggans. More recently, these mythical creatures have been joined by the Beast of Bodmin Moor, a puma, panther or wild cat that is blamed for the unexplained slaughter of ponies and sheep on the moor – though little scientific evidence has been forthcoming.

From **Jamaica Inn** (*see p14*) of du Maurier fame, the geographical heart of Bodmin Moor, it's a mile or so's stroll south to **Dozmary Pool**, which on sunny days is visible for miles around as a bright blue diamond. Some say this spot is the watery lair of the Lady of the Lake and the final

resting place of King Arthur's sword, Excalibur, although there are other contenders.

Close to Dozmary are two much larger recreational lakes, offering plenty of scope for birdwatching, fishing and walks year-round. **Colliford Lake** attracts over-wintering wildfowl and is a top spot for natural brown trout fishing, while **Siblyback Lake** has sandy beaches and a watersports centre (01579 346522). South of here, **Dranesbridge** is the starting point of a riverside ramble to **Golitha Falls** – a wooded valley where the rapid waters of the River Fowey hurtle along a deep gorge, and over a series of cascades.

Further west, the villages of Warleggan, Cardinham and St Neot are good starting points for exploring the lush, wooded fringes of the moor. **St Neot** is a delightful place, and worth visiting for its church alone, which boasts a beautiful 15th-century interior with stunning stained glass.

Warleggan is the subject of the film *A Congregation of Ghosts*, released in 2009, which tells the true story of the

Bodmin Moor

Places to visit

There are several interesting churches around Bodmin Moor, including the 16th-century St Mary Magdalene Church in Launceston, with its elaborately carved granite exterior; the Church of St Neot, on the south-western edge of the moor, known for its medieval stained glass; and the high-towered Church of St Nonna at Altarnun, known as the 'Cathedral of the Moor'.

Bodmin Jail
Berrycoombe Road, Bodmin, PL31 2NR (01208 76292, www.bodminjail.org). Open 10am-8.30pm daily. Admission £15; £12.50 reductions.

Until 1862, public executions took place at this infamous jail, with crowds flocking from all over the county to witness the grisly events. The glowering, 18th-century granite building is still a disquieting place to visit, with a grim display of dungeons, cells, pillories, execution blocks and the original hanging pit. Perfect sightseeing, then, for a cold, steely grey day before a walk on the moor. As of 2021 it's been given a fancy £8.5m revamp to bring it into line with national tourist attractions like the London Dungeons – visitors can now participate in such experiences as *The Dark Walk*, a cinematic experience designed to transport you back into a working 18th-century penal prison.

Jamaica Inn
Bolventor, Launceston, PL15 7TS (01566 86250, www.jamaicainn.co.uk). Open Museum summer 8am-9pm daily; winter 11am-4pm daily. Admission £3.95; £2.95 reductions.

At the heart of Bodmin Moor, this inn was an important staging post on the turnpike road for several centuries, and a hotbed of smuggling. It only came to prominence as a tourist attraction, though, when Daphne du Maurier set her bestselling novel here, after frequent visits to the inn in the 1930s. The inn now feels like little more than a tourist trap – all the more so thanks to its location on the A30, which makes it a convenient stop for coaches. Nonetheless, there is some interest to be found here at the Smugglers Museum, containing a quirky collection of smuggling devices from times gone by, and the small du Maurier exhibition (including her desk). There is a dated hotel attached, a pub and a shop (which does, at least, sell the du Maurier classics alongside less useful fridge magnets and trinkets).

Lanhydrock House 💜
Bodmin, PL30 5AD (01208 265950, www.nationaltrust.org.uk). Open House 11am-5pm. Garden 10.30am-5.30pm. Closed in winter. Admission House check on the website. Garden only £10; £5 reductions.

Two and a half miles south-east of Bodmin is one of Cornwall's grandest houses, situated above the Fowey valley. Lanhydrock House was constructed in the 17th century but was rebuilt after a fire in the late 1800s, resulting in a profusion of High Victoriana. The house is now owned by the National Trust, with 50 or so rooms open to the public; allow plenty of time for your visit. One of the few remaining 17th-century interiors is the long gallery, which has a stunning barrel-vaulted ceiling depicting scenes from the Old Testament. Another highlight is the restored Victorian kitchen and servants' quarters. In spring, the bloom of camelias, azaleas, magnolias, rhododendrons and bluebells is breathtaking; footpaths lead from the gardens into the 1,000-acre area of park and woodland beyond.

Launceston Castle
Launceston, PL15 7DR (01566 772365, www.english-heritage.org.uk). Open Apr-June, Sept 10am-5pm daily. July, Aug 10am-6pm daily. Oct 10am-4pm daily. Admission £5.90; £3.50 reductions.

Strategically placed high above town on a grassy mound surveying the Cornish border, this Norman castle must have been a fearsome sight for enemy forces. Much of the original construction has disappeared over the centuries, but enough remains to make the steep trip up to the keep worthwhile. On a clear day the views in every direction are spectacular, taking in deeply undulating valleys and, on the horizons to the east and west, the dramatic profiles of Dartmoor and Bodmin Moor.

Blisland Inn see p21

South Penquite Farm *see p22*

Reverend Frederick Densham, who, influenced by Gandhi and his travels in India, returned to live in the village in the 1930s to preach to a remote and deeply traditional community.

The south-eastern corner of the moor, meanwhile, has some desolate scenery around the peaks of **Kilmar Tor**, **Hawk's Tor** and **Trewortha Tor**, as well as a concentration of Bronze Age remains clustered around **Minions**, the highest village in Cornwall. The most impressive of all the prehistoric sites is the **Hurlers**, just outside the village, which consists of three circles of massive standing stones. Although their original purpose is unknown, local lore recounts that they are men turned to stone for playing the Cornish game of hurling on a Sunday.

South of Minions, near the village of Darite, is a huge Stone Age burial chamber known as **Trevethy Quoit**. To the north, meanwhile, the **Cheesewring** is a quite extraordinary top-heavy pillar of granite slabs that has been eroded by the moorland winds. It's hard to believe that it was formed entirely naturally – or that it isn't about to topple over.

Just beyond the moor's southern fringes is the ancient stannary and market town of **Liskeard**, on the mainline railway. Not in the slightest bit touristy, it is a working town with a traditional centre.

Launceston

Launceston (pronounced 'Lanson' locally), the ancient 'capital' of Cornwall, is a charming, richly historic market town. It acts as the traditional gateway between Dartmoor and Bodmin Moor, and is one of the area's most interesting inland towns for a wander. Although not much of the 12th-century town wall remains, evidence of Launceston's medieval fortifications endures in the shape of **Southgate Arch** (originally one of

Five Artisan Cheeses

Cornish Blue
This is a soft, mild, young cow's milk cheese, more akin to Gorgonzola than traditional British blue cheeses, with a sweet, mellow flavour. It is produced by the Cornish Cheese Co (01579 362294, www.cornishcheese. co.uk), based near Liskeard.

Cornish Yarg
Lynher Dairies Cheese Company (01872 870789, www.lynherdairies.co.uk), near Truro, makes this moist, Caerphilly-esque pasteurised cow's milk cheese. Its unique, delicate taste derives from the rind, which is made from nettle leaves; a delicious wild garlic version is also available.

Gevrik
Meaning 'little goat' in Cornish, Gevrik is a full-fat goat's milk cheese with a clean, nutty flavour and a creamy texture. It hails from the Cornish Country Larder (01637 860331, www.ccl-ltd.co.uk) in Trevarrion, on the north coast.

Menallack Farmhouse
Matured for two months, this hard, full-fat, unpasteurised cow's milk cheese is based on Cheshire. It is produced at Menallack Farm near Penryn, and is available in classic or baby versions. Buy it online from the Cheese Shed (07703 965595, www. thecheeseshed.com).

Trelawny
A traditional farmhouse mould-ripened cheese, made with pasteurised cow's milk, Trelawny has a clean, lemony flavour with a creamy aftertaste. The texture is deliciously moist and slightly crumbly. Buy a block from Lobbs Farm Shop (01726 844411, www. lobbsfarmshop.com) near the Lost Gardens of Heligan.

Things to do

Bodmin & Wenford Railway♥
General Station, Bodmin, PL31 1AQ (01208 73666, www.bodminrailway.co.uk). Open June-Sept daily. Feb-May, Oct-Dec times vary. Check website for details. Tickets £14.95; £7.95-£13.95 reductions; £39.95 family.

Cornwall's only full-size steam railway connects with the mainline at Bodmin Parkway, and can be accessed via the Camel Trail at Boscarne Junction, or the beautifully preserved heritage station of Bodmin General (where the classic GWR brown and cream benches and signage invites sighs about the way rail travel used to be) in the centre of Bodmin. The railway makes a 13-mile round trip through the freshly unfurling countryside – and kids go loco for the Thomas and Santa specials in the school holidays. Adults, however, may be more interested in alighting at Boscarne Junction for the idyllic Camel Valley Vineyard (see *right*), a 25-minute walk away. Full details and timetables can be found on the website.

Camel Trail cycling
Bikes can be hired at nearby East Rose (01208 850674, www.eastrose.co.uk).

Since the extension of the Camel Trail (see *p39 and p66*) a few years back, you can now cycle off-road from Bodmin Moor all the way to Padstow. You can pick up the trail near the village of St Breward.

Camel Valley Vineyard♥
Little Denby, Nanstallon, PL30 5LG (01208 77959, www.camelvalley.com). Open Apr-Oct 10am-5pm Mon-Sat. Nov-Mar 10am-5pm Mon-Fri. Guided tour Apr-Sept 2.30pm Mon-Fri. Grand tour & tasting Apr-Oct 5pm Wed (& 5pm Thur in Aug). Tours £5-£12.

Credited with putting Cornish wine on the map, Camel Valley is one of the UK's leading vineyards. Making the most of the valley's mild climate and fertile slopes, the Lindo family produce a small range of superlative wines. Their most famous offerings are the Cornwall Brut, a multi-award-winning sparkler with delicate fruity notes and fine bubbles, and the Bacchus white, which won silver at the International Wine Challenge in 2020. Tours of the vineyard, usually conducted by one of the winemakers, are fascinating and friendly – and include a taste of the finished product. The vineyard is easily accessible from the Camel Trail (three miles from Bodmin), and is a 25-minute walk from Boscarne Junction station, which you can reach by steam train on the Bodmin & Wenford Railway.

Carnglaze Slate Caverns
St Neot, PL14 6HQ (01579 320251, www. carnglaze.com). Open 10am-5pm Mon-Sat (10am-8pm Aug). Admission £8; £5-£6 reductions; £22.50 family.

Guided tours take visitors underground through three vast caverns, created by slate mining, to reach a huge, blue-green lake. Bring a jumper, as it's chilly even on the hottest of days.

Camel Trail Cycling

Camel Valley Vineyard

Launceston Steam Railway
St Thomas Road, Launceston, PL15 8DA
(01566 775665, www.launcestonsr.co.uk).
Open times vary, check website for details.
Tickets £15; £7.45-£9.95 reductions; family
£32.

Locomotives from the late 19th century chug
along several miles of narrow-gauge tracks
from a small transport museum at St Thomas
Road in Launceston to Newmills. The five-
mile round trip follows the route of the old
Waterloo to Padstow line through the Kensey
valley; tickets are valid for the day, so you
can stop for a picnic. Opening hours are
strictly seasonal, with extra services laid on
in high summer and the half-term holidays.

Launceston Steam Railway

three entries to the town) and the 11th-century **castle** (*see p14*), the seat of the first Earl of Cornwall. In the town centre, the 16th-century **St Mary Magdalene Church** (*see p111*), famous for its ornate carved exterior, is a striking sight.

The town also supports a healthy crop of smart, independent shops, many on the lanes radiating out from the main square. Names to look for include long-established free-range butcher **Philip Warren** (1 Dunheved Court, 01566 772244, www. philipwarrenbutchers.co.uk, closed Sun), the **No 8 Cafe and Deli** (8 Westgate Street, 01566 777369, www. no8launceston.co.uk) and **Charlie Bears** (2 Milford Park, 01566 777092, www.charliebears.com), the shop and HQ for globally beloved collectible bears of the same name.

One of the loveliest of the villages around Launceston is **Altarnun**, where founder of Methodism John Wesley often stayed on his frequent preaching trips to Cornwall. (Wesley Cottage is open to the public, some half a mile from Altarnun in the hamlet of Trewint; www.lamc.org.uk). In the village, a picturesque 15th- century packhorse bridge straddles the River Inney, overlooked by the stunning church of St Nonna (*see p111*).

Camelford & the northern moor

In the moor's north-eastern corner, Camelford is a compact town on the River Camel, often clogged with slow-moving traffic thanks to its position on the tourist-heavy A39. Although its name actually derives from a conflation of 'cam' (meaning crooked) and 'hayle' (estuary), Camelford has become associated over the years with Camelot, legendary court of King Arthur. The myth has been perpetuated by the presence of a carved sixth-century stone at nearby **Slaughterbridge**, which supposedly marks the site of the king's final battle

at Camlann. What's certain is that a battle did take place here in the ninth century between the Saxons and the Celts, but Arthurian enthusiasts insist the stone is evidence of Arthur's fatal wound at the hand of Mordred. The myths and countermyths are explored in full at Slaughterbridge's Arthurian Centre (01840 213947, www.arthur-online.co.uk, closed Nov-Mar).

Camelford also provides easy access to the moor and its highest peaks: **Rough Tor** (1,311 feet), pronounced 'rowter', and **Brown Willy** (1,375 feet). The latter's name is enough to raise a smile in all but the most strait-laced of visitors, but is in fact a corruption of 'bronewhella' or 'highest hill'. Both peaks can be seen for miles around, and offer gobsmacking views over Cornwall from their summits, with the gorse and granite of the moorland giving way to green fields and the sea. Rough Tor, three miles south-east of Camelford, is the more accessible of the two, with a small car park close to its base. There are ruins of a medieval chapel on the summit, and the southern slopes are dotted with Bronze Age hut circles.

Both peaks can be tackled in a day's hiking, starting and finishing at the car park at the foot of Rough Tor (follow signs to Camelford). You can descend Rough Tor on its southern slopes to continue on to Brown Willy. No technical expertise is required for the walk, but bring waterproofs (beware the 'Brown Willy effect', a meteorological phenomenon resulting in heavy rain showers), food and drink, and an OS map.

Where to eat & drink

Self-evidently, Bodmin Moor isn't a wining and dining destination – cosy pints of Cornish ale and hearty cooking are more the order of the day. Almost every village on the moor has its own intimate, fire-warmed inn, one of the nicest of which is the **Blisland**

Inn (*see below*). Other options include the **Old Inn** at St Breward (01208 850711), the highest in Cornwall and also one of the oldest; and the cosy **Crow's Nest** (01579 345930) at Darite, near St Cleer.

For more sophisticated options, look to **Rock** (*see p69*) to the north, or **Lostwithiel** (*see p28*) to the south, both of which are easily accessible by car. The excellent gastropub at **St Kew** (*see p64*) is also not far from the western edge of the moor.

Blisland Inn

Blisland, PL30 4JF (01208 850739). Open 11.30am-11pm Mon-Sat; noon-10.30pm Sun. Lunch served noon-2pm daily. Dinner served 6.30-9pm Mon-Sat; 6.30-8.30pm Sun.

This pretty, old-time pub attracts beer buffs from miles around with its choice of draught real ales. A gentler proposition than the moor's more desolate-feeling inns, the Blisland is bedecked with hanging flowers and faces the tranquil village green, with lots of bench seating outside. Pub food is served, with mains such as sausage in a bap or a Cornish Ploughman's keeping close to the £6-£8 mark.

Where to stay

In Bodmin itself there's a smattering of choices, including the well-regarded **Westberry Hotel** (Rhind Street, 01208 72772) with its pleasant, secluded garden. A short drive south of the moor, near Lostwithiel, the unspoilt farmstead of **Botelet** (*see p43*) offers B&B in season and self-catering year-round.

Belle Tents

Owls Gate, Camelford, PL32 9XY (01840 261556, www.belletentscamping.co.uk). Open Apr-Sept. Rates from £245 a night (min 3 night stay).

Located on the northern edge of the moor, Belle Tents offers a handful of generously furnished, candy-striped bell tents for hire. The set-up is perfect for small groups of campers, as the site is portioned up into three terraces, each with a fully equipped kitchen tent. Tents have proper beds (duvets are provided), raised flooring, carpets and kitchens. The footpath to Rough Tor is close by, and the north coast six miles away.

The Bodmin Jail Hotel

Scarlett's Well Rd, Bodmin, PL31 2PL (01208 822822, www.bodminjailhotel. com). Rates £191-£262 double incl breakfast.

Proof that, in the end, everything will be gentrified, the Bodmin Jail Hotel is the culmination of first phase of a lavish £50m regeneration project, which has also included a glitzy makeover for the Bodmin Jail tourist attraction, and is set to expand to glamping facilities and hospitality academy. At those prices we are not, of course, talking about a cramped bunk and a bowl of gruel: the 70 rooms have been made by knocking three cells apiece together, the beds are luxurious doubles, there's a restaurant (The Chapel) and a 'tavern' (The Jolly Hangman) and you're probably safe to drop the soap. Due to the coronavirus pandemic it's only opening its doors for this first time this spring, but it certainly looks set to be the most memorable spot to overnight in Bodmin.

Cornish Yurt Holidays

Greyhayes, St Breward, PL30 4LP (01208 850670, www.yurtworks.co.uk). Rates £360-£760 per week for 2-6 people. No credit cards.

Each of the three comfortable yurts here has rugs and carpets, lanterns and OS maps, books and games, and a barbecue outside. A compost toilet is tucked into a yurtlet near each yurt, and there's a lovely shared bathroom yurt, with wood-fire water heating, a full-sized bath and a star-spangled view overhead. A solar shower cabin has also recently been added. The yurts are situated on the edge of Bodwin Moor; to get here, you must leave your car and stroll the final (short) stretch on foot.

Geodome Ekopods

The Old Vicarage, St Clether, Launceston, PL15 8QJ (www.ekopod.co.uk, 01275 395447). Open Apr-Oct. Rates from £70 a night.

Forming part of Sawday's glamping collection, these modern white Ekopods – inspired by the domes of the Eden Project – are located on the edge of Bodmin Moor amid meadows and plentiful peace and quiet. Even the fussiest of glampers should feel sufficiently pampered with super king-size double beds, kitchen, bathroom, solar-powered lights, tea and coffee, private terrace and beautiful views – plus a bath or shower. Still, the real indulgence for those seeking an escape from buildings, roads and other people will be the solitude of the setting.

Higher Lank Farm

St Breward, PL30 4NB (01208 850716, www.higherlankfarm.co.uk). Open Mar-Oct. Rates B&B £840-£1,075 per week. Self-catering £800-£2,025 per week, for up to 4 adults & 5 children.

Lucy Finnemore, her husband 'Farmer Andrew' and their four children run 'toddler dream holidays' from their farm near Bodmin Moor. As the idea is to cater specifically for the needs of families with babies and young children, the holidays are reserved for families who have at least one child under six. The en-suite rooms and self-catering Nursery Rhyme Barns come with all the equipment you could ever need: cots, high chairs, toys and even feeder cups (Higher Lank's green policy also means that washable nappies are lent free of charge, and there's a laundering service). The farm has its own woodland walks, as well as farm-themed play areas. But the best fun of all for the young guests is joining in with poultry feeding and egg collecting, giving bottles to spring lambs, grooming and riding the pony and putting the livestock to bed. By arrangement, Lucy provides meals for kids and adults, while substantial, Cornish-sourced breakfasts are included in the room prices. Babysitting can be arranged; parental fantasies of peaceful evenings in country pubs are also indulged.

Pip & Pip's Cabin

Rezare, Launceston, PL15 9NX (07842 199011, www.quirky-holidays-cornwall.co.uk). Rates £330-£450 for three nights for 2 people.

Pip is a diminutive 1930s steamroller wagon, now converted into a snug bedroom with a double bed. The rest of the living quarters (a spacious bathroom, lounge and kitchen) are in the timber-clad Pip's Cabin, just across the clearing. On chilly evenings, light up the woodburner or build a campfire in the fire pit – sometimes the simple things in life really are the best. Check the website for the details of the other options on site, which include a 1940s railway wagon and a converted barn.

Pixie Nook

Warleggan, PL30 4HB (01637 881183 www.uniquehomestays.com). Rates from £950 for 3 nights.

The sign for the tiny village of Warleggan declares that it's 'twinned with Narnia': a bold claim, but you get the impression: it's very enchanting, as is Pixie Nook, a luxurious but tranquil cottage that sleeps two on the edge of the moors. Enjoy boho chic, a crackling log burner, and the tasteful hot tub in the middle of the rambling rose-strewn garden.

South Penquite Farm💜

Blisland, PL30 4LH (01208 850491, www.southpenquite.co.uk). Open May-Oct. Rates from £10 per night. Yurts from £40 a night.

Two grassy fields of this Soil Association-certified organic farm, surrounded by open moorland, have been set aside for camping. The solar-powered shower block is both eco- and user-friendly, with enormous, thoughtfully appointed shower cubicles, while the equally smart loos feature gleaming white circular sinks and pine-clad walls. Campfires are allowed, and children can play table football in the lounge or real football out on the playing field. Visitors hankering for a few extra home comforts can hire one of the four yurts in the bottom field, equipped with woodburners, futons, lamps and gas stoves, and with a table and chairs outside. Book ahead.

The Norman font at St Nonna Church, Altarnun *see p111*

Fowey & the South-East Coast

From Mevagissey up to the Tamar River, this portion of the Cornish Riviera has been a favourite family holiday destination for generations – not least for the endless opportunities it offers for messing about on the water. Every little coastal town has its regatta week, when bunting is put up, fireworks organised and flotillas of colourful sails take to the water.

For those who are prepared to explore, there is a beach for every taste: small, sheltered coves, miraculously empty on account of the lack of car access and toilets; wild and windy expanses; surf breaks; craggy bays, teeming with rock pools at low tide; and good old-fashioned sandcastles-and-cornets beaches.

Beyond the busy tourist strongholds of Fowey, Looe and Mevagissey, the area is replete with hidden treasures: sleepy creeks and tiny beaches, jungly gardens and stately homes, and windswept heights that reward your scramble with fabulous views over clear-watered bays. And whatever you do, don't forget Cornwall's 'forgotten corner': the stunningly scenic and vividly historic Rame Peninsula, right on the border with Devon.

THE RIVER FOWEY

Fowey

You can swiftly identify a newcomer to the south Cornish coast by his stated intention to visit 'Fowee Hall'. It is pronounced 'Foy', and the place is as intriguing as its name. With its steep winding streets and busy little port, located at the mouth of the river of the same name, this natural harbour is always busy with visiting yachts and boats. Regatta week in Fowey, usually the third full week of August, is considered to be one of the best local regattas in the country; the spectacular Red Arrows display over the harbour is a highlight.

With its classy boutiques, galleries, delis and cafés, and smartly painted houses, Fowey makes a well-heeled base for trips upriver and out to the nearby beaches. Taking to the water is a must. It is thought that Kenneth Grahame drew inspiration for *The Wind in the Willows* from the creeks and quiet waters of the Fowey estuary, and most of Fowey would agree with Ratty's sage advice to Mole: 'There is nothing – absolutely nothing – half so much worth doing as simply messing about in boats.'

Fowey was also the home of Daphne du Maurier, whose legacy is celebrated every May with an arts and literature festival. There is also a small **Literary Centre** in the centre of Fowey, next to the church, which has a modest exhibition on Du Maurier, and sells her complete, in-print works; the **Tourist Information Office** (5 South Street, 01726 833616, www.fowey.co.uk) is on the same site. Good holiday reading for romantics would be Du

Maurier's *The House on The Strand*, *Frenchman's Creek*, *Rebecca* or *Jamaica Inn*, all of which are set in and around Cornwall.

Around the estuary

The Fowey estuary offers some of the county's most bewitching waterside scenery, its quiet creeks backed by dense woodland and sprinkled with quaint hamlets. From Fowey, there are foot ferries upriver to pretty **Bodinnick**, the home of the Du Maurier family, and across the river to the old fishing village of **Polruan**, which has perfect views of the pastel-shaded houses of Fowey across the water. The beautiful 'Hall Walk' takes

Fowey see p25

Tamar Bridge see p49

you along the serene banks of Pont Pill creek from Polruan all the way around the river to Bodinnick, where you can catch a ferry back to Fowey.

Stowed away at the head of a tidal creek is the peaceful village of **Lerryn**, which has fantastic woodland walks nearby, picnic tables by the river and the friendly **Ship Inn** (Fore Street, 01208 872374, www.theshipinnlerryn. co.uk). A regular car ferry crosses from Fowey to Bodinnick, giving access to the eastern side of the river, and Looe beyond.

Fowey is within easy reach of several sandy beaches. The cliff-sheltered **Ready Money Cove** is the closest option – an idyllic spot that can be easily accessed on foot from Fowey (head out along the Esplanade). **Polkerris Cove** – great for watersports – is a quick drive away, or a more rewarding walk around the coastal footpath, which takes you past the promontory of **Gribbin Head** and its 84-foot-high red-and-white stripey daymark tower.

The more intrepid should seek out the clear waters and white sands of **Lantic Bay** ❤, a short drive away via the Bodinnick ferry (or a few miles' walk along the cliffs from Polruan). The steep path down to the beach is not suitable for pushchairs and there are no toilets or facilities, but this refusal to pander to modern sensibilities, combined with the scenery, makes this one of the best beaches in Cornwall. To the west of Fowey is the big sandy beach at **Par Sands**, a popular family beach with facilities.

In season, a ferry chugs west along the coast from Fowey to the village of Mevagissey (*see p38*).

Lostwithiel

The attractive town of Lostwithiel, at the head of the Fowey estuary, was a major port for the export of tin back in

Carlyon Beach, St Austell Bay *see p38*

Gorran Haven, Mevagissey *see p38*

Norman times. Today it has a more tranquil, genteel feel, with a pretty church and a five-arched bridge spanning the River Fowey – although the stunning remains of the Norman fortress of **Restormel** (*see p44*), just outside town, are a potent reminder of the town's past strategic importance. Much quieter than its more touristy neighbour Fowey, downriver, Lostwithiel nonetheless supports a number of interesting independent enterprises in its two quaint main streets.

The unofficial antiques capital of Cornwall, the town has a cluster of shops selling objets and artefacts, as well as more modish establishments, such as the **Lostwithiel Antique Centre** (Mill Hill, 01208 873308, www.lostwithielantiquecentre.com), which specialises in retro oddities – from cult film posters to ancient mummies

– to quirk up your home. The characterful organic emporium **Watts Trading** (12 Fore Street, 01208 872304, www.wattstrading.co.uk, closed Sun), selling everything from bamboo towels and candles to eco-friendly toilet cleaner.

The zesty **Bella Mama** deli♥ (24 Fore Street, 01208 872524, www.bellamama.biz) sells Cornish cheese and light lunches, as well as superb cakes and artisanal bread. A **farmers' market** takes place in the community centre (01840 250586) every other Friday from 10 am until 2 pm and Lostwithiel even has its own **food festival** in October, testament to a flourishing interest in local produce.

Where to eat & drink

Michelin-starred chef Nathan Outlaw put Fowey on the map, and his departure in late 2009 was something

Things to do

THE RIVER FOWEY

Polkerris Beach Company
The Pilchard Store, Polkerris, PL24 2TL (01726 813306, www.polkerrisbeach.com). Closed winter.

The RYA-recognised watersports centre, right on the beach at Polkerris, provides training for all levels in windsurfing, sailing and stand-up paddlesurf. It also hires out one- or two-person sit-on kayaks.

ST AUSTELL BAY & AROUND

Pentewan Valley Cycle Hire
1 Westend, Pentewan, St Austell, PL26 6BX (01726 844242, www.pentewanvalleycyclehire.co.uk). Open Easter-Sept. Bike hire from £18 per day.

This cycle hire shop is usefully placed at the start of the Pentewan Valley Trail, a manageable route that takes you through a river valley for around three miles towards St Austell. Alternatively, pedal along the trail to Mevagissey. Bikes are rented by the half- or whole day.

St Austell Brewery Visitor Centre
63 Trevarthian Road, St Austell, PL25 4BY (01726 66022, www.staustellbreweryvisitorcentre.co.uk). Open varies, phone for details. Admission £15.

Revered for its real ales – such as Tribute, Tinner's and Proper Job – the St Austell Brewery is one of Cornwall's most famous independent breweries. Visitors are taken on a tour of the Victorian-built brewhouse, and shown the different stages of the brewing process. There's a small interactive museum at the entrance, and the ticket includes tastings and a pint in the bar.

Wheal Martyn Clay Works
Wheal Martyn, Carthew, PL26 8XG (01726 850362, www.chinaclaycountry.co.uk). Open Jan 10am-4pm Tue-Thur, Sat, Sun. Feb-Easter, Sept-Dec 10am- 4pm daily. Easter-June 10am-5pm daily. July, Aug 10am-6pm daily. Admission £9.75; £5.50 reductions.

The series of white peaks that characterise the landscape around St Austell look, at first sight, like the peaks of some unmapped mountain range. They are, in fact, the piles of a blow to its upwardly mobile dining scene. But in recent years it's got over it big time. Plenty else warrants your attention, with **Q**, **Appleton's** and **Fitzroy** at the forefront of a busy scene that takes in everything from seaside-chic cafés to smart seafood restaurants and historic waterside pubs.

If you're planning a picnic, stock up at **Kittow's of Fowey** butcher and deli (South Street, 01726 832639, www. kittowsfowey.co.uk, closed Sun winter), packed to the rafters with cheeses, cold meats and own-made cheese and pork pies.

Conveniently placed on the road back from Ready Money Beach, with tables and customers spilling out on to the quiet lane in summer, **Pintxo** (38 the Esplanade, 01726 834941, closed Mon-Thur winter) is chic, relaxed Spanish tapas and sherry bar – perfect for a classy post-beach wind down.

Enthusiasts of the great British pub will be amply diverted by the pubs in the area, many of which have soul-soothing locations on the river. In addition to the **Rashleigh** at Polkerris (*see p33*) and the **Crown** (*see p34*), in the peaceful inland village of Lanlivery, it's worth taking a pint stop at the following: the terrace at the **Old Ferry Inn** (01726 870237, www.oldferryinn.co.uk) next to the ferry at Bodinnick for superb river views; the friendly **Russell Inn** (01726 870292) in Polruan, which makes up for its lack of views with a friendly atmosphere, affordable pub food and free Wi-Fi; and the idyllically located **Ship Inn** (01208 872374, www.theshipinnlerryn.co. uk) at Lerryn, with a large beer garden.

of waste deposited by the local china clay industry. This extensive visitor attraction takes you on a journey through the history of china clay, with a modern exhibition and a walking trail around the 19th-century clay works, past old locomotives, wagons and a 35-foot waterwheel, all the way out to a viewing platform at the rim of a working china clay pit. To see everything on this 26-acre site you would need the best part of an afternoon. Another such crater was filled by the Eden Project (see p45), which is accessible on foot or by bike as part of the Clay Trails project (see p39).

LOOE BAY & AROUND

St Mellion International Resort
St Mellion, Saltash, PL12 6SD (01579 351351, www.st-mellion.co.uk). Open Summer 7am-dusk. Winter 8.30am-dusk. Green fees £35-£90. Club hire £35.

One of the two 18-hole golf courses at St Mellion was designed by the world-renowned Jack Nicklaus, and is considered a most demanding course. The resort pumped £20 million into a makeover – including the addition of a new luxury hotel – for the England Open, which it was to host in 2011.

Wild Futures' Monkey Sanctuary
Murrayton House, St Martins, PL13 1NZ (01503 262532, www.monkeysanctuary.org). Open Easter-Sept 11am-4.30pm Mon-Thur, Sun. Admission £9; free-£7 reductions; £25 family.

You'll find fail-safe animal magic at the headquarters of primate protection charity Wild Futures, set in woodland just off the coastal footpath. It was the first place in the world to breed the Amazonian woolly monkey outside its native habitat, and also rehabilitates monkeys formerly kept as pets. Lesser horseshoe bats, visible via live video link, are also resident in the cellar, and there's a play area, Victorian garden and veggie café.

Appleton's

19 Fore St, Fowey, PL23 1AH (01872 228738, www.appletonsrestaurant.com). Open noon-11.30pm Mon-Sat; 10am-4pm Sun. Lunch served noon-3pm Mon-Sat; dinner served 6pm-9pm Mon-Sat; brunch served 10am-3pm Sun.

Jamie Oliver's Fifteen may be no more, but some of its spirit lives on via the current, eponymous venture from its former head chef, Andy Appleton, who held the role for nine years. As with Fifteen, the cusine is modern Italian, based on locally sourced ingredients: try the octopus and chickpea starter or the gnocchi with Cornish mushrooms, or just swing by the bar for one of ten types of negroni.

Dwelling House ♥

6 Fore Street, Fowey, PL23 1AQ (01726 833662, www.thedwellinghouse.co.uk). Open Summer 10am-6.30pm daily. Winter 10am-5.30pm Mon, Wed-Sun. No credit cards.

This delectable little period tearoom is a must for cake aficionados, particularly those who swoon at the sight of three tiers of pastel-hued cupcakes. (Think dainty lavender sprigs on light purple icing, a sprinkling of mini marshmallows on a vanilla cream topping, or an artful swirl of chocolate.) Said cupcakes are served on their very own vintage cake stand, and are ideally accompanied by a pot of loose-leaf tea (25 varieties available). Less cute offerings include a superb walnut and coffee cake, sticky toffee pudding and light lunches (cold platters, soup, sandwiches). Forget about nervously clattering teacups and pretension: the staff are charming, the prices reasonable and the menu rather

Lost Gardens of Heligan see p46

sweetly concedes that, while fine leaf tea is a wonderful thing, they understand that sometimes only a strong teabag will do. There's a small walled garden out the back, and Dwelling House is also a B&B, offering double rooms and breakfast for around £80.

Fitzroy

2 Fore St, Fowey, PL23 1AQ (01726 932934, www.fitzroycornwall.com). Open noon-10pm Tue-Sun. Lunch served noon-5pm; dinner served 7.15-9.15pm.

Set up in 2019 by hip north London restaurateurs David Gingell and Jeremie Cometto as their first venture outside the capital, Fitzroy brings sophisticated ideas to traditional Cornish ingredients: during coronavirus lockdown its takeaways kept locals going with fried oyster and seaweed mayo sandwiches and crab soup with wild garlic. In true London style, it's walk-ins only during the day (though you'll need a reservation for dinner).

Pinky Murphy's Café

19 North Street, Fowey, PL23 1DB (01726 832512, www.pinkymurphys.co.uk). Open 9am-5pm Mon-Sat; 9.30am-4pm Sun. No credit cards.

Polka dots, candy stripes and florals come together in chaotic harmony at Fowey's most colourful café. Eclectic furniture creates a carefree, beach-hut vibe – your seat could be anything from a sarong-draped director's chair or a vintage armchair with a crochet blanket to a (cushioned) plastic crate on the tiny outside terrace, shaded by a shocking-green faux-rush parasol. The fun-packed menu takes in big breakfasts, filled ciabattas, veggie platters with fresh dips, excellent own-made cakes, and Pinky's Cream Tease. There's free Wi-Fi too.

Rashleigh Inn

Polkerris, PL24 2TL (01726 813991, www. therashleighinn.co.uk). Open Summer 11am-11pm daily. Winter 11am-11pm

33

Mon-Sat; noon-10pm Sun. Lunch served noon-3pm, dinner served 6-9pm daily.

Ruling the roost in the tiny cove of Polkerris, this thriving pub is housed in the centuries-old lifeboat station on the beach, making it an ideal fuel stop on the coastal footpath. The huge beach-side terrace makes the most of its sea-facing position, while the interior is well kept and traditional – and we can vouch for the very good, reasonably priced crab sandwiches. If you're based in Fowey, consider a circular walk out along the coastal path and back on the inland footpath, making the Rashleigh your halfway point.

Sam's

20 Fore Street, Fowey, PL23 1AQ (01726 832273, www.samsfowey.co.uk). Open/ food served Bistro noon-9.30pm daily. Bar Summer 5-11.30pm Mon-Thur, Sun; 5pm-1am Fri, Sat. Winter 6pm-midnight Fri, Sat.

The retro diner decor, zippy service and unfussy food have made this bistro a Fowey institution – something that will become immediately apparent when trying to procure a table in peak season. No bookings are taken, but the addition of a cool new upstairs bar and the uplifting, rock-inflected soundtrack do at least take the pain out of the wait. There is plenty of fresh, simply cooked fish on the menu, along with chunky chargrilled burgers and children's portions of grown-up meals. Chargrilled whole sardines with Cornish sea salt are a time-honoured classic, as is the Scooby Burger, piled high with pineapple, egg and bacon and held together with a skewer. Sam's on the Beach (The Old Lifeboat House, 01726 812255), up the road at Polkerris, serves pizzas, salads and seafood – and takes bookings. Reserve an upstairs table with a harbour view, or people-watch in the café downstairs.

Where to stay

Crown Inn

Lanlivery, PL30 5BT (01208 872707, www.thecrowninncornwall.co.uk). Rates £50-£99 double incl breakfast.

Those wanting to stay in a 'proper' old country pub in a pretty Cornish village must customarily endure the low-grade furnishings and scratchy linens that seem to go with the territory. But the Crown is a notable, and very good-value, exception: a handsomely preserved 12th-century pub with nine tastefully rustic rooms attached (some in the old outhouses). It

also serves good, fresh food, three real ales at any one time and ten wines by the glass. Guest rooms have solid pine chests of drawers, white cotton sheets, flatscreen tellies and up-to-date (but shower-only) bathrooms. It's a simple package but it's no less appealing for it, especially when you factor in the period drama romance of the village setting, opposite a striking granite church. It's also handily located for visiting the Eden Project, Fowey and the south coast.

Fowey Hall Hotel

Hanson Drive, Fowey, PL23 1ET (01726 833866, www.foweyhallhotel.co.uk). Rates £199-£299 double incl breakfast.

This luxury family hotel is perfectly situated above Fowey, with views up the river in one direction and the open sea in the other. A Queen Anne chateau-style mansion (reputedly the inspiration for Toad Hall in *The Wind in the Willows*), Fowey Hall is the sort of extravagant setting that would usually have parents hovering uncomfortably over their children. Here, however, familes are welcomed wholeheartedly. Under-12s sharing their parents' room are accommodated for free, and the hotel caters for all ages, with the Ofsted-registered Four Bears Den nursery for under-sevens, a baby-listening service, a games room, badminton, croquet and much more. The interior decor is chateau chic (chandeliers, grand fireplaces and the reassuring whiff of expensive leather),

but with contemporary art on the walls, Roberts digital radios in the rooms and a pleasing lack of florals. The Spa has a hot tub overlooking the estuary, treatment rooms and a glass-walled swimming pool, making sure that guests are never without those views.

Old Quay House

28 Fore Street, Fowey, PL23 1AQ (01726 833302; www.theoldquayhouse.com). Rates £230-£370 double incl breakfast.

One of Cornwall's finest boutique hotels, the Old Quay House has just 11 luxurious rooms – so book early. The cliché-free cream and black colour scheme shows style and sophistication, and makes a refreshing change from the usual seaside colours of Cornish hotel rooms. Lovely touches abound: contemporary art in the corridors (for sale); personal service from a small team; and a plethora of little extras, such as a small hot water bottle in your bedroom in winter, a computer for guest use on each level and a mini-fridge in the corridor containing fresh milk for tea. The hotel's unique selling point, though, is its smart riverside terrace, jutting out into the Fowey River, which ripples gently at the sides. Guests can sip a glass of wine on the terrace or dine at the highly competent Q restaurant, serving bistro classics and seafood. As per most old Cornish fishing villages, parking is problematic, but the trade-off is more than fair: who needs wheels when you're this close to the water? No under-12s.

Pencalenick House

Fowey, PL23 1NH (www.whiteblanc mange.com). Rates see website for details.

As holiday lets go, it doesn't get much more private – or dream-like – than Pencalenick House. A stunning modernist property built into the contours of the banks of the Pont Pill creek, it is shrouded in thick woodland, and further camouflaged by a green roof planted with local grasses and a curving, cedar-clad front. Designed by Seth Stein architects, and shortlisted for the Wood Awards in sustainable architecture, the house, available for hire by a maximum of 13 guests, is breathtakingly creative. Inside,

Old Quay House *see above*

South-West Coast Path ❤

At some 630 miles (1,014 kilometres), the South-West Coast Path is the longest national walking trail in Britain, running from Minehead in Somerset right round the coastline of Devon and Cornwall to finish at Poole harbour in Dorset. It encompasses some of the most spectacular coastal scenery in the country – and despite its length, there is hardly a dull mile on the whole route. The path passes through Areas of Outstanding Natural Beauty, Heritage Coasts, Exmoor National Park, a UNESCO Geopark and a Biosphere reserve, not to mention industrial heritage sites, fine seaside towns and picturesque harbours.

The Cornwall part is by far the most extensive section of the trail, encompassing some 300 miles of terrain, from Marsland Mouth on the north coast to Cremyll on the south-east coast. It also provides some of the most challenging walking conditions and most varied scenery – starting with the high cliffs and rugged landscape around Sandy Mouth and the surfing hubs of Bude and Widemouth Bay, and on to Tintagel Castle; moving on to the Camel Estuary near Padstow (served by a series of small ferries). After that, the terrain becomes a little easier, passing by the sand dunes known as 'the towans' between Newquay and Hayle, where you may have to walk on the beach at certain points, before winding round the Penwith Peninsula – full of steep ascents and rocky terrain just beyond St Ives and Penzance. Then comes the greener scenery of the south coast, where forests, rivers and valley estuaries (Helford, Fal, Fowey, Looe and Tamar) make up the views, and there are plenty of rest opportunites at pretty fishing villages and beaches.

In Devon, the path traces the outline of both north and south coasts, climbing to the Great Hangman on Exmoor's edge, the highest point on the whole route. The broad Taw-Torridge estuary involves a lengthy riverside detour, while on the south coast several estuaries have to be crossed; some of these are served by ferries, while one (the Erme) can be waded at low tide. The route passes lighthouses and coastal lookouts, and broad sandy beaches provide contrast to clifftop panoramas. The cliffs are at their most colourful in early summer when wild flowers such as sea thrift are at their peak; later, the intense yellow of gorse fills the scene. In autumn and winter wave-lashed rocks stand out against an often intensely blue sea.

Rumps Point see p68

To walk the whole trail requires at least six weeks, but most people opt to do sections at a time or simply include parts of the coast path in circular day walks. There's no shortage of permutations on using the trail, including catching a bus in order to explore linear stretches of coast path. All the Tourist Information Centres have leaflets about local coastal walks, and there are a number of guidebooks to the whole trail. For more information visit www.southwestcoastpath.com and www.swcp.org.uk.

you'll find Starck fittings, Cornish slate detailing, and glass walls looking on to the calming waters of the creek. And did we mention the private beach, with its own boat? Naturally, Pencalenick is an expensive – make that very expensive – proposition, but what it offers is genuinely one of a kind.

Upton House 💜

2 Esplanade, Fowey, PL23 1HY (01726 832732, www.uptonhousefowey.com). Rates £2,800-£3,385 per week for 2-8 people.

Upton House, in the heart of Fowey (read: enchanting narrow streets and estuary views, but alas no parking), is a fine antidote to the muted oceanic colours and seascapes of Cornish bed and breakfast cliché. Indeed, the revamped corner townhouse is no longer a B&B: you have to rent the whole thing for at least a week. It isn't cheap, but you will get to appreciate the whole building and all four of its bedrooms, which are playfully different in style and colour, each the work of tirelessly imaginative Austrian interior designer Angelique Thompson, who also runs the Upton House design boutique next door, where you can buy the contents of your room. Choose from the all-white Snow Bubble, in which a rotating mirror ball casts snowflake-like light flecks on the wall; the high-camp Flamingo Room, with shocking-pink accents and hand-block-print flamingo wallpaper; 'baroque boudoir' the Scullery, with four-poster bed, stealthily skull-themed wallpaper and a (plastic) skeleton in the closet; and the pièce de résistance, the Loft, with a whirlpool bath, superb estuary views, art deco walnut dressing table and champagne truffles. In the communal areas, chandeliers, feather-trim curtains and a gloss-black piano turn up the glamour. Heart-shaped vanilla porridge with pink-hued sugar and caramelised banana for breakfast? Well, frankly, why not. Life's too short for boring rentals.

St Austell

Unlike the more nostalgically attractive towns of Fowey and Lostwithiel, St Austell has a mainly industrial heritage, and a slightly grittier feel. Ever since the discovery of huge deposits of china clay in the mid 18th century, the town has been at the heart of the area's enormous china clay operation – an industry that, though in decline, is still trading. The landscape around St Austell has been shaped by centuries of intense mining, leaving a collection of surreal-looking white conical mountains and chasmic pits (one of which was famously converted into the world's largest greenhouse by Tim Smit; see the Eden Project, *p45*).

With its down-at-heel atmosphere and tired high-street, St Austell has largely been bypassed by tourists. But its fortunes have improved lately, as a number of regeneration projects zone in on the area: the £75 million White River Place complex opened in 2009, with the county's first new cinema in over 70 years and a rather predictable shopping centre, while the government is moving forward with a plan to build 5,000 homes as part of a new carbon-neutral eco town in former china clay mines.

Charlestown & the coast

An unusually straight road, designed to take horse-drawn clay wagons three abreast, runs down the hill from St Austell to the sea at Charlestown. Built at the end of the 18th century, the port was planned and laid out by Charles Rashleigh, after whom it is named. Its little dock was designed to load china clay and copper ore from the nearby pits and mines on to ships for export. The dock is now home to a collection of old sailing ships, used in film projects all over the world – and the elegant houses of the Georgian new town are also a favourite with film and television location scouts.

To the south-west, **Porthpean** is regarded as St Austell's town beach, and is a local favourite.

Mevagissey

Mevagissey is an ancient port and fishing village that dates back to the 14th century. In the 19th century, pilchards were the main catch here, and the fish were salted and stored in cellars in the town and exported. The painted cob and slate houses cling to the hillside overlooking the two harbours, and the old fish cellars have been converted into tourist-oriented shops and eateries. These days, the fishermen supplement their income by taking visitors out on fishing trips; there is shark fishing for the adventurous, and mackerel trips for families who want to catch their own supper.

Polstreath beach, a lovely stretch of sand and shingle, lies below the cliffs on the north edge of town, reached by 200 steps. More accessible is the beach at Pentewan to the north, which marks the start of a cycle trail that winds through a wooded river valley towards St Austell (*see p38*). Nearby **Portmellon Cove**, a 20-minute walk south along the coastal footpath from Mevagissey, has a pretty, sandy stretch – and further south, **Gorran Haven** is another fishing village with two safe, sandy village beaches, good for swimming and snorkelling.

The **Lost Gardens of Heligan** (*see p46*) are a short drive (or bus ride) from Mevagissey proper, where there is also the excellent, family-run **Lobbs Farm Shop** (01726 844411, www.lobbsfarmshop.com).

Where to eat & drink

St Austell and its surrounding towns on the coast don't go in for destination dining as a rule, with restaurants generally geared towards fleeting tourist trade. For the top tables, you're better off heading just up the coast to Fowey or along to Lostwithiel. One top spot in the area, however, is the **Eden Project Café**, which serves simple but delicious casual fare (deep-filled baguettes, brunch, smoothies and the like). *See p45.*

In Mevagissey, try Portuguese-themed **Alvorada** (2 Polkirt Hill,01726 842055, closed Sun-Tue winter) for tapas, or **Salamander** (4-6 Tregoney Hill, 01726 842254, www.salamander-restaurant.co.uk, closed Mon, Sun winter) for a more formal setting.

Fountain Inn

3 Cliff Street, Mevagissey, PL26 6QH (01726 842320). Open noon-midnight daily. Lunch served noon-2pm daily. Dinner served 6-9pm Mon-Sat.

There's nothing flashy about the Fountain, but therein lies its charm. A smugglers' haunt of old, the plant-covered inn dates back to the 15th century, making it the oldest pub in Mevagissey. The tidy, well-kept bar displays well-preserved original features: low oak beams, a fine open fireplace and smooth, old slate floors. Simple pub food is served: go for the fish and chips, then smuggle yourself away for a few hours in the corner with a pint.

Where to stay

Cornwall Hotel, Spa & Estate

Pentewan Road, Tregorrick, St Austell, PL26 7AB (01726 874050, www.thecornwall.com). Rates £139-£385 double incl breakfast. Rental of Woodland Homes starts at £2,190 per week (peak season), 2 bedrooms.

St Austell was plotted on the tourist map by the Eden Project but is something of a desert when it comes to accommodation. The arrival of the Cornwall – a mini resort crafted from a 43-acre parkland estate

Cornish Cycle Trails

Camel Trail

Setting off from Padstow, on the North Cornish coast, the 17-mile Camel Trail (www.sustrans.org.uk) follows a disused railway line along the Camel Estuary to Wadebridge, then on to Bodmin and Poley's Bridge. The first stretch, to Wadebridge, affords wide open views across the mud flats (bring your binoculars and look out for wading birds) and water; the second cuts through wooded river valleys, en route to the western fringes of the moor. There are bike hire outfits in Padstow, Wadebridge and Bodmin, if you haven't brought your own set of wheels (*see p66*).

Clay Trails

The Clay Trails, or China Trails, weave across the still-operational clay-mining districts surrounding St Austell (*see left*). It's a tranquil landscape of woodland and open terrain, punctuated with crumbling brick chimneys, clay pits and mines; the trails are also a nice way to reach the Eden Project. The trails consist of three main routes: the five-mile Wheal Martyn Trail, past the China Clay Country Park; the relatively easy four-mile Bugle to Eden Trail; and the three-mile St Blazey to Par Beach Trail. Recent additions to the network include the Green Corridor, linking the Wheal Martyn trail with St Austell. For further information, see www.claytrails.co.uk or www.sustrans.org.uk.

Mineral Tramways

This ambitious project has opened up almost 40 miles of trails, following the tramways and railway lines that once served the region's thriving tin and copper mines. The best-known trail is the 11-mile Coast to Coast Trail between Devoran on the south coast and Portreath on the north coast. Tracing the route of the horse-worked Portreath tramroad and the Redruth and Chasewater Railway, which opened in 1825, it passes through picturesque heathland, woodland and historic mining sites. It also links in with other Mineral Tramway routes, such as the Tolgus Trail and Wheal Busy Loop. There are bike hire shops and refreshment stops along the route; for a map, see www.cornwalls.co.uk/sports-and-activities/mineral-tramways-trails.htm.

– has gone some way to bridging the gap. There are a handful of rooms in the mansion with period features but the most spacious rooms are in the wood-clad new build, each of which has a south-facing private terrace overlooking the grounds; there is also a collection of self-catering Woodland Homes for rent (and time-share). The design can feel a little on the corporate side, but rooms are consistently comfortable and well appointed, with down toppers on the beds, super-soft linens and requisite big tellies. All guests have access to the Clearing Spa, which has an infinity-style indoor pool, sauna and fitness centre, plus tennis courts. It's a two-mile drive out of St Austell town centre, and a short drive from the beaches of the south coast. There's also a restaurant, lounges, a children's playground and no shortage of open green space in which to roam.

Llawnroc Hotel

Chute Lane, Gorran Haven, St Austell, PL26 6NU (01726 843461, www. thellawnrochotel.co.uk). Rates £115-£175 double incl breakfast.

The Llawnroc (that's Cornwall backwards) is a new hotel on the site of an old pub by the same name – an impressive stone fireplace in the restaurant is one of few clues as to its past life. The look is more aspirational than you'd expect from a small, unassuming Cornish village – oversized zebra-print chairs in reception, decorative Moët bottles – but there can be no arguing about the warmness and efficiency of the service, nor the comfort of the rooms. Mega beds, thick fluffy towels and rainforest showers are all present and correct. There are two on-site restaurants – a bistro and a fine-dining restaurant, both featuring seafood from the hotel's fisherman (if there's line-caught seabass on the menu, don't hesitate). Note that Wi-Fi doesn't extend to the guest rooms (ethernet access only) and the mobile signal is fleeting. All the better to down tools, and head to the sandy beach, just a few winding streets away. The Llawnroc places you within easy reach of the Lost Gardens of Heligan, the Eden Project, and the coves and creeks of the Roseland Peninsula.

Lower Barn ♥

Bosue, St Ewe, PL26 6ET (01726 844881, www.lowerbarns.co.uk). Rates £130-£200 double incl breakfast.

The location might be profoundly rural (though if you have a car, it is very convenient for the Lost Gardens of Heligan and the Eden Project), but there's nothing rustic about the styling at this boutique B&B. The four big guest rooms are decorated in bold, vibrant colours, and guests are lavished with soft white dressing gowns, high-end linens, Sanctuary toiletries, chocolates on the pillow and a flatscreen TV, with a selection of DVDs – there's even a hot tub bubbling away in the garden. Inevitably, Lower Barn isn't the cheapest B&B on the market, but you'd struggle to find a hotel offering these sorts of extras in this price range. Dinner (pre-book and BYO) is served in the Shack, a fairy light-lit hideout in the garden. The Hideaway and the Garden Suite are the most private of the rooms; the former is particularly popular with honeymooners, being tucked away down the garden with a super-king-size bed and a freestanding bath.

Pier House Hotel Charlestown

Harbour Front, Charlestown, St Austell, PL25 3NJ (01726 67955, www. pierhousehotel.com). Rates £130-£180 double incl breakfast.

This small hotel, right on the harbourside in the enchanting port of Charlestown, just along from St Austell, can be spotted in numerous film and television productions. It is warm and friendly, and the renovated rooms (as a rule, the ones with sea views) are great value, with muted tones and new bathrooms. The restaurant extends to a large patio, where you can watch the world sail by.

Trevalsa Court

School-Hill, Mevagissey, PL26 6TH (01726 842468, www.trevalsa-hotel. co.uk). Rates £105-£230 double incl breakfast.

Mevagissey's most attractive hotel stands high on the cliffs above the village (and directly on the coastal footpath), with all but two of the 13 rooms offering open sea views. Once a seaside home, Trevalsa was built in the late 1930s but has the feel of an older, more extravagant country manor, on account of its mullioned windows and oak panelling, which were incorporated from a historic mansion in Leeds. The owners have freshened up the rooms and public areas, adding turquoise and pink accents, Designers' Guild rugs and curtains, and modern new bathrooms. The two-and-a-half-acre subtropical gardens are a delight in summer, and it's a short walk down some steep steps to the lovely beach below.

YHA Eden Project

Eden Project, PL24 2SG (0345 371 9573, www.yha.org.uk). Phone for rates.

The closest you'll get to staying in actual Eden, the YHA Eden Project offers 58 stylishly lo-fi en-suite bedrooms made from shipping containers (in keeping with the site's ethos of sustainability). They're actually called 'snoozeboxes', so don't get your hopes up about the size, but they're pretty cool, and in a very literal sense at the Eden Project. It's being refurbished in 2021.

LOOE BAY & AROUND

Looe

In contrast to upscale Fowey, with its multi-million-pound riverside properties and chichi interiors boutiques, a feel of pre-gentrification British seaside prevails at Looe, with buckets and spades, fudge and bags of chips unashamedly courting the summer trade. What it may lack in sophistication, however, it does make up for with a fantastic town beach and a memorable setting – not to mention the bonus of landing some of the freshest fish around, thanks to its day boats.

The bustling port occupies both sides of the valley at the mouth of the river, with narrow streets of old fishermen's cottages twisting and turning steeply up on either side. Once distinct settlements, East and West Looe are connected by a seven-arched 19th-century bridge; from here, Fore Street runs on the eastern side of the estuary as far as Buller Quay and the busy harbour. Tourists began arriving in Looe in the early 19th century to bathe on the surrounding beaches, but the town didn't really begin to draw the crowds until the building of the railway in 1879. The delightful **Looe Valley Line** (*see p117*) still runs from the mainline station at Liskeard, its one carriage following the river to the sea.

A busy fish market is still held on the east side of the harbour – but if you're keen to make your own catch, check out the blackboards along the quay for fishing trips. Looe is the centre for shark-fishing in the UK, but mackerel fishing and pleasure boating are also widely available. For exclusively Cornish produce, don't miss the **Purely Cornish Deli** (18 Fore Street, 01503 262680, www.purelycornish.co.uk), and its farm shop just outside town at St Martins.

One of the most popular boat excursions is to **Looe Island** (otherwise known as St George's), lying a mile offshore and measuring a mile in circumference. Once the site of a Celtic monastery, the island was bought in the 1970s by two sisters, who lived alone there for over 20 years. Now uninhabited and owned by the Cornwall Wildlife Trust, it has become a fascinating nature reserve.

Beyond the harbour, the protective arm of the **Banjo Pier** extends out into the bay, marking the western end of popular East Looe Beach. Further east and accessible via the coast path is **Millendreath**, not to mention endless little coves and rock pools. The coast path continues east from here to the sandy beach at **Seaton** and to the linear clifftop villages of **Downderry** and **Portwrinkle** on the edge of Whitsand Bay. West of Looe, meanwhile, there's **Hannafore Beach** – good for rockpooling and snorkelling.

Polperro

During the 19th century, the harbour village of Polperro – four miles from Looe – was a prosperous smuggling port, with many fishermen stashing contraband among the hauls of pilchards. Although the village is still a quaint sight, in midsummer it is suffocatingly touristy, as its tiny streets are jammed with daytrippers surveying the endless fudge displays and ye olde tea shoppes.

The village still supports some fishing vessels, which unload their catch on to the quay, and out of season Polperro is a pleasant place for a wander, particularly for a pint at the shipshape Blue Peter Inn (*see p43*).

For walkers, however, the major attraction is the jagged stretch of coastline between Polruan and Polperro, owned almost entirely by the National Trust and thus blissfully unexploited. Nearby is the sleepy village of **Porthallow** – the halfway point in the 630-mile South-West Coast Path, marked by a sculpture – and the pink-grey rocks at Talland Bay.

Where to eat & drink

For snacking in Looe, you can rely on the quality of **Sarah's Pasties** on Buller Street, and the artisanal ice-cream sold at **Treleavens** (Fore Street, 01503 220969, www.treleavens.co.uk, closed Jan, Dec). One kitchen worth a visit is **Blue Plate** (Main Road, 01503 250308, www.blueplatecornwall.com, closed Mon, Sun), just east of Seaton at Downderry. As well as more formal dinners, you can stop by from 5pm for a selection of tapas-style dishes to share – a bowl of Fowey mussels, say, or four mini burgers with a scattering of mini fries.

Other respected restaurants in the area include the **Plough on the Quay** (01503 269088, www.ploughon thequay.co.uk), a small, well-respected establishment with a street food-inflected menu; and **Couch's Great House Restaurant** (Saxon Bridge, 01503 272554, www.

Looe Harbour. See p41.

Portwrinkle see p42

couchspolperro.com) in Polperro, run by Ramsey- and Blanc-trained chef Richard McGeown.

Blue Peter Inn

Quay Road, Polperro, PL13 2QZ (01503 272743, www.thebluepeterinn.com). Open 8.30am-11.30pm daily. Breakfast served 8.30-11.30am. Lunch served noon-2.30pm. Dinner served 6-9.30pm daily.

A genuine find in over-touristed Polperro, the Blue Peter is an old, whitewashed fisherman's pub lodged into the cliff. The topsy-turvy angles, tiny blue windows and low ceilings create a jolly, ship-like vibe – you can even buy a 'I've been wrecked at the Blue Peter' T-shirt before you disembark. There's a tiny amphitheatre of a terrace overlooking the quay, which should be bagged if at all possible.

Talland Bay Beach Café

Talland, PL13 2JA (01503 272088, www.tallandbaybeachcafe.co.uk). Open Apr-Oct daily.

There's nothing else at secluded Talland Bay beach, bar this beach café, but it has all the provisions you're likely to need: crab sandwiches, cream teas, 11 flavours of Roskilly's ice-cream and beach-going essentials such as buckets and spades, sun cream, windbreaks and puzzle books. It even rents sit-on kayaks by the hour, in the right weather.

Where to stay

On the whole, Looe and Polperro's accommodation is in desperate need of an update, with floral-filled B&Bs and guesthouses making up the majority of the rooms. A notable exception is the boutiquey **Talland Bay Hotel** (Porthallow, 01503 272667, www.tallandbayhotel.co.uk), which combines a lighter, more contemporary feel with fine modern Cornish food from chef Nick Hawke.

Botelet ♥

Herodsfoot, PL14 4RD (01503 220225, www.botelet.com). Self-catering £600-£1,500 per week for 5 people. Yurts £450 per week for 2 people. No credit cards.

There is a uniquely unspoilt feel to Botelet – a 300-acre farm sequestered down a long, muddy lane a few miles from Lostwithiel. Arriving at the farmhouse is like stepping into another century: reclaimed granite standing stones mark the driveway, and everything from the traditional Cornish hedging to the slate roofs, ancient trees and wooden gates is wonderfully time-weathered. The Tamblyn family have been working this land for the best part of two centuries and place great value on its heritage, restoring the buildings with a gentle touch and farming the land sustainably. Self-caterers can choose between the Grade II-listed Manor House,

Charlestown Shipwreck & Heritage Centre

THE RIVER FOWEY

Restormel ♥

Lostwithiel, PL22 OEE (01566 774911, www. english-heritage.org.uk). Open July, Aug 10am-6pm daily. Apr-June, Sept 10am-5pm daily. Oct 10am-4pm daily. Admission £6.50; £3.90-£5.90 reductions.

The highly evocative relics of this Norman circular keep and moat are probably the best-preserved remains of their kind in the country. Located just upriver of Lostwithiel, with commanding views over the River Fowey, its lawns are a lovely spot for a picnic. The shop sells kids' swords and chainmail vests for would-be valiant knights.

ST AUSTELL BAY & AROUND

Caerhays Castle

Caerhays, Gorran, PL26 6LY (01872 501310, www.caerhays.co.uk). Open Gardens mid Feb-early June 10am-5pm daily. House Tours mid Mar-early June noon, 1.30pm & 3pm Sat, Sun. Admission Garden & House Tour £13; £6 reductions. Garden only £10; £5 reductions.

In the spring, members of the public may take a tour of the romantic grounds of Caerhays Castle, designed by John Nash in the early 19th century – and one of few remaining Nash castles in the country. It's a spectacular sight, as the vast collection of magnolias, rhododendrons, camellias and azaleas explode into colour. As if the scene weren't impressive enough, Caerhays overlooks the secluded beach at Porthluney Cove. If you are visiting at a time when the estate is closed to the public, you can still get a good view of the castle, framed by age-old woodland, from the road.

Charlestown Shipwreck & Heritage Centre
Quay Road, Charlestown, PL25 3NJ (01726 69897, www.shipwreckcharlestown.co.uk). Open Mar-Oct phone for details.

The Shipwreck & Heritage Centre is housed in old china clay loading premises on the waterfront, and visitors can walk through the tunnels that the clay wagons trundled along before their contents were tipped into the holds of the waiting ships. The centre has a fascinating mix of objects rescued from shipwrecks, along with exhibitions relating to local life, and an intriguing collection of old diving equipment. Younger visitors can play with remote-controlled boats in a miniature port and dock.

Eden Project ♥
Bodelva, PL24 2SG (01726 811911, www. edenproject.com). Open July, Aug 10am-6pm daily. Feb 10am-6pm daily. Jan 10am-4pm Mon-Thur; 10am-9pm Fri; 9.30am-9pm Sat; 9.30am-6pm Sun. Mar-June, Sept-Dec 10am-4.30pm daily. Admission £28.50; £23.50-£26 reductions.

Believe the hype: this place is amazing. All ages love the Eden Project, and it's well worth braving the queues and crowds to explore the largest greenhouses on earth. The vast 'bubble-wrap' domes of the Rainforest and Mediterranean biomes house a world of natural wonders – lush jungle greenery, coffee plants, cocoa beans and rubber plants, as well as herbs, vines, clementines and olive trees – while the Core is home to Eden's inspirational Educational Centre. The brainchild of Dutch-born entrepreneur Tim Smit – whose first Cornish project was the Lost Gardens of Heligan (*see right*) – Eden rose from the barren depths

Eden Project

Places to visit

of a disused china clay pit into a project of extraordinary vision.

The message at Eden is green, but the tone tends to be more factual than moralising: a razed section of Amazonian rainforest, a fraction of what is destroyed every ten seconds, brings home the reality of soya production, while olive oil is bigged up as a sustainable superfood. You can also travel to the Eden Project in an environmentally friendly way. Green buses run from many local resort towns, offering a discounted journey and entrance ticket. Even better, cycle: arrive at the biomes feeling healthy and virtuous – and claim a £4 discount for your effort. The Eden Project is on three different cycle trails; see p39.

There need never be a dull moment for kids, with an array of home-grown play structures and hideaways, stepping stones and rope swings, sandpits and tunnels – not to mention sing-songs, workshops and trails. In winter there is ice-skating in the arena, which in summer hosts a series of big-name gigs at the Eden Sessions, see p7.

Lost Gardens of Heligan ♥

Pentewan, PL26 6EN (01726 845100, www. heligan.com). Open Summer 10am-6pm daily. Winter 10am-5pm daily. Admission £17.50; £8.50-£11 reductions; £48 family.

The romantically named Lost Gardens of Heligan were once part of a historic estate owned by the Tremayne family. The gardens fell into decline when 16 of the 22 gardeners were killed during World War I, and lay neglected for the best part of a century. They were rescued from oblivion in the mid 1990s, when Tim Smit (later the brains behind the Eden Project, see p45) and John Nelson set about restoring them. The project not only gives a sense of the dedication of the 18th- and 19th-century plant-hunters, but also conveys a wider message of ecological sustainability. There are jungle boardwalks, tranquil woodland hikes and, at the heart of the project, the garden itself – not just a showpiece but a productive enterprise. On-site facilities include a farm shop, a tearoom and a picnic area.

Restormel see p44

Mevagissey Model Railway

Meadow Street, Mevagissey, PL26 6UL (01726 842457, www.model-railway.co.uk). Open Apr-Oct 10am-5pm daily. Admission £5; £3.50-£4 reductions; £15 family.

Trainspotters of all ages unite in this dinky Mevagissey attraction. Around 30 visitor-operated model trains roll through all sorts of landscapes, including an Alpine snowscape, gritty urban scenes, seaside settings and a Cornish tin mine. Kids adore the interactive Thomas the Tank Engine section, and the great shop.

RAME PENINSULA

Cotehele

St Dominick, PL12 6TA (01579 351346, www. nationaltrust.org.uk). Open House Mar-Oct 11am-4.30pm Mon-Thur, Sat, Sun. Garden 10am-dusk daily. Admission House & Garden Check website for latest ticket prices. Garden only £8; £4 reductions; £20 family.

This granite-built Tudor manor is set in a particularly beautiful portion of the Tamar River valley. Acquired by the Edgcumbe family in 1353, the house was largely rebuilt in the early 1500s and has altered very little since. Arranged around three courtyards, the buildings contain an impressive array of tapestries, richly carved furniture and Tudor armour. Stroll through the parkland to reach an 18th-century folly tower, where you can climb the dingy stone staircase for fantastic views of the Tamar valley. Strolling through the grounds, you will eventually reach the restored quay, with an exhibition centre at the bottom, and the *Shamrock*, a beautiful sailing barge built at the turn of the 20th century.

Cotehele

Mount Edgcumbe House

Cremyll, PL10 1HZ (01752 822236, www. mountedgcumbe.gov.uk). Open House & Earls Garden Apr-Sept 11am-4.30pm Mon-Thur, Sun. Country Park 8am-8pm daily (8am-6pm winter). Admission House & Earls Garden £8; £4-£6 reductions; £18 family.

Council-owned since the early 1970s, this vast country park and stately home on the banks of the Tamar was once the seat of the Edgcumbe family, who laid out its formal gardens, deer park and orangery. The house, built in the 16th century and restored after it was gutted during the Blitz, is open for visits, and the wider parkland is open to all free of charge, year-round; the views across to Plymouth across the sound are superb. Also on the site are the National Camellia Collection and the Orangery Restaurant.

Port Eliot

St Germans, PL12 5ND (01503 230211, www.porteliot.co.uk). Open mid Mar-early July 2-6pm Mon-Thur, Sat, Sun. Admission House & Grounds Check website for latest ticket prices.

The Port Eliot Estate, Grade I-listed both inside and out, has a richly layered history that spans more than 1,000 years. Still the home of Lord and Lady St Germans, Port Eliot now opens to the public for 100 days a year, thanks to a deal struck with the government in 2008 in lieu of inheritance tax (masterpieces by Sir Joshua Reynolds, on display, were also donated). The medieval priory was significantly redeveloped by Sir John Soane in the 18th century, while the gardens and parklands were the work of the great landscape designer Humphrey Repton. During the open days, visitors can take in the faded grandeur of the house – still endearingly unmodernised – and roam freely in the grounds, which border the Lynher estuary. The 6,000 acres of parkland were once the venue for the Elephant Fayre arts festival and, more recently, the Port Eliot literary festival. Did not open in 2020 due to water damage.

Rame Head *see p49*

dating back to the 17th century and with masses of intriguing original features (including a private walled garden, composed of remains that appeared in the Domesday Book), or the 19th-century Cowslip Cottage, a whitewashed hideaway with a big farmhouse kitchen table and open fireplaces. In summer you can rent an antique-strewn yurt in the meadow. The setting could hardly be more rural, with no sound or light pollution, and the lack of mobile phone signals seals the deal for a holiday away from it all.

Commonwood Manor

St Martins Road, East Looe, PL13 1LP (01503 262929, www. commonwoodmanor.com). Rates £95-£145 double incl breakfast.

Looe's smartest rooms can be found at Common Manor, a spotless white guesthouse with views over the river and woodland below. The rooms (some of which have fantastic river views) are refined and light in tone, with traditional but not fuddy-duddy decor. The staff are exceptionally warm and accommodating, the restaurant is accomplished and among the six acres of lush gardens is a heated swimming pool.

Highertown Campsite

Lansallos, PL13 2PX (01208 265211, www. nationaltrust.org.uk). Rates £7-£9 per night for 1 person.

Set in the blink-and-you'll-miss-it hamlet of **Lansallos**, half a mile from the Cornish coast, Highertown offers stripped-down camping: one lush field by an old granite church (*see p110*), with room for 16 tents. Owned by the National Trust, it's an eco-conscious place, with solar-heated water in the showers and washing-up tap (bring a stash of 20p coins), recycling facilities and two compost loos (there are conventional toilets too). The sand and shingle Lansallos Cove is a 15-minute walk through the woods, although the nearest shops, pubs and restaurants are several miles away, so bring supplies.

RAME PENINSULA

Cornwall's 'forgotten corner' – as the Rame Peninsula is often dubbed – is also one of the county's most beautiful areas. Bafflingly overlooked by tourists and travel guides, the south-eastern tip of Cornwall, on the Devon border, is the stuff of daydreams: romantic creeks, historic country mansions and snug waterside villages that give way to wild, unspoilt cliffs. It is perhaps the out-of-the-way location, and the proximity of Plymouth across the water, that has saved this small peninsula from development – most people dart straight over the **Tamar Bridge** rather than detour into the meandering country lanes, which culminate in a breathtaking dead end when they reach the sea.

For the ultimate in slow travel, take the ferry over from the Barbican in Plymouth right on to the beach at **Cawsand** (5 sailings daily, Easter to Oct, 07971 208381, www.cawsandferry. com). Apart from being a valuable service, it is also a scenic trip – and dolphins sometimes swim with the boat in summer.

Among the sweetest places in all of Cornwall are the twin villages of **Kingsand** and Cawsand, which were once divided down the middle by the old border between Devon and Cornwall. Despite their peaceful atmosphere and seclusion (access is via rambling country lanes), the villages have a quietly sophisticated air, with a couple of smart deli-cafés and a plethora of well-preserved pubs.

Inland, the village of **St Germans**, with its 16th-century almshouses and 12th-century church (*see p110*), is the idyllic setting for the **Port Eliot Estate**, now open to the public for several months of the year (*see p47*). A walk along the River Tiddy from St Germans quay affords lovely glimpses upstream, through the

splendid arches of the railway viaduct.

From here, it is a fantastic walk south around the coast to the timeless drama of **Rame Head**, where there's a candlelit 11th-century church on top of the promontory, and stunning views over the sheer cliffs and white waters of Whitsand Bay. This enormous cliff-backed beach stretches for three miles at low tide; note that swimming can be dangerous due to hidden rip currents (there are lifeguards at Freathy, Tregonhawke, Sharrow and Tregantle). Tregantle Beach is often closed for use as a firing range by the MoD, which occupies a fort up on the cliff.

North from the peninsula stretches the long and winding Tamar Valley, the official division between Devon and Cornwall. It has been designated an Area of Outstanding Natural Beauty on account of its woodlands, quiet waters and rich wildlife, but also for its fascinating industrial heritage; in the late 19th century, mining activity made the river and its quays a hive of activity. The best place to take in the scenery and the history is **Cotehele House** (*see p47*) and, on the river below, the National Trust-preserved Cotehele Quay (free entrance), which is home to the *Shamrock*, a 57-foot ketch-rigged vessel constructed in 1899. The nearby village of Calstock can be easily spotted on account of its spectacular 120-foot-high viaduct, bridging the valley.

Where to eat & drink

The villages of Cawsand and Kingsand are well equipped with good pubs. Among them are the cosy **Devonport Inn** (The Cleave, Kingsand, 01752 822869, www.devonportinn.com), right on the water; locals' choice includes the **Rising Sun** (The Green, Kingsand, 01752 822840, closed Mon), and the aptly named **Halfway House**

Writers associated with Cornwall

Sir John Betjeman (1906-1984)

The former Poet Laureate's immense fondness for Cornwall stemmed from childhood holidays. The county he eventually chose to call home is vividly evoked in his poems, including 'Greenaway' and the lovely 'Cornish Cliffs' ('And in the shadowless, unclouded glare/Deep blue above us fades to whiteness where/A misty sea-line meets the wash of air'). Another poem, 'Trebetherick', remembers the town in which he lived and died. He is buried in the churchyard at St Enodoc's church. See p68.

WJ Burley (1914-2002)

William Burley was a prolific writer, penning some 800 books, but was best known for his crime fiction set in Cornwall, featuring the detective Charles Wycliffe. The books were made into a popular TV series, *Wycliffe*, filmed in the county and broadcast in the mid 1990s. Born in Falmouth, Burley spent most of his life in the village of Holywell, near Newquay. See p82.

Susan Cooper (born 1935)

Two of the books in Susan Cooper's *Dark is Rising* series – *Over Sea, Under Stone* (1965) and *Greenwitch* (1974) – are set in Cornwall, and make heavy use of Arthurian legend and local folklore. The highly acclaimed books for teenagers follow the Drew children's adventures as they are drawn into the struggle between the Light and Dark, during their holidays in the village of Trewissick – a made-up town closely based on Mevagissey, on the south coast, where Cooper used to holiday as a child. See p38.

Daphne du Maurier (1907-1989)

Born in London, du Maurier lived in Cornwall from the age of 20, and the county's landscapes were a huge influence on her work. The family holiday home was in Bodinnick, near Fowey. An annual literary festival is held in Fowey in the writer's honour. Du Maurier later moved to the then-derelict estate of nearby Menabilly; the secluded house was, most famously, the inspiration for Manderley, in *Rebecca*, and also featured in *My Cousin Rachel* and *The King's General*. See p25 and p27.

(Fore Street, 01752 822279, www. halfwayinnkingsand.co.uk), which stands on the old border between Devon and Cornwall. The village's smart deli and café, **The Old Bakery** (Garrett Street, 01752 656215, www. theoldbakery-cawsand.co.uk, closed winter), is worth a stop for cakes, bread, pastries and – on weekend evenings – bistro food.

The Canteen at Maker Heights

Millbrook, Torpoint, PL10 1LA (01752 659069, www.makerheights.org.uk). Open 9.30am-4pm Tue-Sun. Lunch served noon-3.30pm.

Maker Heights is an old Napoleonic-era barracks – high up and out of the way – that's been turned into a creative hub for the Rame Peninsula, full of bustling artists' studios. It also boasts a notable restaurant: Nick Platt's Canteen offers affordable rustic food that hearkens back to his old gig at the River Cottage (at rather more modest prices), plus the most spectacular Sunday lunch in the region. It's super informal: no reservations, no official website, and if you want to look at a sample menu best head to the photos of its chalkboard on its Insta feed.

Finnygook Inn

Crafthole, PL11 3BQ (01503 230338, www. finnygook.co.uk). Open 11am-11pm Tue-Sat; noon-10.30pm Sun. Food served noon-9pm Tue-Sun. Contact for room rates.

The reopening of this newly spruced-up 15th-century coaching inn, in the coastal village of Crafthole, has added a smart gastropub to the area's growing foodie portfolio. Spruced up with oak tables, shelves of books and chic bathrooms, the Finnygook nonetheless retains a homely, traditional atmosphere, with log fires, sofas, and stacks of newspapers. The bar serves ten wines by the glass and a frequently tweaked menu of classy pub food, such as gourmet fish and chips (local haddock deep-fried in Tamar real ale batter), steak burger with gruyère, and steak and Guinness pie – all served with stacks of local veg. There are half a dozen guest bedrooms upstairs. The quirky pub name can be traced back to the 18th century, when Silas Finny made himself unpopular by informing on local smugglers to the authorities. When the aforementioned crooks were released from prison, they sniffed Finny out and killed him – his 'gook' is rumoured to haunt the neighbourhood.

Rod & Line

Tideford Church Road, Tideford, PL12 5HW (01752 851323). Open noon-midnight daily. Food served noon-10.30pm daily.

A fine antidote to homogeneous pubs throughout the land, the Rod is a quirky hideaway – it's small, dark and friendly, and the low, beamed ceiling provides minimal head clearance. Pull up a church pew for a pint of Tribute ale and some of landlord Mike's legendary chilli crab claws from Looe, pheasant or game pie. Off-season, there's a popular late Sunday lunch at 5pm.

The View ♥

Treninnow Cliff Road, Millbrook, PL10 1JY (01752 822345, www.theview-restaurant.co.uk). Open Apr-Oct 11.30am-2pm, 7-9pm Wed-Sun.

If surfer-chef Matt Corner were in the business of chasing stars, rosettes and accolades, we get the impression he has more than enough talent to catch them. As it is though, he's more interested in serving superb local fish and seafood without extraneous frills. You might find such clean-cut delights as line-caught sea bass with crab risotto and lime, or watercress risotto with green-rinded Cornish goat's cheese, or panna cotta with roasted pear. The interior decor is starkly chic – pine chairs, white tablecloths and white walls hung with local contemporary art. And then, of course, there's the view: a soul-stirring panorama from high on the cliffs out into Whitsand Bay, across to Rame Head and out west as far as the Lizard on a clear day. Widescreen windows maximise the vista, and service is flawless. One of Cornwall's rising stars.

Patrick Gale (born 1962)

Probably the most acclaimed present-day writer associated with Cornwall, Gale has lived near Land's End since 1987. Cornish landscapes feature in his first novel – *The Aerodynamics of Pork* – and have made a progressively stronger presence in his works with time, featuring in *Rough Music*, *A Sweet Obscurity* and, in particular, his 2007 novel *Notes from an Exhibition*.

Winston Graham (1908-2003)

Graham is best known for his 'Poldark' saga – 12 novels set in 18th-century Cornwall, which he wrote over half a century, between 1945 and 2002. In the 1970s, *Poldark* became an extremely popular BBC TV series, with scenes filmed across the county and locals often hired as extras for the crowd scenes. Poldark returned to television with five more series between 2015 and 2019. The author himself was born in Manchester, but moved to Perranporth (see *p98*), on Cornwall's north coast, at the age of 17, and lived there for more than 30 years.

Rosamunde Pilcher (1924-2019)

Born in the village of Lelant, not far from St Ives, Pilcher was known for her romance novels, and started her career writing for Mills & Boon under the pen name Jane Fraser. Her most famous book – *The Shell Seekers* – was written later in her life (published in 1987) and depicts the relationship between the protagonist, Penelope Keeling, and her grown-up children, over several decades; it's set in both London and Cornwall, and has been adapted for the stage and television.

Arthur Quiller-Couch (1863-1944)

Quiller-Couch was born in Bodmin. His first novels – including *Dead Man's Rock*, a romance set in Cornwall – were published under the pen name 'Q' while the writer was studying at Oxford University. He later moved back to Cornwall, setting up home in Fowey. He edited the *Oxford Book of English Verse, 1250-1900*, and he also completed Robert Louis Stevenson's novel, *St Ives*. Quiller-Couch's final work – *Castle Dor* – was unfinished upon his death, but later completed by Daphne du Maurier.

Where to stay

The Rame Peninsula is delightfully undeveloped, which means accommodation tends to be small-scale and individual in style. But nowhere, perhaps, is quite so quirky as a stay in a dinky old train carriage, which is what's on offer at the **Old Luggage Van** at sleepy St Germans station (Nut Tree Hill, 01503 230783, www.railholiday.co.uk). The Finnygook Inn (*see p50*) in Crafthole has traditional-chic rooms available.

Blue Monkey
Garrett St, Cawsand, PL10 1PD (07813 070269, www.www.bluemonkeycornwall. com). Rates £799-£3,599 per week for 2-10 people.

Luxurious it may be, but this large self-catering seaside cottage is cheerily family friendly, and offers pretty much everything you need to have a fun time, from fizz on arrival to complimentary kayaks and paddleboards. The friendly owners will even sort you out with a bespoke concierge service, if that's the way you want to go. Sleeping up to ten, it's got the woodburner and barbecue needed to help those summer nights go with a bang, but the real outdoor appeal are the three sandy beaches within easy walk.

Rame Barton
Rame, PL10 1LG (01752 822789, www. ramebarton.co.uk). Rates B&B from £250. Self-catering £1,140 per week for 3-6 people.

Interior designer Karen Cardew and ceramicist husband Paul spent two years rejuvenating this magnificent 18th-century listed farmhouse on the Rame Peninsula, just shy of Rame Head

itself. The two self-catering apartments (within the house) are immaculately clean and comfortable, but it's the two B&B rooms that really catch the eye. Spacious, stylish and with glamorous touches (mirrored bedside tables, elegant heavy curtains and even a silver toilet lid), they are the ultimate style-conscious country retreat. Breakfast is served in the deep-red dining room. Budding potters can try their hand in Paul's studio next door, or just take a tour of his collection of eccentric teapots – as well as the NatWest pigs, which he designed some 25 years ago.

Westcroft ♥
Market Street, Kingsand, PL10 1NE (01752 823216, www.westcroftguesthouse. co.uk). Rates £120-£180 double incl breakfast.

With the word 'boutique' now in such free currency, its impact has been been lost in a sea of fancy fonts and scented candles. But at the Westcroft, an unpretentiously hip B&B housed in a waterfront Georgian coaching inn, the concept is passionately embraced. Warm hosts Sarah and Dylan McLees-Taylor seem to have an innate sense of what their guests might want and when: if you're travelling with a small child, a cot, blankets and a pile of toys appear as if by magic. Nor are there any time limits on breakfast; they will even leave a pot of tea and fresh croissants on the step as a first course before you surface. Of the three rooms, the top-floor Clocktower Suite is the most romantic, with a claw-foot bath for two, views of the stars from the French antique bed and the sound of the waves hitting the shore. But it is the treats sprinkled throughout that really set Westcroft apart: fishing nets for children, pillowcases sprinkled with lavender water and home-made cake. What's more, one of Britain's most exquisite peninsulas lies just outside the door.

Megagissey *see p38*

Padstow & the Atlantic Highway

Such has been its rise to fame as restaurant capital of the region, Padstow scarcely needs an introduction. True to its reputation, the culinary repertoire of this pretty fishing village is nothing if not impressive, with Rick Stein's original Seafood Restaurant now joined by an array of boutique bistros, wine bars and dining rooms more in keeping with the offerings of a prosperous city than a West Country fishing village. Suffice to say, if you like food, you can't go wrong in Padstow and Rock, where you'll find a handful of master-chefs, scrupulously sourced local produce, and more top-notch eateries than you can poke your knife and fork at.

Moving up the Atlantic Highway, more prosaically known as the A39, the shifting yellow sands and blazing blue of the Camel Estuary give way to decidedly more daunting scenery: jagged, black cliffs plunging deep into gale-ravaged seas, wind-pummelled moorland and steeply cut valley villages. Crowds and tourist tat notwithstanding, there is no better place from which to survey the rugged landscape than the ruined castle of Tintagel, cast out on a lonely island and perpetually bludgeoned by Atlantic storms. Even if some aspects of Tintagel seem ridiculous, the wild, rock-girt fortress itself can't fail to impress.

Following Thomas Hardy's 'wandering western sea' towards the Devon border, the Atlantic Highway threads all the way to Cornwall's north-eastern corner and the breezy seaside resort of Bude.

PADSTOW & AROUND

An unparalleled destination for gastronomy, estuary views and coastal charm, Padstow is the epitome of fishing-village-turned-chic. A warren of smart cobbled streets lead to the hubbub of the harbour, an animated mix of crabbers, netters, working boats, yachts and pleasure cruisers, with slate-hung, red brick and grey stone cottages trimming the edges, accommodating pasty shops, boutiques, chippies, pubs and increasing numbers of classy restaurants. The Tourist Information Centre by the quay (North Quay, 01841 533449, www.padstowlive.com, open daily) is a good starting point for exploration.

Evidence suggests that Padstow has been used as a port since the 16th century, though the decline of shipping here is down to the Doom Bar – shallow sandbanks at the mouth of the estuary on which many ships have foundered. But the fishing industry survives in Padstow, not least

Mother Ivey's Bay *see p57*

Padstow

thanks to a leap in interest in premium local produce in recent years, so you'll find plenty of activity in and around the busy working port.

While the Stein 'theme park' can become slightly infuriating (you have to look hard to avoid his stamp on everything from your T-shirt to your beer bottle), to his credit he was the first chef to showcase the calibre of Cornish produce to the foodie world. This in turn has given rise to a whole host of noteworthy restaurants, and Padstow is now considered to be the best place to eat out in Cornwall.

At the expense of more practical retail outlets for local residents, upmarket tourism has also brought an influx of boutiques and galleries. For contemporary pieces, have a browse in the **Padstow Gallery** (Parnell Court, 01841 532242, www.padstow gallery.co.uk) and the **Drang Gallery** (South Quay, 01841 533114, www. thedranggallery.com). Inevitably, there's no shortage of sailing and surf labels (Musto, White Stuff, Fat Face et al), but there are also more original finds to be had among the decor, craft and jewellery outlets. In the unlikely event that you will be cooking for yourself in Padstow, try the **Padstow Farm Shop** (Trethillick Farm, 01841 533060, www.padstowfarmshop. co.uk) on the outskirts of the town. One of the county's best farm outlets, it supplies many of Padstow's top restaurants.

One of the UK's most vibrant May Day festivals is **Padstow's 'Obby 'Oss**, which celebrates the rite of spring. Two 'Oss'es – monstrous effigies made out of hoop-work, tarpaulin and sprays of horsehair – are paraded through the streets to the accompaniment of song, accordions and drums. The pulsing rhythms go on until midnight, marking the continuation of a tradition going back around 900 years, and the resilience of the community.

Although Padstow's narrow, winding streets create a picture-postcard setting, they are ill-equipped to deal with peak-season traffic – so ditch the car and explore on foot or by bike (or boat). There are wonderful walks along the estuary and out to Stepper Point, or you can walk or cycle inland along the famous Camel Trail (*see p66*), a flat, traffic-free path leading inland to Wadebridge and on to Bodmin.

There is a regular foot ferry across the water to **Rock** (*see p68*) during daylight hours, and a water taxi (South Slip, 01208 862815) for those staying out late. And while Rock and Padstow out-smug each other across the Camel Estuary, the stolid market town of Wadebridge looks on to see fair play from the inland tip.

The Seven Bays

Padstow and the Camel Estuary have no shortage of scenic riches, but the real drama is to be found nearby on the Atlantic coast and its 'Seven Bays' – a string of impressive sandy beaches that lace the cliffs together all the way from Porthcothan to the entrance to the Camel Estuary. Just north of Bedruthan Steps (*see p83*), Porthcothan offers an eye-popping sequel to its neighbour, with cliffs, caves and blowholes. Other highlights include the skeletal remnants of a German war ship buried into the sands at Booby's Bay, the pristine white sands of **Mother Ivey's Bay**, and the breakers bulldozing into **Constantine** and **Treyarnon** – two more surfers' favourites that join at low tide to create a vast sandy expanse (swimming is not always safe on account of rip tides). A walk on to Trevose Head, edging out into the ocean, makes for spectacular views all around.

Places to visit

PADSTOW & AROUND

National Lobster Hatchery
South Quay, Padstow, PL28 8BL (01841 533877, www.nationallobsterhatchery.co.uk). Open Summer 10am-7.30pm daily. Winter 10am-4pm daily. Admission £4.95; £2.50-£4.50; £12.95 family.

This hatchery, a charitable enterprise, nurtures giant crabs and lobsters for release into the Cornish seas as a means to conserve stocks. You get to see baby lobsters up close, and learn about the crustaceans that end up in the Stein kitchens. Those so inclined can even adopt a baby lobster for £2.50, and watch on the website for news of when (and where) it was released into the wild.

BUDE & AROUND

Bude Castle Heritage Centre
The Castle, Bude, EX23 8LG (01288 357300, www.thecastlebude.co.uk). Open Easter-Oct 10am-5pm daily. Nov-Easter 10am-4pm daily. Admission £3.50; £2.50-£3 reductions; £10 family.

Victorian inventor Sir Goldsworthy Gurney

had this neo-Gothic castellated home built into the dunes in 1830. Now a state-owned heritage centre, Bude Castle houses a short but interesting exhibition on the history of Bude and its canal, as well as an art gallery showing temporary exhibitions. Exhibits include the grand railway clock that stood in Bude station before it was closed in 1966 (and subsequently destroyed), and a male figurehead salvaged from an Italian ship that foundered along this stretch of coast in 1900. Famous as the first man to make the long journey from London to Bath in a steam carriage, Gurney also revolutionised lighthouses by combining oxygen with revolving mirrors to intensify illumination and create a flashing beam. His genius is honoured by a stark illuminated spike, known as the Bude Light, in the grounds of his former home, which uses fibre optics to create a nightly zodiacal pageant.

TINTAGEL & BOSCASTLE

Museum of Witchcraft
The Harbour, Boscastle, PL35 0HD (01840 250111, www.museumofwitchcraft.com). Open Easter-Oct 10.30am-5.30pm Mon-Sat; 11.30am-5.30pm Sun. Admission£7; £5 reductions.

This spooktastic collection of witchy history has been giving children (and easily perturbed adults) the heebie-geebies for 50 years, with its weird and wonderful collection of spells, tableaux, pickled foetuses, charms, curses, paintings, woodcuts and satanism and shapeshifting paraphernalia. Assorted witches' equipment such as cauldrons and herbs and nasty devices used to persecute witches complete the collection.

Old Post Office
Fore Street, Tintagel, PL34 0DB (01840 770024, www.nationaltrust.org.uk/tintageloldpostoffice). Open Apr-Sept 10.30am-5.30pm daily. Oct-Mar 11am-4pm daily. Admission £3; £1.50 reductions; £7.50 family.

The National Trust looks after the Old Post Office, a restored Victorian post room set in a charming 600-year-old slate Cornish longhouse, surrounded by pretty cottage gardens.

Tintagel ♥

Tintagel, PL34 0HE (01840 770328, www. english-heritage.org.uk). Open Apr-Oct 10am-5pm daily. Nov-Mar 10am-4pm Sat, Sun. Admission £15.70; £9.40-£14.10 reductions; £40.80 family.

Like many of Cornwall's most beautiful places, the blackened remains of this ancient castle reward visitors who come out of season – a blustery day in December is the perfect time to experience its full power. The fact that it's a bit of a challenge to reach (there are 100 steps, a lot of uneven ground and a vertiginous bridge over the rocky valley to Tintagel Head to contend with) makes it all the more exciting. What's left of the 13th-century castle – steep stone steps, stout walls and a lofty space where the Great Hall once stood – contributes to the drama. Tintagel was thought to have been a trading settlement in the fifth century (pottery has been unearthed to back this up). Less empirically, the site is rumoured to be where the legend of King Arthur was born, resurrected by Victorian poet Alfred Lord Tennyson in his *Idylls of the King*. The potential for fantastic stories and family games of noble knights and holy grails are endless, and the views are unfailingly stirring.

Tintagel

Ten Cornish Artists

Works by many of the artists mentioned below are owned by Tate St Ives (*see p158*).

Elizabeth Forbes (1859-1912)

Canada-born Forbes (née Armstrong) came to London in the 1870s, moving to Cornwall in the 1880s, where she met her husband, fellow painter Stanhope Forbes. Their Newlyn School of Painting, set up at the turn of the 20th century, was a joint enterprise. Forbes, known for her paintings of local children, became one of the most established female artists of the time.

Stanhope Forbes (1857-1947)

Forbes was born in Dublin, but moved to Cornwall at the age of 27, where he lived until his death in 1947. He was a key member of the Newlyn School, which focused on Impressionist-style landscapes (particularly scenes depicting fishermen), natural light and figurative painting.

Terry Frost (1915-2003)

One of Britain's most prominent abstract artists, known for his distinctive use of circles, lines and colour in his painting. Frost attended Camberwell School of Art and subsequently St Ives School of Art. After working briefly as an assistant to Barbara Hepworth, he moved to Newlyn, his home for the remainder of his life; the Cornish landscape and the sea were an inspiration for much of his work.

Barbara Hepworth (1903-1975)

One of Britain's most prominent sculptors, Hepworth was also a key member of the St Ives School and the breakaway Crypt Group. Hepworth purchased the Trewyn Studio in St Ives in 1949, where she worked and lived – it's now the Barbara Hepworth Museum & Sculpture Garden (*see p158*). Hepworth was married to fellow artist Ben Nicholson (*see p61*) between 1938 and 1951; she died in a fire in her studio in 1975.

Patrick Heron (1920-1999)

Heron moved to west Cornwall in 1925. After training at London's Slade, he returned to Cornwall to draw, and subsequently became an assistant at the Bernard Leach Pottery in St Ives, where he met Ben Nicholson and Barbara Hepworth; he started to develop his own abstract style from his home at Zennor.

Port Isaac

Roger Hilton (1911-1975)
One of the pioneers of British abstract art, and a prominent member of the St Ives School, Hilton was born in London and studied at the Slade. He started to spend long periods in west Cornwall during the 1950s, moving there permanently in 1964. His work, unusually, became less abstract in his later years.

Peter Lanyon (1918-1964)
Born in St Ives, Lanyon was a painter, printmaker and sculptor known for his abstract paintings that clearly referenced Cornish landscapes, and for his constructions. He was a central member of the Crypt Group (a breakaway group of St Ives School artists), alongside Ben Nicholson and Barbara Hepworth, and subsequent founding member of the Penwith Society of Arts in the late 1940s. St Ives remained his home for much of his life.

Bernard Leach (1887-1979)
Known as the father of British studio pottery, Leach was born and brought up in Asia, and was greatly influenced by Far Eastern – particularly Japanese – approaches to pottery. In 1920, he set up the Leach Pottery School (still open today, partly as a museum; see p158) in St Ives, with Japanese potter Shoji Hamada. Together they promoted pottery that emphasised the fusion of Western and Eastern techniques and philosophies.

Ben Nicholson (1894-1982)
A pioneer of the Constructivist movement during the 1930s, and a key figure in British abstract art in the 1940s and '50s, Nicholson's paintings and prints are easily recognisable thanks to his distinctive geometric style. Many of his most famous works are lino cuts (often of domestic crockery), carvings and painted reliefs. He was inspired by the direct style of the paintings of Cornish fisherman Alfred Wallis.

Alfred Wallis (1855-1942)
One of Cornwall's most famous artists, known for his direct, 'naïve' style that was much celebrated by the St Ives group; Wallis, based first in Penzance and later in St Ives, was a fisherman for much of his life, taking up painting in his late 60s. Having limited funds (he lived in poverty), he used industrial paint and cardboard as a canvas.

Where to eat & drink

From its beginnings at the flagship Seafood Restaurant, 'Padstein' now sees the celebrity chef's signature on three restaurants, a fish and chip shop, a deli (South Quay, 01841 533466 ext 432, www.rickstein.com), coffee shop (Lanadwell Street, 01841 533901), gift shop (8 Middle Street, 01841 532221), accommodation (*see p65*) and a seafood school (*see p66*).

Although Stein turned heads towards the area's perfect marriage of top-quality produce and stunning scenery, he is by no means the only name in town with a strictly 'source local' manifesto and a smart dining room to boot. The best of a very good bunch are reviewed below, but you might also consider a hot steak pasty from **Chough's** by the quayside (The Strand, 01841 532835, www.cornishpasty.com, open daily).

In Wadebridge, coffee geeks should stop at **Relish** (Foundry Court, 01208 814214, www.relishcornwall.co.uk, closed Mon, Sun), whose barista Jack Hudspith won a top ten place in the UK Barista Championships; there is an excellent deli next door stocking a wide range of Cornish goodies.

Cornish Arms ♥
Churchtown, St Merryn, PL28 8ND (01841 520288, www.rickstein.com). Open 11.30am-11pm daily. Lunch served noon-3pm, dinner served 6-9.30pm daily.

When news broke that Stein had acquired the fine old village pub in St Merryn, it was hard not to envisage, with inescapable cynicism, a chic makeover, a gastrofied menu and prices pitched at global voyagers, not villagers. To his credit, Stein hasn't taken that route. The menu is made up of simple British pub fare (real beef burger, ploughman's, fresh tomato soup with tapenade, apple pie) prepared with care, and the decor is traditional and rustic, with old black-and-white photos on the wall, and bottles of ketchup and malt vinegar sitting prosaically on each wooden table.

London Inn
Lanadwell Street, Padstow, PL28 8AN (01841 532554, www.londoninnpadstow. co.uk). Open 11am-11pm Mon-Sat; noon-10pm Sun. Lunch served noon-2.30pm daily. Dinner served 6.30-9pm Mon-Sat.

Originally three fishermen's cottages cuddled into the inner streets behind the quay, this is a proper local boozer. It's a fine place to nurse a traditional Cornish ale – just don't expect a trendy wine list or plump sofas to sit on. What you will find, however, is plenty of local character, as well as lots of local characters.

Paul Ainsworth at No. 6 ♥
Middle Street, Padstow, PL28 8AP (01841 532093, www.paul-ainsworth.co.uk). Food served May-Sept noon-2pm, 6-10pm Tue-Sun. Oct-Apr noon-2pm, 7-10pm Tue-Sat.

Keeping Stein's Seafood Restaurant well and truly on its toes, Paul Ainsworth's

No. 6 holds Padstow's only Michelin star. Bedecked in a glamorous, contemporary style (nautical trimmings blessedly absent) with black and white checked floors, cool crockery and suited waiters, the restaurant is as well dressed as the food. Sweet chilli and spiced avocado accompany perfectly seared carpaccio of tuna, and Launceston lamb is made daringly complex courtesy of sweetbreads, liver and kidneys. Every dish is beautifully presented and bursting with innovative flavour. A sorbet palate cleanser, for example, comes with popping candy, and a dessert of caramelised banana is served with peanut butter ice-cream. For a more casual, more affordable outpost of the Ainsworth empire, try his family-orientated Caffè Rojano (9 Mill Square, 01841 532796).

Pescadou

Old Custom House, South Quay, Padstow, PL28 8BL (01841 532359, www. oldcustomhousepadstow.co.uk). Lunch served noon-2pm, dinner served 7-9pm daily.

As the name suggests, this is a place for fish-lovers. Mixing classic and contemporary influences in both design and cuisine, Pescadou tailors its menu around the best of what is caught on its doorstep (it has a prime harbourside position). And even if it's not plucked from the ocean outside, pickings such as the succulent Fowey river mussels won't be sourced from too far away. While the menu attempts to range beyond seafood, options such as steak-frites or risotto are never going to sound as exciting as a whole Padstow lobster or half-shell scallops with lemongrass and lime, fresh from the day boat.

Prawn on the Lawn

11 Duke St, PL28 8AB (01841 532223, www.prawnonthelawn.com). Open noon-10pm Tue-Sun.

Sister restaurant to the Islington establishment of the same name, Rick and Katie Toogood's laid-back restaurant-slash-fishmonger offers exquisitely fresh seafood in an ultra-informal setting. Crab, oysters and seafood platters are constant menu fixtures, but the rest is delightfully at the mercy of the day's catch, and can vary wildly. Note that due to coronavirus, the restaurant has decamped to a marquee on nearby Trerethern Farm until October 2021.

Rick Stein's Café

10 Middle Street, Padstow, PL28 8AP (01841 532700, www.rickstein.com). Breakfast served 8-11am, coffee & cake served 10.30am-noon, lunch served noon-3pm, dinner served 6.30-9.30pm daily.

One of the more relaxed and affordable venues under the Stein banner, this is the sort of place you can be just as happy slurping coffee behind a newspaper as dressed up for Sunday lunch. The fresh, nautical decor befits its location, with stripy cushions and watery paintings adorning wood-panelled walls, and there's a small courtyard for sunny afternoons. The seafood, even in its simplest form, is fantastic, with globally inspired favourites such as Thai fish cakes, grilled cod with spicy noodles or skewers of squid with cumin, coriander and lime. Breakfasts of

Cornish Arms

own-made granola compote with berries, Stein pastries and trademark *huevos rancheros* see this tiny space heaving in high season.

St Kew Inn
St Kew, PL30 3HB (01208 841259, www.stkewinn.co.uk). Open 11am-11pm Mon-Sat; noon-10.30pm Sun. Lunch served noon-2pm daily. Dinner served 6.30-9pm Mon-Sat; 6.30-8.30pm Sun.

The St Kew Inn's idyllic setting, in a village some four and a half miles from Wadebridge (think handsome church, soothing river, age-old cottages) conjures up scenes from a period drama, and the pub's beamed interior offers the sort of simple, trend-resistant comfort that makes you want to linger all night. Since the pub's former chef, the Michelin-starred Paul Ripley, departed last year, St Kew has become less renowned for its food, and has lost some of its impressive following, yet the place is often still buzzing with locals, part-time locals and tourists settling in for an evening of St Austell brewery ales served straight from the barrel. The simple menu features gastropub classics, such as sirloin steak, and beer-battered fish and chips, while more interesting dishes appear in the form of Porthilly mussels, and beetroot tagliatelle with dill and truffle oil.

St Petroc's Bistro
4 New Street, Padstow, PL28 8EA (01841 532700, www.rickstein.com). Lunch served noon-2pm, dinner served 6.30-10pm daily.

Set in the fifth-oldest building in Padstow, St Petroc's has blended its traditional rustic character with a contemporary Stein twist. A simple bistro menu bears all the hallmarks of the man himself, but his signature seafood theme is supplemented by a meat-heavy grill section and various vegetarian dishes. The menu changes daily according to what's in, what's left and what's been caught, and although it makes light reading it caters for all tastes – and comes with an affordable price tag. The ribeye steak with béarnaise sauce is cooked to perfection, and the sea bass

with roasted veg says everything about the superb quality of local fish that Rick Stein has been raving about for years.

Seafood Restaurant
Riverside, Padstow, PL28 8BY (01841 532700, www.rickstein.com). Lunch served noon-2pm, dinner served 6.30-10pm daily.

The jewel in the crown of the Stein empire, the flagship establishment is the place to book if you're out to impress and there's no limit to your budget. The seafood is beyond reproach, from simple Padstow lobster and oysters sourced from the Duchy Oyster Farm on the Helford River to innovative combinations such as sea bass with tomato, butter and vanilla vinaigrette, mackerel stuffed with ginger and chilli masala or salmon marinaded with passionfruit, lime and coriander. With a sleek reception desk, a stylish seafood bar in the centre of the room and opinion-dividing modern art on the walls, the Seafood Restaurant looks and feels like a destination restaurant – Cornwall's first, back in 1975, and still one of the best. Flaws are few, but will inevitably be judged heavily at these prices: whichever way you look at it, £9.95 is a lot to pay for a dessert.

Stein's Fish & Chips ❤
South Quay, Padstow, PL28 8BL (01841 532700, www.rickstein.com). Restaurant & Take-away Lunch served noon-2.30pm, dinner served 5-9pm daily.

The impressive choice of fish varieties on offer here blows your average fish and chip shop out of the water. The pebbled counters, shell-framed mirrors and clean interior create a comfortable beachy atmosphere – although it's all too easily packed out by the hordes of families clamouring to sample the Stein reputation. Ultimately, it's the food that matters, and the quality of the fish is impeccable. Expect generous portions of plump, juicy fillets encased in a perfect golden batter (or grilled if you prefer), served with steaming hot, crisp-shelled chips and a slice of fresh lemon – to eat in (in boxes) or take away. It's worth the wait.

Where to stay

There's no shortage of accommodation in Padstow, but as peak season sees the whole area bursting at the seams, book in advance.

Cornish Tipi Holidays♥

Tregeare, nr Pendoggett, PL30 3LW (01208 880781, www.cornishtipiholidays. co.uk). Rates £485-630 per week for 2-6 people in a tipi. Wild camping in meadow £40 per tent or camper per night for 1-6 people. £7.50 per child per night.

Amid the ferns, bluebells and gently nodding foxgloves of this wooded 16-acre site stand 28 canvas tipis, arranged in convivial clusters (the 'village fields') or in leafy clearings, for those seeking romantic seclusion. At the centre of the site is a long, crystal-clear lake, where campers can swim, fish or go boating. Campfires are allowed, and tipis are equipped with camp stoves, coolboxes, rugs, lanterns and kitchenware – though you'll need to bring your own camp beds, bedding, towels and torches. The coast is a few minutes' drive; Wadebridge, some ten miles away, is the nearest town.

Old Custom House

South Quay, Padstow, PL28 8BL (01841 532359, www.oldcustomhousepadstow. co.uk). Rates £105-£185 double incl breakfast.

Standing right on the quayside, the Old Custom House is a listed building that has been refurbished to create an intimate contemporary hotel. Most of the rooms boast harbour views, so you can wake up to the early morning light flooding the estuary. The superior rooms are elegant and spacious, emphasising the seaside location with sand-coloured furniture and framed drawings of shells. The only downside to being smack-bang in the middle of town is being perched right above the pub.

Padstow Townhouse

16-18 High Street, Padstow, PL28 8BB (01841 532093, www.paul-ainsworth. co.uk). Rates £245-£285 double incl breakfast.

Behind the door of an elegant cottage at the top of the town, Paul Ainsworth's first venture into accomodation is set back from the bustle of Padstow's harbourfront. Formerly the eight-room Tregea Hotel, the six-suite Townhouse boasts bigger and plusher rooms, lavishly decked out and given names like Toffee Apple and Bon Bon. This being Ainsworth, the food is a major feature: all sorts of indulgent snacks and drinks are left out in The Kitchen Pantry for guests to help themselves to and make a note of via an honesty system. There's also parking, which is rare in Padstow.

Prospect House

4 New Street, Padstow, PL28 8EA (01841 532700, www.rickstein.com). Rates £220-£299 double incl breakfast.

The latest four guest rooms in the Stein empire are also the most private – hidden away behind St Petroc's Hotel & Bistro, but accessed via an independent entrance (guests are given their own key). The style is slick and contemporary, with subdued, natural shades, black and white seascapes on the walls and, in the best rooms, deluge showers, glass-encased gas fires and huge baths. A superb breakfast is served a few metres up the road at St Petroc's.

St Edmund's House♥

St Edmunds Lane, Padstow, PL28 8BY (01841 532700, www.rickstein.com). Rates £386 double incl breakfast.

There are some stylish rooms above the Seafood Restaurant and at St Petroc's, but the best accommodation in the Stein stable is at St Edmund's House. Think a Hamptons-style beach house, with six minimalist yet luxurious rooms overlooking private gardens and the Camel Estuary. Each room bears the name of a local bay, etched into its driftwood door sign, plus four-poster beds, en-suite marble bathrooms, oak flooring and an air of seaside luxury; ground-floor rooms also have a private deck. Once you've sunk into the bath with the twinkling estuary in view or reclined by the bay windows, you won't want to leave the comfort of your self-contained retreat – but you're forced out for breakfast, which is served in the Seafood Restaurant (*see p64*).

Things to do

PADSTOW & AROUND

Camel Trail 💙
(01872 327310, www.sustrans.org.uk).
Cornwall's best-known cycle trail follows
a disused railway line between Padstow,
Wadebridge, Bodmin and Poley's Bridge,
which was once used to transport slate and
sand. The entire trail is flat and manageable
– and therefore ideal for families – but the
most popular and scenic portion hugs the
estuary between Padstow and Wadebridge
for five miles. You can hire bikes from
Bridge Bike Hire in Wadebridge (01208
813050, www.bridgebikehire.co.uk), whose
range includes child and adult trailer bikes,
tandems and bikes for special needs, or
at Padstow Cycle Hire (South Quay, 01841
533533, www.padstowcyclehire.com). In
2006, two extensions to the Camel Trail
were completed, one up into Bodmin and
the other towards Bodmin Moor. See p39.

Cornwall's Crealy Great Adventure Park
*Trelow Farm, Tredinnick, PL27 7RA (01841
541286, www.crealy.co.uk). Open varies;
check their website. Admission £18-£20.*
Theme park-lovers will do well at Crealy;
once you've invested in a family ticket, you
can come back as often as you like for the
next week. Children love it, and adults are
rather beguiled by the animal attractions,
which include noble shire horses, sucky-
mouthed koi carp that feed from your hand,
bunnies, calves, piglets, lambs, guinea pigs,
ferrets and bumptious goats. The rides are
especially good for tinies, and there's a
big sandpit, helter skelter and adventure
playground, as well as mini diggers to ride
and two indoor playzones. A little safari
train takes you though the 100 acre-slice
of woodland and meadows in which Crealy
sprawls. Check out the glorious sunflower
maze. Take your own picnic rather than
shelling out for the café offerings.

Harlyn Surf School
*23 Grenville Road, Padstow, PL28 8EX
(01841 533076, www.harlynsurfschool.
co.uk). Open Apr-Oct; times vary, phone for
details. Lessons from £45.*
Small student to instructor ratios are
promised at Harlyn Surf School, whose
dizzying array of courses ranges from
intensive learn to surf weekends to
summer surf camps for kids and teenagers.
Instruction in the art of paddleboarding –
easier to master than surfing, and involving
a reassuringly wide board – is also offered.

Padstow Boat Trips
www.padstowboattrips.com.
Zoom off on a high-speed boat trip (Oct-
Easter), or experience the gentler thrill of a
fishing trip or cruise from Padstow harbour.
Prices vary: see the website for details of
the various operators, or visit Padstow's
Tourist Information Centre (01841
533449).

Rick Stein Cookery School
*Riverside, Padstow, PL28 8BY (01841
532700, www.rickstein.com). Dates vary,
check website for details. Lessons from £195
per day.*
Stein's esteemed Cookery School offers
one-, two- or four-day courses in a wide
range of international cuisines (including
Japanese sashimi and sushi, Thai fish and
French fish). Students get to work with
some of the freshest seafood around, in
a combination of hands-on sessions, chef
demonstrations and, most importantly,
tasting sessions. All in all, something of a
dream sequence for foodies.

ROCK, POLZEATH & PORT ISAAC

Camel School of Seamanship
*The Pontoon, Rock, PL27 6LD (01208
862881, www.camelsailing.co.uk). Open
Summer 10am-5pm daily. Winter by
arrangement only. Courses from £210 for
two days.*
This family business offers sailing taster
sessions and longer courses on the Camel
Estuary, along with power-boat instruction.
More experienced sailors can also hire
Wayfarer dinghies.

Camel Ski School
*The Pontoon, Rock, PL27 6LQ (01208
862727, www.camelskischool.com). Open
Easter-Oct 9am-dusk daily. Courses from £15
per person.*
For a bit more welly on the water, the
Camel Ski School offers waterskiing and

wakeboarding tuition. It also owns a floating café – the Island – which you can drop into via you own boat, or pay £10 to be picked up and dropped from anywhere in Padstow or Rock, grabbing a cup of floating Joe on the way.

Era Adventures
Valley Caravan Park, Polzeath, PL27 6SS (01208 862963, www.era-adventures. co.uk). Open times vary, check website for details. Activities prices vary; check website for details.

Daredevil activities offered by this Polzeath-based adventure company include surfing (and surf safaris), mountain biking, kite surfing, sea kayaking, rock climbing and power-boating.

St Enodoc Golf Club
Rock, PL27 6LD (01208 863216, www. st-enodoc.co.uk). Open 8am-dusk daily. Green fees £17.50-£47.50. Club hire £25.

St Enodoc Golf Club in Rock incorporates two beautifully sited courses on the edge of the estuary, one of which allows unrestricted access for visiting players. Also enjoying a spectacular position over Constantine Bay is Trevose Golf Club (01841 520208, www.trevose-gc.co.uk), which has extensive country club facilities.

Surf's Up!
21 Trenant Close, Polzeath, PL27 6SW (01208 862003, www.surfsupsurfschool. com). Open Jan, Mar-Dec 10am-dusk daily. Lessons from £35.

This friendly surf school offers lessons and coaching for all levels, from nervous novices to accomplished surfers looking to polish their technique.

BUDE & AROUND

Big Blue Surf School
Summerleaze Beach, Bude, EX23 8HN (01288 331764, www.bigbluesurfschool. co.uk). Open phone for details. Lessons from £30.

Taking full advantage of Bude's varied beaches, this well-established surf school

operates at Middle Beach and Crooklets, as well as Summerleaze. Half-day introductions are good value at £25 – and the more sessions you book in for, the lower prices drop.

Bude Sea Pool
Summerleaze Beach (01208 262822, www. cornwall.gov.uk). Open May-Sept 10am-6pm daily.

Not as elaborate as the art deco Jubilee Pool in Penzance, Bude's sea pool was built into the rocks on Summerleaze Beach during the lido boom of the 1930s – and is filled and emptied twice a day by the tides. There's a lifeguard in high season. Terraces for sunbathing and a sloping bottom make for a comfortable bathing experience, but the occasional encounter with a crop of slimy seaweed – not to mention the all-natural temperature – lend it the invigorating feel of a wild swim.

Bude Surfing Experience
Adventure International, Belle Vue, EX23 8JP (07779 117746, www.budesurfingexperience. co.uk). Lessons Easter-Sept 10am & 2pm daily. Oct-Easter by arrangement. Lessons from £29. No credit cards.

Expert tuition for beginners, groups and experienced surfers, with hot showers and indoor changing rooms.

Tamar Lakes
Near Bude, EX23 9SB (01288 321712, www. sw lakestrust.org.uk). Open 24hrs daily. Watersports Centre & Café Apr-Oct times vary, phone for details. Admission free.

Straddling the border with Devon are the reservoirs and campsite at Tamar Lakes. The lower lake is a nature reserve, with a small car park and pedestrian access along the dam, connecting with the towpath beside the former Bude Canal. The larger upper lake has a car park and visitor centre with a café and offers watersports facilities, with the chance to try sailing, windsurfing and kayaking. Walkers can follow a path right round the lake, and coarse fishing permits are sold at the visitor centre.

Treverbyn House

Station Road, Padstow, PL28 8DA (01841 532855, www.treverbynhouse.com). Rates £120 no breakfast (2021 season only). No credit cards.

Occupying a grand Edwardian house, Treverbyn is an elegant B&B with coveted views over the estuary. For a romantic weekend, hide out in the stylish decadence of the Turret Room, or choose a room with a cosy open fire for a winter retreat. Traditional furnishings complement period features, but the rooms are bright, airy and comfortable. Usually a delicious breakfast with organic own-made preserves is served in your room. However, due to coronavirus restrictions no breakfasts are being offered in 2021.

ROCK, POLZEATH & PORT ISAAC

Rock to Polzeath

Facing Padstow across the river, and easily accessed by ferry, is the tiny village of Rock. It's actually very sandy, but takes its name from the quarry that used to provide the rocky ballast for sailing ships emptied of cargo across the river. Increasingly popular with wealthy folk from the city since it became associated with royalty (William and Harry came here for watersports, and hundreds of public school pupils followed suit), Rock is reputed to be the home of more millionaires than anywhere else in Cornwall, and has to endure the label 'Kensington-on-Sea' – which irritates the locals no end.

It is lovely, however – especially out of season, when the beach that stretches along the side of the Camel all the way around to **Daymer Bay** ★ at low tide is empty of all but dog walkers, hardy windsurfers and lots of pre-schoolers, unrestricted by term dates and enchanted by the rock pools. You can get to Rock's beaches via a scenic coastal walk or across the 18-hole golf course at St Enodoc,

named after the diminutive church with a crooked steeple nestling prettily in the valley. **St Enodoc Church** (*see p110*) is probably best known through its association with poet John Betjeman, who is buried in the graveyard alongside sailors and fishermen who lost their lives on the infamous Doom Bar at the entrance to the Camel Estuary.

The estuary is superb for watersports, and Rock has several clubs (*see p66*). The nearby holiday village of **Polzeath**, overlooking Padstow Bay, is a good place for novice surfers and bodyboarders, as the waves are gentle and the sand is fine. A beautiful, two-mile walk around the edge of the bay from Rock, Polzeath offers an attractive – and considerably more down-to-earth – cluster of cafés, surf shops and restaurants, and a large sandy beach. There's a sprinkling of surf schools (*see p67*); for equipment hire, head to **Anne's Cottage Surf Shop** (Polzeath Beach, 01208 863317, www. annscottage.com). From Polzeath, it's a fantastic walk to the remnants of an Iron Age castle at **Rumps Point**.

Port Isaac

Port Isaac may not attract the same hordes of beach-bound holidaymakers as Rock and Polzeath, but it does suffer from an infestation of second-homers. In this pint-sized fishing village, where white slate-hung cottages cling to a steep incline above a 700-year-old harbour, it seems every other home belongs to someone distinctly un-Cornish. Explore the little alleyways between the cottages (look for the one called Squeeze-ee-belly Alley), have a pint overlooking the harbour at the snug Golden Lion pub (*see p70*), and banish all thoughts of estate agents.

There's a sprinkling of one-off shops and galleries, including **Dennis**

Port Gaverne

Knight Fish Merchant in Port Isaac (1 Fore Street, 01208 880498, closed Sun), with an excellent range of fresh fish.

Being part of a working harbour, albeit a very quaint one, the beach at Port Isaac isn't your best bet for a traditional day out at the beach. Adjacent **Port Gaverne** has a sheltered pebbly beach that's better for swimming, but for sand and space, head for Polzeath.

Where to eat & drink

An affluent tourist trade in these parts supports a variety of excellent restaurants – most notably those belonging to Nathan Outlaw, the Fish Kitchen and New Road. Since he relocated from Fowey, Outlaw has built on his reputation as the leading light of Cornwall's restaurant scene: both of his restaurants have a Michelin star apiece (and his old, eponymous gaffe – shuttered due to coronavirus – boasted two).

In addition to the restaurants, pubs and cafés below, the following pubs and cafés make for low-key stops with views: the **Rock Inn** (Rock Road, Rock, 01208 863498), a modern pub-restaurant and café with huge windows and balcony tables overlooking the estuary; the neat **Blue Tomato café & takeaway** (01208 863841) a few doors down, with a small veranda affording views of the estuary; and the **Waterfront** (Beach Road, 01208 869655, www.waterfrontpolzeath.co.uk, closed winter), at Polzeath, with a large deck overlooking the beach.

The Dining Room Rock

Pavilion Building, Rock Road, Rock, PL27 6JS (01208 862622, www.thediningroomrock.co.uk). Dinner served 7-9pm Wed-Sun.

Fred Weedles' intimate, well-regarded Rock restaurant keeps choices simple with its fixed-price, resolutely small modern British menu, on which almost every ingredient is locally sourced and prepared on site. However, changes to the menu are frequent and experimentation can run high: how about a Cornish gouda starter with set custard and baby beetroot? Fred's wife Donna runs the relaxed 30-cover restaurant, which caters to all over ten.

Golden Lion

Fore Street, Port Isaac, PL29 3RB (01208 880336, www.thegoldenlioncornwall. co.uk). Open 11am-11pm Mon-Sat; noon-10.30pm Sun. Lunch served noon-2.30pm, dinner served 6.30-9.30pm daily.

This delightful old village pub overlooks the harbour – and played a starring role in the ITV series *Doc Martin*. It feels comfortingly aged and rickety, with a sloping floor and pictures of ancient mariners and RNLI heroes on the walls. Many of the dishes on the pub food menu feature Port Isaac seafood, and the fish and chips are excellent – an enormous piece of freshly battered haddock, fried to perfection. Crab sandwich and pint of St Austell HSD in hand, make your way to the sweet spot: the small balcony directly overlooking the harbour and beach.

Outlaw's Fish Kitchen

1 Middle St, Port Isaac, PL29 3RH (01208 880237, www.outlaws.co.uk). Lunch served noon-3pm Tue-Sat; dinner served 6pm-9pm Tue-Sat.

Formerly the chilled out, single Michelin star yin to Restaurant Nathan Outlaw's two-Michelin star, fine-dining yang, the cosy Fish Kitchen now probably stands as his marginally fancier restaurant next to the recently opened New Road. Set in a small converted Port Isaac cottage, the picturesque Fish Kitchen – which has just eight tables – is relatively informal, offering a fixed-price £80 seafood menu that changes daily with the catch. Needless to say, it's all absolutely delicious.

Outlaw's New Road

6 New Rd, Port Isaac PL29 3SB (01208 880896, www.outlaws.co.uk). Lunch served noon-3pm Tue-Sat; dinner served 6pm-9pm Tue-Sat.

Restaurant Nathan Outlaw was one of the British culinary scene's highest-profile coronavirus casualties: Outlaw said he could no longer make Cornwall's only two-Michelin star restaurant economically viable under social-distancing measures. It's not a disaster though: he swiftly launched a successor restaurant, New

Road (so called because it's on... New Road) and stated in interviews that he had never really been comfortable with fine dining and was glad to be rid of it. The need to turn the five tables quickly (two sittings at lunch and at dinner) means there's no tasting menu à la Restaurant Nathan Outlaw, but the fixed-price £80 seafood menu is naturally superb, and enough to effortlessly bag New Road a Michelin star in its first year of operation.

Paul Ainsworth's The Mariners

Slipway, Rock, PL27 6LD (01208 863679, www.paul-ainsworth.co.uk). Open 9am-10pm daily. Breakfast served 9am-noon Mon-Sat; pub menu served noon-9.30pm Mon-Sat and 6pm-9.30pm Sun; lunch served noon-5pm Sun.

Paul Ainsworth added this beloved Rock gastropub to his empire in 2019. If you want to mix with the sailing crowd, there's still nowhere better to catch them, although there's a more down-to-earth and family-friendly vibe since Ainsworth took over – there's even a kids' menu! If you're not here to talk boating – or tune into the Kensington-on-Sea scene – you can focus on the stunning views over the water to Padstow, or cosy up by the fire in the bar on a winter's evening. There's laid-back pub food, cream teas on the terrace, an almighty Sunday lunch and thoughtful veggie and vegan menus.

Trevathan Farm

St Endellion, PL29 3TT (01208 880164, www.trevathanfarm.com). Open Mon-Sun 9am-11am and noon-3pm.

A working farm with 11 holiday cottages to let, Trevathan also has a shop with locally produced food and wine, a pick-your-own soft fruit business, plus this jolly tearoom and restaurant. Perched on the hillside outside St Endellion village, the tearoom and conservatory have splendid views over the valley to St Austell. On Sundays it's worth booking in for the roast Trevathan-reared lamb or beef with home-grown vegetables, but during the week you're safe enough just turning up for the daily specials menu of salads, lasagne, fish pie or filled paninis. These may well star the legendary Cornish yarg cheese (also

St Moritz

from May to September and with wooden steamer chairs dotted around it, is a delight. Baths are big, showers torrent forth, handbasins are double-sized and fluffy bathrobes and decent toiletries are provided. Superstar chef Nathan Outlaw has recently moved on from the restaurant, but his replacement Guy Owen's new restaurant Karrek is worth a look with its £85-a-head Cornish tasting menu. Outside, the terrace looks over the gardens and pool to the Camel Estuary and a little gate in the garden sets you on the footpath for the golf course, the beach, dunes and St Enodoc church, evading the ghastly road down to the beach – it's crammed with 4X4s and has little or no pavement.

St Moritz

Trebetherick, PL27 6SD (01208 862242, www.stmoritzhotel.co.uk). Rates £160-£400 double incl breakfast; apartments £745-£1,900 (6-8 guests).

sold in the shop), with its nettle covering. Breakfasts, own-made cakes and cream teas are also on the agenda. The biggest attraction for children is the play area with zip slide, mini diggers and tractors to play on, and a pets corner with rabbits, angora goats, wallabies, guinea pigs, poultry and, in spring, lambs.

When it arrived on the scene in 2007, St Moritz was the first new, purpose-built luxury hotel to be built in Cornwall in over 30 years – a gleaming white, art deco-accented complex, bringing with it up-to-speed decor and facilities. A palpably ambitious affair, St Moritz matches its chic looks and ocean-facing views with plenty of substance: exceedingly comfortable

Where to stay

In Port Isaac, the Slipway Hotel (The Harbour Front, 01208 880264, www. portisaachotel.com), above the bar-restaurant of the same name, has an unbeatable location next to the beach; its ten rooms are chintz-free and comfortable.

St Enodoc Hotel

Rock, PL27 6LA (01208 863394, www. enodoc-hotel. co.uk). Rates £170-£360 double incl breakfast.

This family-friendly hotel is a bastion of taste and decorum, without being frosty. From the airy reception and adjoining lounge with slate floors and original art, you climb up stairs and landings carpeted in candy stripes to equally bright rooms. The grounds are pleasantly landscaped and the sheltered outdoor pool, heated

St Enodoc Hotel

beds, switched-on staff, and a superb leisure area equipped with pool, jacuzzi, hammam, steam and a Cowshed spa. Families take note: St Moritz is proactively child-friendly, with a kids' play room (Wii and Xbox present and correct), a baby pool and basics such as cots and high chairs at the ready. St Moritz mightn't be the place to live out any nostalgic dreams of simple fishermen's cottages and log fires, but there's plenty of characterful old Cornwall within easy striking distance, not to mention Rock and Padstow close by.

BUDE & AROUND

Less standoffish than Padstow, and considerably more innocent than Newquay, Bude is a gusty, open-planned resort town high up in the north-east of the county. While developing its prospects as a lively seaside resort with a **jazz festival** (01288 356360, www.visitbude.info) – sadly not taking place in 2021, but it should return for 2022 – a long-standing surf scene and a good family beach, this is a town that still values its industrial past, having recently ploughed over £5.5 million into a major regeneration of the **Bude Canal**.

An early 19th-century construction built to carry the calcium-rich sand of the coast to the infertile uplands of Exmoor, the canal was part of a grand plan to link with the upper Tamar, thus joining the Bristol and English Channels. But the railway arrived long before that ambition could be realised, and the canal rapidly declined (as, eventually, did the railway, with the Bude branch line closed by the 1960s). The canal is now an attractive asset, with rich birdlife and wildlife, and towpaths for walking and cycling, and pedalos and rowing boats for hire; the new **Tourist Information Centre** (The Crescent, 01288 354240, www. visitbude.info) has more details and an exhibition on the canal's history.

Most of all, though, visitors come for the expansive beaches in the vicinity, where Atlantic breaks create a splendid swathe of surf. The most central of Bude's beaches is the wide, sandy **Summerleaze**, with its own seawater swimming pool (*see p67*) and a saddlebacked breakwater. Just to the north, **Crooklets** is the site of numerous surfing and lifesaving competitions, while **Sandy Mouth**, beyond, lives up to its name with a sweep of sand and rock pools. Offshore reefs create some good surf at the narrow sandy cove of **Duckpool**, a little further on. To the south is the mightily impressive span of **Widemouth Bay**, whose golden sands and reliable waves attract hordes of beachbums.

Morwenstow

Ducking out of the bullying Atlantic gales, between Bude to the south and Hartland Point to the north, Morwenstow fits tidily into a small wooded combe close to the Devon border. The tiny hamlet is most famous for its connection to the eccentric, opium-smoking Victorian vicar Reverend Stephen Hawker, who served at the parish chuch (*see p111*) and is credited with the introduction of the Harvest Festival in English churches. Hawker's presence looms in the stepped mock-Tudor gables and Gothic windows of the Morwenstow Vicarage, where each chimneypot mimics the spire of a church. The Grade I-listed church itself, set against the ocean backdrop, is a memorable sight.

Where to eat & drink

As you move up the coast away from the gastro epicentre of Padstow, the number of notable restaurants thins out, giving way to centuries-old inns and cosy tearooms, ideal for breaks from the scouring Atlantic winds.

Among the most attractive pubs in

Bude Canal and Beach

the area is the **Bush Inn** (01288 331242, www.thebushinnmorwenstow. com) in Morwenstow, a rugged 13th-century pub just back from the coastal footpath. Once the smugglers' boozer of choice, the inn is thought to have provided the inspiration for Daphne du Maurier's *Jamaica Inn* – and the snug, pared-down old bar is instantly evocative of past times. The Bush also has three comfortable country-styled bedrooms, with views, for B&B.

2 Belle Vue Avenue

2 Belle Vue Avenue, Bude, EX23 8BS (01288 489376, www.2-belle-vue-avenue. business.site). Open 6pm-11pm Wed-Sat.

You don't go to Bude for the ultra-fancy food of some of its near neighbours, but this discreet little gem of a bistro is a nice alternative to the surfer vibes found in the town's higher profile eateries. 2 Belle Vue Avenue offers sun-soaked Mediterranean cuisine, expertly done, but has also done a mean line in takeaway sandwiches during the coronavirus lockdown – the Philly cheesesteak is improbably terrific – that it would be nice to think will carry on after.

Bay View Inn

Widemouth Bay, Bude, EX23 0AW (01288 361273, www.bayviewinn.co.uk). Open 9am-11.30pm daily. Summer Breakfast served 9-10am, food served noon-9pm daily. Winter Breakfast served 9-10am daily. Lunch served noon-2.30pm, dinner served 5.30-9pm Mon-Fri. Food served noon-9pm Sat, Sun.

A pub with light-hearted, surfy aesthetics, the Bay View Inn is set on the coastal road, a few miles from Bude. It's worth a stop for good, crowd-pleasing food (sticky toffee

Five Cornish ales

Betty Stogs

Truro-based Skinner's makes this bestselling 4% pale amber bitter, which has won Champion Best Bitter and Champion Beer of Britain. To celebrate the accolade, the brewery redesigned the label to feature busty Betty with the Union Jack.

Tasting notes Mid-strength golden bitter, with fruity notes and hoppy overtones.

Chalky's Bite

Rick Stein challenged Sharp's Brewery in Rock to make a beer with individuality to 'stand alongside the Belgian greats'. The result – named after Stein's late canine companion – is a 6.8% beer of immense character, with a refreshing hint of wild Cornish fennel and higher than average levels of (natural) carbonation, making it a great accompaniment to seafood and fish. It is served in Stein's numerous enterprises in Padstow, among other outlets.

Tasting notes A distinctive, triple-fermented golden beer, perfect as an aperitif or with seafood.

pudding, Cornish fillet steak and chips, fish pie) and exhilarating views across the panorama of Widemouth Bay. Sit on the wide decking for maximum effect. There are several rooms for B&B (£105-£150 double incl breakfast) upstairs.

Life's a Beach

Summerleaze Beach, Bude, EX23 8HN (01288 355222, www.lifesabeach.info). Open Summer 10.30am-4.30pm, 7-11pm Mon-Sat; 11am-4pm Sun. Winter 7-11pm Thur, Fri; 11am-4pm, 7-11pm Sat; 11am-4pm Sun. Lunch served Summer 10.30am-3.30pm Mon-Sat; 11am-4pm Sun. Winter 10.30am-3.30pm Sat; 11am-4pm Sun. Dinner served Summer 7-8.45pm Mon-Sat. Winter 7-8.45pm Thur-Sat.

Every crowd-pleasing Cornish beach worth its salt has a cool café-restaurant, and Bude's town beach, Summerleaze, is no exception. Overlooking the crests rolling in off the Atlantic from its clifftop seat, Life's a Beach is a multi-purpose chill-out zone for hungry families, surfers

and the salty-haired of all ages by day, serving ice-creams, lattes and laid-back lunches (burgers, baguettes, bruschettas). Come the evening, the prices, cuisine and atmosphere are all more bistro than beach café – and local seafood dominates proceedings.

Rectory Tea Rooms

Rectory Farm, Crosstown, Morwenstow, EX23 9SR (01288 331251, www.rectory-tearooms.co.uk). Open phone for details.

Opposite Morwenstow Church, the Rectory Tea Rooms has been serving up cream teas for some 60 years – during which time the art of the afternoon tea has been lovingly perfected. The house blend of loose leaf tea is Smuggers' Choice, and the plump scones and jams are own-made. There is a lovely garden area, and the interior is steeped in history – the house dates back to the 13th century, and the beams, flagstone floors and fireplaces are original. There is also a window serving ice-creams and soft drinks in season, and the tea rooms recently introduced Sunday roasts to the menu.

Where to stay

Beyond the Camel Estuary, classy hotels become more scarce, with self-catering cottages and B&Bs dominating. In addition to the accommodation reviewed below, try the **Edgcumbe in Bude** (19 Summerleaze Cres, 01288 353846, www.edgcumbe-hotel.co.uk). Attached to The Deck restaurant, it offers Nordic-inspired rooms and sea views at modest prices. **Bangors Organic** (Bangors House, Poundstock, Bude, 01288 361297, www. bangorsorganic.co.uk), one of only a handful of B&Bs certified organic by the Soil Association, has a number of spacious, tastefully rustic rooms, and serves its own organic produce at breakfast and in the restaurant.

Beach Hut

Nr Widemouth Bay (01637 881942, www. uniquehomestays.com). Rates £1,495-£3,650 per week for 2 people.

Beach huts don't get much more desirable than this one, managed by the eminently luxurious Unique Homestays brand. The wooden Beach Hut in question sits in splendid isolation on the fringes of a remote north coast beach. The look, both inside and out, is stripped-down seaside chic, with white wood-panel walls, natural wood floors and cream-painted furniture. However, the real excitement is right outside your door – the sea, stars, cliffs and solitary silence. Sleeps two.

Beach Modern

Various locations around Bude (01288 275006, www.beachmodern.com). Rates see website for details.

A total of four luxury self-catering properties come under the slick Beach Modern umbrella, all within easy reach of Bude's beaches. The biggest (no.28) sleeps up to 20 people, and all are stylishly minimalist, with lashings of white.

Elements Hotel & Bistro

Marine Drive, Bude, EX23 0LZ (01288 352386, www.elements-life.co.uk). Rates £89-£160 double incl breakfast.

Bude's only boutique hotel sits high on the cliffs between Bude and Widemouth Bay. Despite clean, contemporary styling in the 11 rooms, there is an easygoing, surfy feel to the place, with epic views of the jagged coastline from the decking area, a heated drying room for beachware and wetsuits, and even storage space for surfboards. You can book yourself a surf package or borrow the hotel's foam boards. The bistro is a bright, competent affair, with the daily-changing menu taking inspiration from the day boats.

The Deck

19 Summerleaze Cres, Bude EX23 8HJ (01288 353846, www.thedeckbude.co.uk). Open 4-8.30pm Tue-Sat. Closed Jan.

With its roaring barbecue, surfer clientele and, you know, deck, this popular Bude spot offers plenty of hearty dude food. There's burgers, steaks, and its signature hanging skewers: enormous, ingredient packed sticks of barbecued goodness, running the gamut from seafood, to meat feast, to the all-important surf and turf. It's not ultra-sophisticated but it's fresh and tasty and prepared with love, and should plug even the most ravenous post-surf appetite.

TINTAGEL & BOSCASTLE

It's best to visit Tintagel on a turbulent day. Not only will you see vast blooms of spray coming off the beach, but the straggling village blends in with its bleak setting. Surrounded by moorland and crashing seas, its dark slate cottages look both menacing and mystical. But most visitors to Tintagel come to see its spectacular ruined castle (*see p58*), the mythical

Doom Bar

Sharps' legendary bitter is named after the notoriously dangerous sandbank of the Camel Estuary. It's an award-winning 4.3% ale, widely drunk in Cornwall for its warm, distinctive flavours and smooth consistency.
Tasting notes Delicious hints of spice and all things nice, but easy-going enough to be a session beer.

Spingo

Crafted on a small scale by the Blue Anchor (*see p126*) in Helston, thought to be the UK's oldest brew-pub, Spingo is a strong, dark ale. It comes in four incarnations: IPA, Middle, Bragget and, the strongest, Special (6.5%) – we recommend the copper-coloured Middle. Other than at the Blue Anchor, it is served at the Dock Inn (01736 362833) in Penzance. Bottles can be bought in Helston's Oliver's. Worth the pilgrimage.
Tasting notes: Sweet and strong with unusual, memorable flavours.

Tribute

St Austell Brewery first brewed this premium 4.2% pale amber beer for the solar eclipse in 1999, and it is now its hugely popular flagship beer, drunk throughout the West Country.
Tasting notes Bronze-coloured, refreshing light citrusy notes.

birthplace of King Arthur. Despite the boisterous commercialism that has attached itself to Arthurian legend, the remnants of Tintagel castle – set against the vivid green-turquoise of the surrounding sea (so coloured due to the copper content in the sand) – are by any measure an extraordinary sight.

The surrounding coast is just as wild and menacing – renowned for ferocious storms, heavy seas and shipwrecks. South of Tintagel, the waves at **Trebarwith** test the skills of surfers, with the hump of Gull Rock looming offshore; the beach, a long stretch of sand backed by cliffs and caves, all but disappears at high tide.

The village of **Boscastle**, three miles north of Tintagel, is an altogether more quaint sight. A tiny natural harbour at the end of a deep, narrow valley (or combe), where the River Jordan reaches the sea, Boscastle has endured worse onslaughts than a tide of holidaying humanity; in 2004, it was practically washed away by flash floods, when some 440 million gallons of water poured through the village in one day. Miraculously, no one was seriously hurt, but some ancient cottages were irreparably damaged.

The scenically placed village has tearooms, pubs and knick-knack shops, as well a new **visitors centre** (01840 250010, www.visitboscastleand tintagel.com) on the harbour, which contains a well-executed exhibition on the history and geography of Boscastle, as well as some interesting exhibits relating to Thomas Hardy and his connection with the area. Hardy first visited Cornwall in 1870, when contracted to work as an architect on nearby St Juliot's Church, where he would meet and court Emma Gifford, later to be his wife (make your holiday reading Hardy's A Pair of Blue Eyes, inspired by the area around Boscastle). A scenic footpath leads out of

Boscastle several miles through the Valency valley to the church in question.

Off the road between Tintagel and Boscastle (the B3263) you'll see signs for **Rocky Valley**. A parking place leads you to this beauty spot and towards **St Nectan's Kieve**, where a 60-foot waterfall plunges into a deep rock basin – considered a sacred place since pre-Christian times, and reputed to be one of Cornwall's most haunted locales.

Where to eat & drink

Tintagel is largely given over to lacklustre pubs and tearooms, unsubtly themed to appeal to the thousands of tourists traipsing through in search of traces of King Arthur. For more accomplished dining or just a quiet pint of local ale, try the 18th-century Mill House Inn, below.

Mill House Inn

Trebarwith, PL34 OHD (01840 770200, www.themillhouseinn.co.uk). Open 11am-11.30pm daily. Lunch served noon-2.30pm, dinner served 6.30-8.30pm daily.

This 18th-century corn mill is set in pretty woodland, halfway up the valley from the surfing beach at Trebarwith Strand – and completely removed from the throng of Tintagel proper, a mile or so down the road. The old pub itself is an informal place with slate floors and a wood-burning stove for chilly days, while the newer restaurant behind is a more refined (but still family-friendly) affair, with light wood floors and white tablecloths. Dishes throughout are made from locally sourced meat, fish and vegetables, with the bar menu featuring the comforting likes of Cornish bangers and mash, snakebite-battered haddock and chips, and wild mushroom and spinach penne pasta. The restaurant menu is more cosmopolitan and elaborate, showing imaginative use of ingredients: own-cured veal and saffron-smoked mozzarella, leek-roasted organic sea trout with rosemary and Cornish potato soufflé, and lavender panna cotta, for example. Sharp's ales (as well as beers from the local Tintagel brewery) are served throughout, and bands play in the pub. There are also eight guest rooms (£85-£140 double incl breakfast).

Where to stay

The Mill House Inn (*see above*) has eight attractive rooms, with rustic wooden furniture and white linens.

Avid readers of Thomas Hardy's novels might be interested in staying a night or two at the Old Rectory (01840 250225, www.stjuliot.com) at St Juliot, near Boscastle. Rooms are traditional but light and airy, and it's all set in three acres of lush grounds. This is where Hardy stayed while working on the local church in 1870, and where he courted his wife-to-be.

Boscastle Hostel

Palace Stables, Boscastle, PL35 0HD (0845 371 9006, www.yha.org.uk). Open Apr-Nov. Rates from £16.40 per night for 1 person.

Located next to the water in Boscastle's lovely harbour, this comfortable little hostel is housed in a former stables, once occupied by the horses that pulled the boats ashore. The force of the 2004 floods devastated the hostel's interior, but it has been fully refurbished and looks reborn. Modernisations include a number of great three- and four-bed family rooms, sparkling bathrooms and a self-catering kitchen.

Boscastle House💜

Tintagel Road, Boscastle, PL35 0AS (01840 250654, www.boscastlehouse. com). Rates £125 double incl breakfast.

The young, charming owners of this boutique guesthouse, overlooking the steep combe of Boscastle, have injected some much-needed style into the mainly weary-looking hotel options in this corner of Cornwall. Boutique accents abound – outsized floral wallpaper, statement colour accents, rich fabrics – and each of the rooms sports a different colour

scheme, ranging from fresh greens and creamy tones to Beaujolais-red. Rooms are unusually spacious, with features that normally command a more substantial price tag: roll-top baths, wrought-iron beds, walk-in showers, chandeliers and a beauty treatment menu. There is no restaurant, so technically this isn't a hotel – but nor is it a suffocatingly intimate B&B, since the rooms feel appealingly independent. Other bonuses include complimentary tea and cakes on arrival, a croquet lawn at the front and a stylish guest lounge.

Orchard Lodge

Gunpool Lane, Boscastle, PL35 0AT (01840 250418, www. orchardlodgeboscastle.co.uk). Open Feb-Oct. Rates from £931 for 7 days.

Orchard Lodge is a bright newcomer in Boscastle, offering five scrupulously well-kept and contemporary B&B rooms – think fresh cream carpets, sparkling white bathrooms and thick towels. A member of CoaST (Cornwall Sustainable Tourism Project), the Orchard Lodge shows remarkable committment to local sourcing at breakfast: the milk is from nearby Delabole, the apple juice from Liskeard, the smoked fish from Widemouth Bay and, most impressively, the sausages are made from their own pigs, kept on an organic farm down the road. Note that discounts are offered to those arriving on foot, by bike or by public transport.

Tintagel Youth Hostel

Dunderhole Point, Tintagel, PL34 0DW (0845 371 9145, www.yha.org.uk). Open Apr-Nov. Rates from £16.40 per night for 1 person.

This place is wonderfully remote, and people who've stayed here say it feels as if it's on the edge of the world. The views out to sea are incredible, so you can understand why competition for the two four-bed and two six-bed rooms is so fierce during school holidays. Tintagel Hostel has a little shop where you can buy the wherewithal for a cook-up in the kitchen (no meals are served). It's staffed mainly by volunteers, who are friendly and helpful.

Newquay & the Atlantic Coast

The north coast is what one might call 'classic Cornwall': great sashes of bright sand, melodramatic cliffs and crags, and an endless supply of Atlantic breakers. We'd probably even go so far as to say that this stretch of coast has the greatest concentration of fine beaches in the country.

But while scenic beauty explains how the north coast came to be the engine house of Cornwall's booming tourist trade, historically the area was defined by the twin industries of fishing and mining. Ivy-choked mine stacks punctuate the landscape around Camborne, Redruth and St Agnes, while Newquay was built on the once-lucrative pilchard trade. Now much of the area earns its crust, directly or indirectly, from leisure and tourism. Property developers throng, keen to cash in on the stunning views and the SUV-loads of families, surfers and partygoers who wend their way down the Atlantic highway to luxury hotels, B&Bs, holiday cottages, campsites, surf shacks and – less happily for the Cornish – second homes.

The largest resort on the north coast (and in all of Cornwall) is Newquay, the self-proclaimed surf capital of Britain and, less attractively, party central for binge-drinking school leavers and single-sex groups. But for all those who pile in for a potent mix of sticky shots, late-night drinking and cheesy clubs, there are plenty of others who come despite it – more interested in watersports, walking and, increasingly, chic retreats and restaurants.

NEWQUAY & AROUND

Newquay

When, in separate incidents just weeks apart, two teenagers fell to their deaths from the cliffs after an evening of underage drinking in 2009, it stoked the smouldering debate over Newquay – its unbridled property development and rampant construction, but, most of all, the rivers of underage, post-exam drinkers that flow through every summer to behave badly in someone else's backyard. Nobody is betting against this continuing post Covid.

While the discussion rages on – the police calling for a clean-up, others enjoying the funfair – Newquay's natural assets retain an indelible appeal. For an idea of the raw materials that first made Newquay a resort, make your way to the western side of the harbour; from here, you can take in the entire sweep of cliff-vaulted beaches across the bay.

Newquay was known as Towan Blystra (sandy hill) until adventurous Elizabethans built the Newe Keye for their sailing vessels in the 15th century. With the development of mass tourism and the thriving surf

Bedruthan Steps *see p83*

NEWQUAY & THE ATLANTIC COAST

scene, the basis of the town's original claim to fame, the humble pilchard, tends to get forgotten. Yet until the early 20th century, it was plentiful shoals of small herring that provided Newquay's income.

Above the western side of the bay perches the **Huer's Hut**, which provided shelter for the pilchard watcher. His job was to cry 'Heva!' through a long horn when he saw the silvery fish, then direct the sailors as they manoeuvred their boats around the entire shoal. Millions of plump fish were netted from the boats, and the whole town would turn out to offload the hauls.

Newquay's insignia is still two pilchards, even though the town lost its pilchards when they took it into their fishy heads to change their migration pattern. This, combined with the coming of the railways in the 19th century, put paid to maritime trade and sent the area into a steep financial decline, until the arrival of mass tourism buoyed it up once again.

Although you wouldn't believe it from the downmarket town centre, eminently stylish recent additions to Newquay's eastern beaches – the striking **Scarlet hotel** (*see p92*) in Mawgan Porth – herald a shift upmarket. Even more irrefutable evidence of Newquay's gentrification has arrived in the shape of Prince Charles's plan to develop his second ideal village project here, dubbed 'Surfbury' and based on the original Duchy of Cornwall venture in Poundbury, Dorset.

Great surf accounts for a huge chunk of Newquay's visitors and also for some of the biggest summer events in the South-West, including the English National Surfing Championships and Relentless Boardmasters. The attraction here is not just the consistent swell, but also the sheer number and variety of surf beaches – making it possible to choose a beach

to make best use of prevailing conditions. *See p92*.

The beaches

Tourist blurb often makes mention of Newquay's chain of 11 golden beaches. While the numbers depend a little on your definition of 'Newquay' and 'beach', there seems little point in splitting hairs: by anyone's measure, this short stretch of coast has an embarrassment of beaches.

In the town centre, **Towan Beach**, next to the harbour, is the busiest stretch of sand in high season, backed by watersports-hire outfits and beachside tat markets. Beyond the harbour, the road continues past the Huer's Hut to the Towan Head clifftop, where the views are terrific. On the west side of the headland is **Little Fistral Beach**, followed by **Fistral Beach** proper – a west-facing strand that bears the full brunt of the Atlantic, where a 'surf's up' vibe prevails.

At the far end of the beach, **East Pentire Head** overlooks the Gannel Estuary as it noses out to sea. On the south side of the estuary – reached by ferry from the **Pentire** hamlet (10am-6pm daily, summer only) – the village of **Crantock** is a secluded suburb with a large, north-west facing beach, bordered by grassy dunes; close by, sandy **Porth Joke** is small and idyllic. Beyond the protrusion of the Kelsey Head, **Holywell Bay** is another popular stretch with parking, toilets and cafés, backed by the gentle peaks of a vast dune system.

Travelling north from Newquay harbour, Towan Beach makes way for **Great Western**, **Tolcarne** and **Lusty Glaze** (the latter being by far the best name for a beach we've ever heard), all of which join into one mile-long stretch at low tide. Tolcarne has been in and out of the news since 2003, when a proposal to build an artificial surf reef here was aired. That plan appears to have been blown out of the water by Newquay's bigger cheeses, much to the disappointment of the many wetsuited entrepreneurs who ply their trade here. In a new twist, Bournemouth constructed its own artificial reef in 2010, designed to turn out perfect waves – though it was subsequently closed in March 2011 after two of the reef's sandbags were damaged by a passing boat and never reopened.

Porth Beach, with **Porth Island** at its northern side, was the site of an Iron Age settlement, and is linked to the mainland by a footbridge. It's quiet compared to Watergate Bay round the corner, but it does have ice-cream shops, toilets and cafés. Beyond Trevelgue Head, before reaching Watergate, is hidden Whipsiderry Beach, a quiet, rugged beach with access via steps in the cliff.

Newquay's most fashionable beach has to be **Watergate Bay**, a watersports resort and chic dining destination. Here, you can ride the waves and master the arts of kitesurfing, wave-skiing or paddle-surfing at the Extreme Academy (*see p86*), or the chilled-out Beach Hut (*see p85*), before crashing out at the hip hotel (*see p95*).

Bedruthan Steps & Mawgan Porth

Cornwall may be famous for its rocky coast, but Bedruthan Steps takes cragginess to new extremes. Here, the beach plays second fiddle to the towering rock stacks – some chiselled and pyramid-like, others resembling barnacle-encrusted turrets. According to legend, they were the stepping stones of a giant.

Surveyed from the top of the cliff, this is an intimidating spot; you can watch the scenery being carved before your eyes. As the ocean pummels the cliffs, new rocky outcrops are slowly formed by the constant crumbling. (In 1980, for instance, the distinctive

crown of the Queen Bess rock stack was lost to the waves.) And so it follows that visitors are advised to steer clear of the cliff edges – both above and below – which are gradually collapsing. Closed from November to February, Cornwall's stormiest season, Bedruthan Steps is not for the faint-hearted, even in clement weather. The steep path down to the beach may induce vertigo, and the return journey will give your lungs a workout. Refreshment is on hand in a small National Trust café by the car park.

As you get swept away by the romance of it all, don't get swept away by the incoming waves – at high tide, much of the beach disappears. And don't even think about swimming or surfing here. Though a few hardened locals do bring their boards, they take their life in their hands: Bedruthan is very much a case of beauty with cruelty. The currents are treacherous and the rocks can be deadly.

If the stone staircase is too perilous, take in the scene from the coastal footpath above. Gentle on the legs yet with plenty of drama, the cliff-top walk between Carnewas Point and Park Head is superb, and the remains of Redcliff Castle – an Iron Age fort – are near the path.

Bedruthan Steps has but one hidden neighbour: Mawgan Porth, a sheltered, sandy beach resort tucked into the next valley, and a better bet for a proper day at the beach. It is also now home to one of the county's hottest hotels, the recently opened eco-luxe **Scarlet** (*see p84 & p92*).

Where to eat & drink

Jamie Oliver's Fifteen may have sadly been and gone, but as Newquay has smartened up it has inexorably gastrified, with current leading light probably Paul Harwood's Michelin-rated **Fish House** (*p85*) on Fistral Beach.

Green and glamorous

How the Scarlet reinvented eco-chic.
One minute, Mawgan Porth was muddling along in a distinctly untrendy way – a few holiday lets, a low-key pub and a shop – the next, one of the country's hottest new hotels landed on the edge of the cliff, drawing the attention of travel editors nationwide – not to mention legions of eco worriers, architects and foodies. Although it has been some years since ecology and style were mutually exclusive, it is still rare to come across such hefty eco credentials (the realm of biomass heaters, not just botanical toiletries) so close to the cutting edge, particularly in the seemingly paradoxical field of eco luxury.

You'd need hours, if not days, to read the specifics of the Scarlet's (see p92) environmental policies and its from-scratch architecture, but a few key points warrant highlighting. All power comes from renewable sources; carbon emissions are over 70% less than the average for a building of its size; grey water and rain water are both harvested; the ventilation heat-exchange system removes the need for air-con; heating comes care of a wood-chip, carbon-neutral biomass boiler; and so the list goes on...

By any measure, the architecture is dazzlingly creative, achieving that much sought-after but rarely realised blending of building and landscape. An infinity pond at the entrance leads the eye seamlessly into the seascape behind; the natural outdoor swimming pool is strewn with granite boulders and cleaned by the reedbeds; reclaimed wood from Plymouth harbour creates the divisions between private terraces; and, best of all, two deep-red hot tubs stand outside on the cliff, silhouetted against the sea. Each of the 37 rooms has ocean views; splash out on one of the upper categories and you might get your own private garden and a spiral staircase leading up to a little roof terrace. The styling is low-key luxe: think rich, tactile fabrics, statement light fittings and gorgeously sleek bathrooms.

At the helm in the restaurant is Jeremy Medley, who previously headed Northamptonshire's renowned Oundle Mill, and who recently took over from local chef Ben Tunnicliffe. While we wouldn't go quite so far as to call the food avant-garde during Tunnicliffe's reign, you could come expecting a sprinkling of surprises, and Medley continues this creative spirit. This being an eco hotel, local ingredients take centre stage in dishes such as roast sea bass with nettle gnocchi and purple sprouting brocolli, or rabbit and damson stew with suet dumplings.

In a departure from standard high-dining attire, the staff wear Thai-style fisherman

His former boss Rick Stein's family-friendly, Eastern-inspired seafood restaurant **Rick Stein, Fistral** (*p92*) is a near neighbour, while also worth a look is ultra-friendly brunch mecca the **Fore Street Cafe Bar** (38 Fore St, 07956 642324), while Australian-influenced (!) restaurant **Bush Pepper** (6 Fore St, 01637 852530, www.bushpepper.co.uk) has a thoughtful and inventive menu that largely steers clear of Antipodean-themed novelty (except that you can buy a kangaroo steak).

Newquay town centre is decidedly unrewarding when it comes to food – burgar bars, boozy curryhouses and Mexicans, fudge and ice-cream vans dominate.

Beach Hut
Watergate Bay, TR8 4AA (01637 860877, www.watergatebay.co.uk). Food served 10am-4pm Mon-Thur, Sun; 10am-9pm Fri, Sat.

The family-friendly Beach Hut, once a bucket and spade shop, retains a lighthearted, beachside vibe. Being part of the über-slick Watergate Bay brand, it's a fashionable spot, with smart rattan chairs, stripped wooden floors and mood lighting. Nonetheless, staff won't bat an eyelid at the sight of sandy flip-flops or boardshorts. Fresh fish, Fowey river mussels, burgers, steak, salads and mugs of hot chocolate for après-surf comfort troughing are the order of the day, but a sprinkling of Asian dishes hit the spot too – our chicken and prawn laksa didn't shy away from serious spice. A wholesome children's menu runs from grilled free-range chicken with chips and peas to fish with new potatoes and peas, and there is a takeaway window – often with a snaking queue in high season – for those who want to picnic on the beach.

Fish House
5 International Surfing Centre, Headland Rd, Newquay, TR7 1EW (01637 872085, www.thefishhousefistral.com). Open noon-9pm daily.

trousers and Clarks shoes, and there is a compellingly creative feel to the place. Like the rest of the hotel, the restaurant's decor would be stylish even for Soho – so for a distinctly unhip coastal community near Newquay, it's clean off the trendometer. Scarlet-coloured textile lampshades and metal chairs patterned like tree branches set the tone, and there are glorious sunset views across the sea.

The lovely, lantern-lit Ayurvedic spa offers a naturally inspired menu of treatments, with refreshingly realistic aims (wellbeing, not wrinkle reduction) and hanging canvas pods for post-treatment cocooning. Throughout, there's an intelligent, conceptual feel to the place – the *Rough Guide to Happiness* takes the place of the Bible, engaging art hangs in public spaces, and the welcome book requests guests don't bark down their mobiles in communal areas. But there are a few unusual decisions that seem bound to frustrate: there is no reception area, just a grouping of fashionable sofas and a lot of confusion, and there's no Wi-Fi, in a didactic bid to induce you to relax (cables are available from reception). Overall, though, this is a deeply desirable hotel, and for many the very embodiment of 'new Cornwall': creative, sustainable and drenched in coastal cool.

Beach Hut see p85

Things to do

NEWQUAY & AROUND
For more on the surf scene in Cornwall, including surf schools, see p92.

Adventure Centre
Lusty Glaze Beach, Lusty Glaze Road, Newquay, TR7 3AE (01637 872444, www. lustyglazeadventurecentre.co.uk).

Turning Lusty Glaze beach into a giant adventure playground, this centre offers abseiling, rock climbing, surfing, coasteering and a spectacular zip wire across the beach. The Cliffhanger is Lusty Glaze's newest adrenaline-pumping activity, taking you on a high-rope traverse over crashing waves, caves and cliffs.

Cornwall Karting
St Eval, Pl27 7UN (01637 860160, www. cornwallkarting.com). Open Mar-Oct 10am-6pm Mon-Sat. Nov-Feb hours vary; check the website for details. Admission from £24; £12 reductions.

The largest circuit in the South-West offers four circuits and five types of kart (catering for all ages, from three up). Speed freaks will want to check out the pro karts, which max out at 70mph.

Extreme Academy
Watergate Bay, TR8 4AA (01637 860543, www.watergatebay.co.uk).

Watergate's adventure sport centre has wind- and wave-driven pursuits covered, with traction-kiting, kitebuggying, waveskiing and paddlesurfing, as well as good old-fashioned surfing. Alternatively, book an 'Extreme Day' to pack them in (£85 per person).

There's no denying that the 2019 loss of Jamie Oliver's Fifteen – probably the most famous restaurant in Cornwall after Rick Stein's Seafood Restaurant – was a blow for Newquay. Still, it was hardly the end of the town's culinary aspirations, and indeed Fistral Beach is currently something of a mini foodie Mecca. The leading light is probably former Rick Stein protégé Paul Harwood's Michelin Guide-rated Fish House, a small, rustic restaurant offering superlatively fresh seafood and seafood curries at reasonable prices. The light lunch menu is particularly kind on the wallet – check out the many permutations of seafood taco.

Lewinnick Lodge
Pentire Headland, Newquay, TR7 1NX (01637 878117, www.lewinnicklodge. co.uk). Open 9am-11pm daily. Breakfast served 9-11.30am, lunch served noon-5pm, dinner served 5-10pm.

There is hardly a shortage of restaurants in Cornwall with sea views, but there aren't many, if any, that allow you to wine and dine literally on the top of a cliff (practically overhanging the Atlantic, if you venture out on to the decking area).

Lappa Valley Railways
St Newlyn East, Newquay, TR8 5LX (01872 510317, www.lappavalley.co.uk). Open Apr-Oct. Tickets £13.95; £11.95 reductions; £47.50 family.

The stars of this family attraction, set in a wooded valley, are the miniature steam trains. Varying in size from the 15in-gauge Zebedee to the tiny, seven-inch-gauge petrol-powered Mardyke Miniature APT, they chuff around merrily, taking families from the café and pedal car track to the boating lake and crazy golf, then round to the play castle and brick path maze. The railway used to carry wagonloads of ore from the East Wheal Rose mine, which now houses an exhibition.

ST AGNES, PERRANPORTH & THE COAST
For more about cycling or walking the network of Mineral Tramways in the area, *see p39.*

Bike Barn
Elm Farm Cycle Centre, Cambrose, TR16 5UF (01209 891498, www.cornwallcycletrails. com). Open 10.30am-5.30pm daily. Cycle hire from £20.

This bike hire centre near Portreath, right on the Coast to Coast cycle trail, offers mountain bikes (some with suspension), tandems, child trailers and free parking.

Perranporth Golf Club
The Clubhouse, Budnic Hill, Perranporth, TR6 0AB (01872 572454, www.perranporth golfclub.com). Open dawn-dusk daily. Rates from £25.

A scenic links course, on the cliffs above Perranporth.

Watergate Bay see p83

Places to visit

NEWQUAY & AROUND

Blue Reef Aquarium
Towan Promenade, Newquay, TR7 1DU (01637 878134, www.bluereefaquarium.co.uk). Open Mar-Oct 10am-5pm daily. Nov-Feb 10am-4pm daily. Admission £12.50; £9.50-£11.50 reductions; £42 family.

These days, every seaside resort worth its salt has an aquarium for rainy days and, to its credit, Newquay's is a modern, child-friendly affair. Highlights of the 'undersea safari' include the jellyfish nursery; the displays of captive-bred species, such as clownfish and seahorses; Turtle Creek and Turtle Rescue; and, most excitingly, the Underwater Tunnel. Local marine life is also bigged up, with mock-ups of rocky Cornish habitats created for lobsters, spider crabs and conger eels.

Dairyland Farm World
Near Newquay (A3058), TR8 5AA (01872 510246, www.dairylandfarmworld.com). Open Farm World Apr-Oct 10am-5pm daily. Admission £8.95; free-£6.95 reductions; £34.50 family. Bull Pen Nov-Mar 10am-6pm Thur, Fri; 10am-5pm Sat, Sun. Admission free-£3.95 (weekdays); £5.75 (weekends).

Dairyland was born in 1975, when the Davy family, owners of Tresilian Barton Farm, decided to upgrade their milk production using a form of milking parlour pioneered in America, called the Rotary. A source of fascination for the public, the milking parlour attracted increasing numbers of visitors and became the UK's first farm-themed tourist attraction. Today, there's an indoor fun centre as well as playgrounds, climbing nets, pat-a-pet, pony riding, animal feeding and pet parades – not to mention the farm museum, nature trail and gift shop. For all this, the attraction still centres on the working dairy farm, and the milking demonstration educates supermarket-nourished children. And if the sun isn't shining, there's always the Bull Pen, a massive indoor play centre.

Newquay Zoo
Trenance Gardens, Newquay, TR7 2LZ (01637 873342, www.newquayzoo.org.uk). Open 10am-5pm daily. Admission £12.60; free-£10.60 reductions.

Opened in 1969 as a pets' corner in the ornamental gardens, Newquay Zoo was a small and undistinguished affair until

Trerice

about 20 years ago, when new ownership and redevelopment upped the ante. It's now a much-loved small zoo, with a strong conservation and captive breeding programme for red pandas, pied tamarins, Humboldt penguins and lynx, among others. The tropical house contains a slice of jungle that can be viewed both from ground- and first-floor level; every so often, a man-made rainstorm deluges it to keep it steamy. Recent additions have been the Philippines' species area, where spotted deer and curious-looking warty pigs, both endangered species, make themselves at home, and the three-acre African Savannah exhibit, where zebra, wildebeest and nyala antelopes roam.

Trerice

Kestle Mill, nr Newquay, TR8 4PG (01637 875404, www.nationaltrust.org.uk). Open Feb-Nov 11am-5pm daily. Admission to gardens £5; £2.50 reductions; £12.50 family.

Down a winding country lane, a few miles inland from Newquay, the Elizabethan country manor house of Trerice and its sleepy, sheltered grounds is an idyllic scene. Beyond the Dutch-gabled, limestone façade are a series of handsome rooms filled with portraits and tapestries, including the Great Hall, with a musicians' gallery where players could be heard but not seen. The Great Barn café at the back is an attractive space.

REDRUTH & CAMBORNE

East Pool Mine

Pool, TR15 3NP (01209 315027, www.nationaltrust.org.uk). Open Apr-Oct 11am-5pm Mon, Wed-Fri, Sun (open Sat July, Aug). Admission £6.10; £3 reductions; £15.20 family.

Despite the uninspiring approach through a Morrisons car park, the hulking engine-houses at this historically significant visitor attraction stand in the heartland of Cornish mining. Inside, you can get up close to the Cornish steam-powered beam engine, invented by local boy Richard Trevithick; at over 52 tonnes, it's an arresting piece of equipment. Across the road you can watch one in motion. Narrated with a tone of Cornish pride, the short film on hard-rock mining shown in the low-key Heritage Centre acts as a reminder that this rundown area,

now the butt of many a local joke, was once one of the most innovative and prosperous industrial areas in the world. Richard Trevithick's cottage is in nearby Penponds (open 2-5pm Wed).

King Edward Mine

Troon, Camborne, TR14 9HW (01209 614681, www.kingedwardmine.co.uk). Open May-Sept 10am-5pm, days vary. Admission £9; £2 reductions. No credit cards.

Up until a few years ago, this site was used by the Camborne School of Mines as a training mine and, as a result, it is one of the oldest intact mining complexes in Cornwall. There is an old-fashioned but absorbing museum, a guided tour of the machinery in action in the mill – some of the last such examples in the world – and a small shop. The site is also home to the Mineral Tramways Heritage Project, a network of cycling trails, and the starting point for the circular, seven-and-a-half-mile Great Flat Lode Trail.

ST AGNES, PERRANPORTH & THE COAST

Outside St Agnes, the Blue Hills Tin Stream (Wheal Kitty, 01872 553341, www.bluehillstin.com, closed Sun, closed Nov-Easter) visitor centre recreates early methods of tin smelting and casting.

Healey's Cornish Cyder Farm

Penhallow, Truro, TR4 9LW (01872 573356, www.healeyscyder.co.uk). Open Apr-Dec daily. Jan-Mar Mon-Fri. Times vary; check website for details. Admission free. Tours £6.50; £4.50 reductions.

As well as being the place to stock up on Cornish Rattler (Cornwall's most popular cider), apple brandy, fruit wines and scrumpy of varying strengths, all made on site, the Cyder Farm is a cheery visitor attraction. You'll have to pay for the full distillery tour and museum, and the tractor ride around the orchards, but the pretty courtyard, farmyard, shire horse stables, jam room and Mowhay café-restaurant are open to all. Just down the road, **Callestick Farm** (01872 573126, www.callestickfarm.co.uk, free), of ice-cream fame, is open to visitors in summer.

Ten top surf spots

Fistral Beach

Fistral Beach in Newquay is a long, straight beach, whose consistent waves have made it a popular spot for surfers. It's home to the British Surfing Association, the Newquay Surf Life Saving Club and the Newquay Boardrider Club, and is also known for its international competitions and surf museum. SurfGSD surf school (07739 536122, www.surfgsd.com) caters for all levels.

Gwithian

The surf breaks very slowly at this gently sloping beach, located at the northernmost point of St Ives Bay. With rideable surf year-round and relatively warm waters, it's a good spot for novices. Contact Gwithian Academy of Surfing (01736 755493, 01736 757579, www.surfacademy.co.uk) for lessons.

Harlyn Bay

This large, crescent-shaped beach near Padstow, backed by dunes, has a good expanse of sand at low tide and is a safe place to learn the ropes, with tuition from Harlyn Surf School (01841 533076, www. harlynsurfschool.co.uk, closed Nov-Mar). In summer, the lack of swell might deter the more advanced.

Holywell Bay

This tranquil, clean, family-orientated spot – the National Trust's flagship beach – has some of the best surf in Cornwall, without the crowds of nearby Newquay. Hone your technique at the Holywell Bay School of Surf (01872 510233, www. holywellbayschoolofsurf.com, closed Nov-mid May).

Perranporth

Ten miles south of Newquay's beaches, and much less crowded, Perranporth has long stretches of sand and a good variety of waves. The Perranporth Surf School (07974 550823, www.perranporthsurf school.co.uk) can provide instruction, and lifeguards man the beach between May and September.

Although the exterior isn't particularly prepossessing, once inside this large bar-restaurant is a smart perch for dinner or drinks, with contemporary decor, a sunny soundtrack, cut-above Med-influenced brasserie fare and huge cliff-top views from the Pentire Headland. Prices are reasonable, and the wind-in-the-hair feeling makes it worthy of a stop. It's also accessible via the footpath from Fistral Beach.

Rick Stein, Fistral

Fistral Beach Complex, Headland Rd, Newquay TR7 1HY (01637 808437, www. rickstein.com). Open noon-9pm daily.

The Stein empire has extended its tentacles to Newquay with this casual, well-priced restaurant. Fish is the order of the day, of course, but his Fistral Beach gaff has something of a USP, insofar as the menu is explicitly influenced by Stein's travels around India and the Far East. It's also super-affordable: at time of writing, nothing on the menu would set you back more than a tenner, be that a fish chilli burger, sea bass pho, or freshly caught, sustainable fish battered or grilled.

Scarlet

Tredragon Road, Mawgan Porth, TR8 4DQ (01637 861800, www.scarlethotel. co.uk). Lunch served noon-2.15pm, dinner served 7-9.30pm daily.

You'll find accomplished cooking and top-notch local ingredients at this hotel/restaurant, Cornwall's newest eco-conscious epicentre of cool (*see p84*).

Where to stay

With the exception of the Headland Hotel (*see p94*) and the Bay (*see p95*), central Newquay has a distinct dearth of classy accommodation. Instead, it's mainly given over to grotty guesthouses and budget surf lodges (crashpads involving bunk beds, cramped conditions and low prices).

Probably the most upmarket of the lodges is the **Reef Surf Lodge** (10-12 Berry Road, 01637 879058, www. newquayreefsurflodge.co.uk), with flatscreen TVs beaming out surf videos, and a bar area; meanwhile, **Base Surf Lodge** (20 Tower Road, 01637 874852, www.basesurflodge.co.uk) overlooks Fistral Beach. A guesthouse alternative to the rowdy surf lodge scene is an en-suite room at **Trewinda Lodge** (17 Eliot Gardens, 01637 877533, www.trewindalodge.co.uk).

Beach Retreats

01637 861005, www.beachretreats.co.uk. Rates from £395 per week.

If the lace curtains and earthenware jugs of mainstream Cornish holiday homes don't do it for you, browse the 60 polished properties on the books at this north coast self-catering specialist. Some of its houses and apartments feature such luxuries as a pool, jacuzzi, barbecue area or domed ceilings – but even on a lower budget you can count on clean, stylish decor. Locations include Watergate Bay, Porth, Fistral, Mawgan Porth and the Camel Estuary.

Bedruthan Steps Hotel

Mawgan Porth, TR8 4BU (01637 860555, www.bedruthan.com). Rates £139-£285 double incl breakfast.

In the age of rampant greenwashing, it's getting harder to separate eco-chat ('We try to use locally sourced ingredients where possible.') from eco-commitment ('We guarantee that 70% of the produce used in our restaurant is locally sourced.'). The Bedruthan Steps Hotel, occupying an enviable cliff-top perch between Newquay and Padstow, falls into the latter category, putting its money – three million pounds, to be precise – where its mouth is to become the first independent hotel in the country to bag the toughest green accreditation of all: the serious-sounding ISO 14001. What makes this feat all the more impressive is that the team aren't running a dinky boutique B&B, but a four-star resort hotel with 101 bedrooms, a 280-seat restaurant, a bar, a spa (with steam rooms, treatments, a sauna and pool), tennis courts and conference facilities. Private villas and B&B apartments are also available.

Porthleven

Located north of Kynance Cove, between Land's End and Lizard Point, Porthleven is one for experts and hardcore locals, and is known for having the best reef break in the country. It can be a dangerous place for novices, however.

Praa Sands

One of West Cornwall's most popular beaches, Praa Sands has an appealingly unpretentious vibe – and is the proud host of the World Crap Surfing Championships, usually held in December. Surfers are catered for by Stones Reef Surf Shop (01736 762991) on the beach, and by a lively après-surf scene.

Sennen Cove

A stone's throw from Land's End, Sennen Cove is a stronghold of free surfing – the belief that grace and fun define a surfer, rather than competitive success – and is good for both beginners and serious surfers. Lessons and board hire are available from Sennen Surfing Centre (01736 871227, www.sennensurfing centre.com, closed Nov-Mar) and the Smart Surf School (01736 871817, www.smartsurf.co.uk).

Whitsand Bay

In south-east Cornwall, Whitsand Bay has sheer, lofty cliffs, dramatic scenery and extensive stretches of sandy beaches, suited to beginners and intermediates. Discovery Surf School (07813 639622, www.discoverysurf.com) runs classes here in summer (mainly July and August).

Widemouth Bay

In North Cornwall, three miles south of Bude, Widemouth Bay offers varied conditions and is frequented by beginners and intermediates, who aren't quite ready to tackle the largest waves. Raven Surf School (01288 353693, www.ravensurf.co.uk), set up by former surfing champion Mike Raven, offers instruction here, and at nearby Summerleaze Beach in Bude. RNLI lifeguards patrol its sands in high season.

Bedruthan's child-friendly credentials are almost as momentous. Widely considered to be one of the UK's most family-friendly hotels, it has a variety of indoor and outdoor play areas and no less than five Ofsted-inspected children's clubs (for which extra charges apply). Children and babies can take tea separately from the aged Ps, and there is also a family dining area.

Fistral Beach Hotel and Spa

Esplanade Road, Pentire, Newquay, TR7 1PT (01637 852221, www.newquay-hotels.co.uk). Rates £50-£150 double incl breakfast.

Recently revamped at great expense, and incorporating the Fistral Spa, the Bay is now Newquay's smoothest mid-range choice. In an elevated position on the Pentire Headland, nicely removed from the scrum of Newquay proper, the Bay has 90 rooms. The best rooms feature oversized bathtubs looking out over the sweep of Fistral Beach; bring binoculars to get a close-up of the surfers cruising in or wiping out. The grey exterior doesn't inspire, but inside the decor is contemporary, and the staff attentive and on the ball. The 'check in and chill out' spa packages clearly appeal to couples, who kick off their stay with an Espa body massage and a snooze in the low-lit relaxation area. A few doors down, the Esplanade Hotel (01637 873333) is the Bay's family-oriented sister establishment, and home to the Quiksilver Surf School.

Harbour Hotel

North Quay Hill, Newquay, TR7 1HF (01637 873040, www.harbourhotel.co.uk). Rates £205-£235 double incl breakfast.

Five en-suite rooms with balconies make the most of the Harbour's enviable location, looking out into Newquay Bay. The decor goes in for traditional aesthetics, with a scattering of antiques and iron bedsteads, but whatever it looked like you'd be spending most of your time surveying the view. A welcome oasis of calm, directed at the chardonnay rather than alcopop crowd.

Headland Hotel

Fistral Beach, Newquay, TR7 1EW (01637 872211, www.headlandhotel.co.uk). Rates £185-£415 double incl breakfast.

Looming over Little Fistral Cove from its own promontory, this imposing hotel may look familiar, thanks to its role in the unsettling film adaptation of Roald Dahl's *The Witches*. But despite its size, Victorian grandeur and purported ghosts, there's nothing sinister about Carolyn and John Armstrong's hotel. Service is friendly, the guest rooms are classically elegant and the views inspirational. The Headland has ten acres of grounds, as well as two heated pools, a sauna, a small gym, snooker, croquet and a nine-hole golf approach course and putting green. Alongside the hotel is a 'village' of 40 nicely appointed holiday cottages (think contemporary but cosy interiors) overlooking Newquay Bay and Little Fistral beach. The cottages can be rented for a minimum of three nights and enjoy access to the hotel's facilities.

Sands Resort Hotel

Watergate Road, Porth, TR7 3LZ (01637 872864, www.sandsresort.co.uk). Rates £55-£100 double incl breakfast.

With the sandy pleasures of Porth Beach to the fore, rolling green farmland aft and vast tracts of play area in the middle, Sands is well positioned and equipped to keep holidaying families happy. This gives it the air of a holiday village rather than a top banana hotel, but the children won't be complaining as they work their way through the treats and diversions laid on for them. Sands is a big, bright block of a hotel, with a playground, mini golf, a large outdoor pool, a maze and tennis courts out back. Inside are games rooms, playrooms, an indoor pool, various lounge areas, an entertainments hall called the Atlantic Suite and a large, canteen-like restaurant. During school holidays, guests can arrange for their kids to be whisked away and organised into Ofsted-inspected clubs, divided by age. While their progeny are thus diverted, grown-ups can let their hair down at the Ocean Breeze Spa, where treatments run from quick manicures to unhurried massages.

Wheal Coates tin mine *see p98*

Scarlet💟

Tredragon Road, Mawgan Porth, TR8 4DQ (01637 861800, www.scarlethotel. co.uk). Rates £250-£685 double incl breakfast & dinner.

Newquay's hippest hotel is the place to sample luxurious eco-living (*see p84*).

Watergate Bay Hotel💟

Watergate Bay, TR8 4AA (01637 860543, www.watergatebay.co.uk). Rates £260-£900 double incl breakfast.

The grand old Victorian exterior of the hotel at Watergate Bay now conceals a series of super-chic rooms and suites, decorated in hip beach-house style with solid oak floors and juicy pink pinstripes, as well as extras such as Wi-Fi, plasma screen tellies, DVD players, MP3 player docks, L'Occitane freebies and thick towelling robes. The Coach House has decidedly smaller, less la-di-da suites with no views, as a budget option.

One of the original players in the child-friendly hotel game, Watergate provides all sorts of school holiday activities (animal encounters, discos, arts and crafts), as well as heated pools, tennis and squash, and indoor games rooms. Younger children can have an early supper and bedtime, while parents dine later while tuning into the baby-listening service. On site, there's the Living Space bar-café, with its huge, sea-facing terrace and laid-back food, or the smarter Brasserie. A few paces away is the Beach Hut (*see p85*), which falls under the Watergate Bay brand. The Extreme Academy surf school and surf equipment hire (*see p86*) is also part of the resort. With so many bases covered, you may struggle to find reasons to leave the bay.

REDRUTH & CAMBORNE

The advent of cool Cornwall has, for better or for worse, completely bypassed Redruth and Camborne. Those chasing chic retreats or celebrity chefs will find nothing to detain them in these parts, but as the capital of the once-mighty Cornish mining industry, a hotbed of industrial innovation, and for a taste of the 'real' Cornwall, the area merits further investigation.

During the 1850s this was a hugely

Trevaunance Cove *see p98*

important mining area, at one point producing some two-thirds of the world's copper. However, the discovery of cheaper deposits of ore overseas at the end of the 19th century heralded the start of the decline of Cornish mining, and a steep drop in the area's fortunes. Evidence of the region's mining heritage is everywhere; following the once-profitable underground mineral lodes, the landscape is dotted with granite stacks, engine houses and old industrial buildings. Most are derelict, but some have been turned into fascinating heritage centres (*see p91*).

Self-evident, too, are the signs that the conurbation of Camborne, Redruth and Pool now has some of the lowest incomes in the country. One particularly poignant reminder of the area's struggling economy is the graffiti scrawled on the walls outside the closed South Crofty mine, the words taken from Robert Bryant's folk song: 'Well Cornish lads are fishermen/And Cornish lads are miners too/But when the fish and tin are gone/What are the Cornish boys to do?'. South Crofty (not open to the public) was the last Cornish mine to close in the late 1990s, leaving hundreds jobless. Plans to reopen the mine have been aired over the past few years, although debate rumbles on. In the meantime, the £29 million Heartlands project has been awarded to the area, with the aim of creating a vast cultural park and rebooting the local economy.

Aside from some dignified civic architecture and a handsome old Cornish thoroughfare in the shape of Redruth's Fore Street, the streets of Redruth and Camborne – lined with lacklustre low-cost chains and charity shops – provide few reasons to dawdle. More cultural interest can be found in the historical sites out-of-town: the National Trust-owned **East Pool Mine** and the **King Edward Mine** (for both, *see p91*). Then there's the **Mineral Tramways** project – a network of old industrial tram and rail routes that are perfect for traffic-free biking or walking (*see p39*).

Beyond the towns, the moorland is bracing, with wrecked engine houses and swathes of bracken creating a desolate scene. Dominating the whole

region is the ragged, boulder-strewn summit of **Carn Brea**, 738 feet above sea level. One of Cornwall's most stirring yet seldom-visited vantage points, it is crowned by a towering Celtic cross, visible from miles around, and a slightly surreal folly castle (home to a Middle Eastern restaurant in the evenings).

The life of local inventor Richard Trevithick (1771-1833), is celebrated on Trevithick Day, the last Saturday in April. Trevithick was the creator of the first beam engine, allowing the mining of much deeper shafts.

Where to eat & drink

Redruth and Camborne offer few, if any, restaurants of note. The best option is probably the **Stones Krowji café** (West Park, www.stonesbakery. co.uk, closed Sat, Sun). Part of local arts and studio space Krowji (www. krowji.co.uk), it's run by Falmouth's much-loved Stone's Bakery, and offers good coffee, cake and sandwiches. Part of local arts and studio space Krowji (www.krowji.co.uk). Good, traditional pasties don't come much better than at **Berrymans** (www.

cornish-pasty.co.uk), a third-generation-owned bakery with outposts in Redruth, Camborne and Perranporth.

Where to stay

Redruth and Camborne come up very short on good hotels. Your best bet in Redruth town centre is probably the comfortable but stiflingly old-fashioned **Penventon Park Hotel** (West End, 01209 203000, www. penventon.co.uk); otherwise, head out to the coast for better picks.

ST AGNES, PERRANPORTH & THE COAST

The coast north of Redruth and Camborne is dotted with popular surfing beaches, notably **Porthtowan**, a small community with an excellent, wide beach that's also home to the invariably buzzing **Blue** bar (*see p98*). Nearby, the old mining harbour village of Portreath – which once shipped out thousands of tonnes of copper ore to Wales for smelting – is now an unassuming place, in possession of a sandy beach and a scattering of surf shops and cafés; most tourists, however, know it as the start or finish of the **Coast to Coast cycle trail**, part of the **Mineral Tramways** project (*see p39*).

St Agnes & Chapel Porth

The largest settlement on this stretch of coast is a few miles east at St Agnes, a fishing village that grew in significance in the late 18th century, when the harbour at Trevaunance Cove began exporting copper and tin, and importing coal for the local mines. A model of the harbour is among the historical exhibits on display at the one-room **St Agnes Museum** (Penwinnick Road, 01872 553228, closed Nov-Easter).

Today's straggling town, half a mile inland, centres around the Victorian parish church and a chummy squeeze of galleries, shops (butcher, baker, post office, groceries) and cottages. A little further down is **Stippy Stappy hill,** beloved of photographers for its steep row of wisteria-clad stone cottages.

At St Agnes's small but dramatic **Trevaunance Cove**, there is a tangible sense of the force of nature. The stony remains of a harbour embedded in the cliff – the last of five harbours built here, all eventually obliterated by winter storms – can be seen to the left, and crumbling granite cliffs loom high overhead. It's a popular surfing spot, with a couple of cafés down on the shore and the lively **Driftwood Spars pub** (*see right*).

To gain some perspective on the impressive landscape, climb up to the heathery summit of the **St Agnes Beacon** (629 feet) for one of Cornwall's best views. Beyond the steep cliffs of Porthtowan and Portreath – drizzly days excepted – you can make out the dark lump of Godrevy Head and even St Ives, a staggering 22 miles west. From here, you also get a good view of the remains of the **Wheal Coates** tin mine, embedded in the cliffs and with its engine house silhouetted against the sea. Probably the most scenically placed of all the mine stacks on Cornwall's coast, or at least the most photographed, this old tin mine can also be seen up close from the coastal path just east of Chapel Porth, against a vivid purple heather backdrop.

The nearby beach at **Chapel Porth** is something of a secluded gem, completely undeveloped save for a tiny National Trust café, serving, among other simple fare, a famed hedgehog ice-cream cone – a fantastically calorific affair involving a thick layer of clotted cream and a coating of chopped roasted hazelnuts. Low tide opens up huge stretches of sand to the east and west, but take

care not to get cut off as the tide rises. Each year in September, Chapel Porth hosts the **World Bellyboard Championships**. A niche event in which retro wooden boards are ridden with no wetsuit, no leash and no fins, it's free to enter and open to all.

Perranporth

Architecturally, the holiday town of Perranporth is a less than alluring sight; a sprawling mass of chalets, bungalows, new-builds and older terraces, joined by chippies, kebab shops and brassy pubs. But it's worth pushing past first impressions and on to the vast expanse of smooth golden sands beyond – which, at low tide, stretches several miles around Perran Bay to the west. Surf is good here, with the bay receiving steady swell – in particular at Penhale Sands, at the north end of the bay.

Where to eat & drink

Blue

Eastcliff, Beach Road, Porthtowan, TR4 8AD (01209 890329, www.blue-bar.co.uk). Open 10am-11pm Mon-Fri, Sun; 10am-midnight Sat. Food served 10am-9pm Mon-Fri; 10am-9pm Sat, Sun. (Closed dinner Mon, Tue in winter.)

Burrowed into the dunes at Porthtowan, Blue has the rare pedigree of being a locals' hangout that is popular year-round. Serving post-surf comfort food par excellence, in the shape of burgers, stone-baked pizzas, beer-battered pollock and chunky chips, it also draws crowds for its weekend gig nights. The alcoves built into the front give views on to the beach and out to sea, and there's also a beachside terrace. The feel is youthful and laid-back, but it attracts the surfer-haired of all ages.

Driftwood Spars

Trevaunance Cove, St Agnes, TR5 0RT (01872 552428, www.driftwoodspars. com). Lunch served Apr-Oct noon-2.30pm, dinner served 6.30-9pm daily. (Closed dinner Nov-Mar Mon-Wed, Sun.)

An honourable classic, the Driftwood – down by the beach at St Agnes – is a sprawling and perennially lively old inn dating back to the 17th century. Its array of rooms and nooks mean you can, to a degree, choose your vibe: cosy pints in the dark-beamed old bar downstairs, games of pool next door or lunch with sea views in the hotel's bright, pine-filled upstairs restaurant. The same menu of solid pub classics and fish dishes is served throughout. Several of the pub's own microbrews are on tap at any given time; bottles are also sold at the Into the Brew shop opposite. The Driftwood hosts a beer festival every year – check online for details.

Schooners Bistro

Trevaunance Cove, St Agnes, TR5 0RY (01872 553149, www.schoonerscornwall. com). Food served noon-9pm daily.

The straight line of brown leather bucket chairs by the bar, all facing seawards, seems like a logical design reponse to this sort of view – Schooners is bang on the beach at Trevaunance Cove, looking directly out to sea and the surf action. The nautically themed upstairs restaurant is smarter, venturing into more upmarket territory, but downstairs and on the terrace there's an ambience of post-surf informality, with worn wooden floors, order-at-the-bar service and warming hot chocolate with marshmallows. A simple daytime menu (ham, egg and chips, crab sandwiches, tapas) keeps everything under a tenner.

Watering Hole

Perranporth Beach, Perranporth, TR6 0JL (01872 572888, www.the-wateringhole.co.uk). Open Summer 9am-11pm daily. Winter 9am-11pm Fri-Sun.

Perranporth's venerable beachside venue stands in the middle of the Perran's wide sands. There is a menu of standard-issue bar food – burgers, steaks, Mexican beach fillers – but this is more of a beer-at-sunset spot. The views are fantastic, and this is just about as close to the sand as you can get.

Where to stay

In St Agnes, the Driftwood Spars (*see p98*) has decent-value rooms with not-so-subtle nautical theming, and the **St Agnes Hotel** (Churchtown, 01872 552307, www.stagneshotel. co.uk) has six neutral-toned en-suite guest rooms at budget prices in the heart of the village.

More upmarket is the **Rose-in-Vale** (Mithian, 01872 552202, www.rose-in-vale-hotel.co.uk), an idyllic Georgian country manor hotel with formal, flowery furnishings and a candlelit restaurant, set in 11 acres of wooded grounds.

Atlantic House

Quay Road, St Agnes, TR5 0RP (01872 553546, www.atlantichousecornwall. com). Rates £1,500-£2,950 per week for up to 10 adults.

A world away from the chintz of some of St Agnes's more traditional options, Atlantic House used to be award-winning B&B the Aramay until the owners decided to go down the self-catering route. It remains chic and atmospheric, with five high-spec en-suite bedrooms (32-inch TVs, quality linens, bathrobe and slippers) and a pleasantly secluded location midway between the beach and the village.

Beacon Cottage Farm

Beacon Drive, St Agnes, TR5 0NU (01872 552347, www. beaconcottagefarmholidays.co.uk). Open Apr-Sept. Rates £24-£34 per night for 2 people.

On the lower slopes of the St Agnes Beacon, not far from the cliffs, this campsite has uninterrupted vistas across miles of dramatic Cornish coastline – so the potential for a pitch with a view is high. The facilities are excellent and the crowd generally quiet and respectful, leaving just the sound of the wind racing across the moor to sing you to sleep, and the birds to wake you up. Chapel Porth, some 15 minutes on foot via the coastal path, is the nearest beach.

Falmouth & the Roseland Peninsula

The surf lessons, blustery cliffs and stag-do image of holidays in Cornwall may dominate the headlines, but the creeks, inlets and coves in and around the Carrick Roads estuary are another world – quietly beautiful, romantic and largely untouched. The merging of rivers, protected from the Atlantic swell by the protrusion of the Lizard Peninsula, has created endless watery escapes: silent wooded creeks, soft-sanded beaches hidden from view and rolling green hills that dip gently into the sea. With the villages of the Roseland also painting an idyllic picture, thanks to their well-kept white cottages, miniature harbours and traditional pubs, it all amounts to a powerful tranquilliser for stressed souls.

The wide waterway dividing Falmouth and the Roseland Peninsula is one of the world's largest natural harbours, and countless ships and sails dot the horizon. Overseeing the entrance is the lively town of Falmouth, currently enjoying its new-found status as Cornwall's most happening town.

FALMOUTH

The town

Seat of the county's first and only university, hotly tipped as Cornwall's boom town and home to the new-this-millennium **National Maritime Museum** (*see p106*), Falmouth has the feel of a town that's on its way up.

Where other Cornish seaside towns tend towards old-fashioned bucket-and-spade charm or cutesy chic (St Ives, Padstow, Fowey), Falmouth has a more youthful, cosmopolitan air, thanks in large part to the creation of University College Falmouth, which specialises in arts, design and media. There's now a plethora of hip bars and cafés, and a full calendar of festivals and events.

Until the 17th century, however, Falmouth was little more than a fishing village. Penryn, two miles to the north-west, was the main town, with Pendennis Castle protecting the mouth of the river. Established as the chief base for the Packet Ships in 1689, which took the first international mail to the Continent and the colonies, Falmouth developed quickly, and its huge natural harbour – the first or last stop before heading out or back across the Atlantic, and a safe haven in bad weather – sealed the town's fortunes.

From the modern, piazza-like Discovery Quay and Events Square, home to the National Maritime Museum, the road narrows into charming **Arwenack Street**, with its pretty Georgian façades, via the attractive granite **Church of King Charles the Martyr** (whose palm-framed square tower, overlooking the harbour, features on many a

Pendower Beach *see p111*

postcard), before becoming Church Street.

At the far end of town, after the usual chain stores, mobile phone shops and estate agents, is the charismatic old High Street. Here you can browse galleries, antique shops and second-hand stores. Buy beautiful bread at **Stones Bakery** (07791 003183, www. stonesbakery.co.uk, closed Mon, Sun); drink coffee and flick through the records at **Jam** (*see p104*); or head for the cobbled enclave of Old Brewery Yard, home to the **Mine restaurant** and the **Chintz Bar** (for both, *see p104*).

On the Moor, a large, continental-style square that serves as both marketplace and bus terminal, is another testament to the town's strong artistic identity: the award-winning **Falmouth Art Gallery** (01326

Gyllyngvase Beach *see p103*

313863, www.falmouthartgallery.com, closed Sun). It houses original works by major 19th- and 20th-century artists – including Alfred Munnings, HS Tuke, JM Waterhouse and Henry Moore – and also features contemporary art exhibitions. It's very family-friendly, with automata, a papier mâché show and children's workshops.

Pendower Beach *see p111*

Opposite are the 111 steps of **Jacob's Ladder**, which ascend the large hill above the town. The steps have no real biblical association – they were installed by Jacob Hamblen, a builder and property owner, to facilitate access between his business (at the bottom) and some of his property (at the top). Once you get your breath back, follow the road to the left around the brow of the hill for a fabulous panorama over the town and across the bay. You can take it all in over a quiet pint at the **Seaview Inn** (Wodehouse Terrace, 01326 311359, www.seaviewinnfalmouth.co.uk).

Out on the promontory stands **Pendennis Castle**, built at the same time (1543) as its twin **St Mawes** (for both, *see p106*), a mile across the estuary. Just below, a road runs all around the point, taking in the docks on the way. In 1860, the foundation of **Falmouth Docks** created a focus for maritime industries, and an extensive ship repair and maintenance industry. Beneath the road that leads around the point, a number of narrow paths weave between the rocks, trees and remains of defensive batteries. The castle road then takes you to the town's three main sandy beaches, which have clear waters and views of the bay: Blue Flag-winning **Gyllyngvase** is the nearest to town, with **Swanpool** and **Maenporth** stretching out to the south (all have public facilities and cafés, and are ideal for families).

In season, consider doing away with parking headaches and use the **Ponsharden Park & Float** (01326 319417, 01872 861910, www.falmouth. co.uk, closed Oct-May), which takes you down the Penryn River by boat, all the way to the quay in the centre of Falmouth.

The **Carrick Roads** is home to the last remaining oyster fishery in Europe that is still dredged under sail and oar, with traditional boats working between October and March. The beginning of the season is celebrated every October with the Falmouth Oyster Festival.

Around Falmouth

Effectively conjoined to Falmouth, but once a harbour town in its own right, **Penryn** has changed considerably since the foundation of the university here. Where you might once have found odd charity shops in which to rummage, you are now more likely to stumble across an offbeat interiors boutique, a gallery or a deli along its narrow main street. Down on the water, new development Jubilee Wharf houses the **Muddy Beach café** (*see p108*).

Across the Penryn River from Falmouth are the attractive and affluent yacht-heavy villages of **Flushing** and **Mylor**, accessible by ferry from Falmouth. The **Long Close Farm Shop** (Tregew Road, www. tregewfarm.co.uk) in Flushing is excellent for seasonal vegetables, although check the website before making a special visit, as its future was uncertain when this guide went to press.

The serene waters and exotic gardens of the north bank of the Helford River – around five miles to the south of town – are also easily reached from Falmouth; *see p139*.

Where to eat & drink

There are bars, restaurants and cafés around every corner in Falmouth. As well as those reviewed in full below, we recommend **Jam** (32 High Street, 01326 211722, www.jamrecords.co.uk, closed Sun, Mon), a café in a record shop; and **Mine** (4 Old Brewery Yard, 01326 211073, www.restaurantmine. co.uk), a friendly little restaurant with a compact menu but great food, and outdoor tables in a cobbled yard. Also in Old Brewery Yard, the **Chintz Bar**

(Dental Surgery, Old Brewery Yard, 07538 006495, www.thechintzbar. com) offers cheese, wine and a huge dollop of wilful quirkiness.

Our pick of the fish and chip outlets is **Harbour Lights** (Arwenack Street, 01326 316934, www.harbourlights.co. uk), a restaurant and takeaway; it's cheery and clean, staff will grill fish on request – and children get their meals in 'beach buckets'.

Watering holes near the water include the **Front** (Custom House Quay, 01326 212168), a small bar on the quay that has a thriving music programme (including Cornish folk nights), and a vast selection of rum and ale; the **Shed** (Discovery Quay, 01326 318502), a colourful, kitschy bar and restaurant, and one of the few places in Falmouth to catch the evening sun; and highly rated seafood restaurant **Hooked on the Rocks** (*see p108*).

Cove Restaurant & Bar

Maenporth Beach, TR11 5HN (01326 251136, www.thecovemaenporth. co.uk). Open Summer 11am-11pm daily. Winter 11am-3pm, 6-11pm Mon-Fri, Sat; 11am-11pm Sun. Food served Summer noon-9.30pm daily. Winter noon-2.30pm, 6.30-9.30pm Mon-Fri, Sat; noon-9.30pm Sat.

This friendly, stylish restaurant, a few paces from the shore at Maenporth, has a café and tapas menu for beach breaks, along with more substantial lunches and dinners. The short but creative menu changes every six to eight weeks to make the most of local ingredients, especially seafood (Falmouth Bay scallops, for instance, or Cornish sole steamed with coriander and lemongrass). There are some well thought out options for vegetarians too, such as red onion and pear tarte tatin with feta and endive salad. The large terrace has gorgeous views over the beach, and the decor is tasteful and minimalist. Off-season, there are regular culinary masterclasses (fish, game, chocolate), which cost from as little as £12.95 per person.

Gylly Beach Cafe *see p108*

Places to visit

National Maritime Museum Cornwall

FALMOUTH

National Maritime Museum Cornwall 💜
Discovery Quay, Falmouth, TR11 3QY (01326 313388, www.nmmc.co.uk). Open 10am-5pm daily. Admission £14.75; free-£7.50 reductions.

Housed in an impressive wooden building, the five- year-old NMM features a huge collection of restored sailing craft and nautical objects, as well as hands-on interactive displays, audio-visuals, talks and special exhibitions, covering all aspects of maritime life, from boat design to fascinating tales of survival at sea (the exhibition on the history of diving is particularly good). One highlight for all ages is the Tidal Zone, where you can go underwater and look out into the harbour through two large windows; stand there for long enough and you'll see the tide rise and fall. Another is the 360 degree views over the harbour and towards Flushing from the top of the 95-foot Look Out. One ticket buys you annual unlimited access – and given the vast scope of the museum, it's worth considering a second visit. There is a stylish glass-fronted café on the first floor, looking out over the water.

Pendennis Castle
Pendennis Headland, Falmouth, TR11 4LP (01326 316594, www.english-heritage.org. uk). Open July, Aug 10am-6pm daily. Apr-June, Sept 10am-5pm daily. Oct-Mar 10am-4pm daily. £12.50; free-£12.20 reductions; £35.10 family.

Sitting fatly on the rocky peninsula overlooking one of Falmouth's best beaches, Pendennis cannot be ignored. It was constructed between 1540 and 1545 to form the Cornish end of the chain of coastal castles built by Henry VIII to counter the threat from France and Spain. In the centuries that followed, the fortress was frequently adapted to face new enemies, right through until 1945. In 1646, prior to the Civil War, the fort played host to the future Charles II before he sailed to the Isles of Scilly, when it withstood five months of siege, before becoming the penultimate Royalist garrison on the British mainland to surrender. Pendennis also saw significant action during World War II. The Guardhouse has been returned to its World War I appearance; underground, there's a network of magazines and tunnels, including the World War II Half Moon Battery, as well as the original 16th-century keep with its recreated Tudor gun.

In summer, battle re-enactments take place on the gun deck, and open-air concerts and plays are performed on the lawn; in July and August, there's the daily ceremonial firing of the Noonday Gun. Christmas shopping and Cornish yuletide events are also held here.

ROSELAND PENINSULA

St Mawes Castle
St Mawes, TR2 5DE (01326 270526, www.english-heritage.org.uk). Open July, Aug 10am-6pm Mon-Fri, Sun. Apr-June, Sept 10am-5pm Mon-Fri, Sun. Oct 10am-4pm daily. Nov-Mar 10am-4pm Sat, Sun. Admission £7.60; free-£6.90 reductions; £19.80 family.

Like its larger sister across the water, Pendennis Castle, St Mawes Castle was built between 1539 and 1543 to defend against attacks from the French and Spanish that never came. When the castle was finally threatened with some serious action in the Civil War, its occupants quickly surrendered it to Parliamentarian forces, hence preserving its immaculate state (it is one of the finest, most complete examples of Henry VIII's south-coast forts).

St Mawes has the same clover-leaf

design as Pendennis, but the three semicircular bastions that surround the four-storey central tower make it the more architecturally distinguished of the two. The castle also enjoys the benefits of its remote location; whereas Pendennis Point sees ice-cream vans, daytrippers and canoodling teenagers crowding the car park day and night, St Mawes enjoys nothing but exposed rocks and fresh, panoramic seascapes.

Tregothnan Estate
Tregothnan, TR2 4AJ (01872 520000, www. tregothnan.co.uk). Tours by arrangement only.

The beautiful old country estate of Tregothnan, not far from Truro, has been owned for 450 years by the Boscawan family. It is now best known for its line of premium tea, grown in its gardens – the first tea to be produced in the UK – and honey (including manuka honey). Private two-hour tours of the historic botanical garden, including a cream tea, cost £65.

TRURO

Royal Cornwall Museum
River Street, Truro, TR1 2SJ (01872 272205, www.royalcornwallmuseum.org.uk). Open 10am-4.45pm Tue-Sat. Admission free.

The county's best exhibition space is a must-visit for anyone interested in Cornwall's history and culture. There is a permanent display on the history of Cornwall, from the Stone Age to the present day, and the museum also has a selection of paintings by Newlyn School artists, a collection of rare mineral specimens, and old master drawings in the De Pass Gallery (John Constable, Van Dyck, Rubens). Attached to the museum is the Courtney Library, which specialises in local history resources, and there's an attractive café by the entrance.

Trelissick ★
Feock, TR3 6QL (01872 862090, www. nationaltrust.org.uk). Open Feb-Oct 10.30am-5.30pm daily. Jan, Nov, Dec 11am-4pm daily.Admission £8; £4 reduction; £20 family.

Gloriously sited on the river and surrounded by (free) walking trails (through the woods, along the water and criss-crossing the estate), Trelissick is a fine example of a

grand Cornish garden. The 30 acres feature an apple orchard and an array of mature trees and plants, many of which are rare and exotic enough to excite the most jaded of gardeners. Only the grounds and gardens are open to the public, together with a café with pleasant courtyard seating, the inevitable NT gift shop, and a rather more charming gallery showing work by Cornish artists and craftspeople. Best of all, the gardens lead down to a couple of ferry landing stages, making them easily accessible from the south coast.

Truro Cathedral
St Mary Street, Truro, TR1 2AF (01872 276782, www.trurocathedral.org.uk). Open 7.30am-6pm Mon-Sat; 9am-7pm Sun. Admission free.

Cornwall's only cathedral, a vast, late 19th-century Gothic Revival edifice, is so imposing it seems to dwarf the rest of this low-rise county capital (indeed, it is said the architect had to build a clearly discernible bend in the nave to fit it into the tight city-centre space). With three Bath stone spires, an ornate façade and some of the world's finest Victorian stained glass, it can't fail to impress. At the time of writing, there were major regeneration plans on the table to breathe new life into the gardens behind the cathedral and restore the central spire.

Gylly Beach Cafe♥

Gyllyngvase Beach, Cliff Road, TR11 4PA (01326 312884, www.gyllybeach.com). Open Summer 9am-midnight daily. Winter 9am-5pm Mon-Wed; 9am-11pm Thur-Sun. Breakfast served 9-11.45am daily. Lunch served noon-5pm daily. Dinner served Summer 6-9pm daily. Winter 6-9pm Thur-Sun.

Despite the slick look – lots of white, blond woods and trendy (though actually very comfortable) white plastic chairs – prices are perfectly reasonable at this bar-restaurant, right on Gyllyngvase Beach. Menu options include gourmet burgers (in Baker Tom's ciabatta) with chunky skin-on chips, and posh fish and chips. But the wide, wraparound beachside terrace at the front, giving far-reaching views of the estuary, is the real draw (fleece blankets are provided on nippy nights). Gylly attracts a mix of well-heeled tourists and locals of all ages, while the serving staff are bright young things who have perfected the art of speedy service.

Hooked on the Rocks

Swanpool Rd, Falmouth TR11 5BG (01326 311886, www.hookedontherocksfalmouth. com). Open noon-3pm and 5pm-9.30pm daily.

Perched about Swanpool Beach with fabulous views, the Michelin Guide-included Hooked on the Rocks specialises in – surprise! – locally caught seafood, with lobsters, scallops and fish fresh from Falmouth Bay. An abundance of outside seating – 16 tables in all – has helped it weather the coronavirus pandemic as well as anyone, although do wrap up warm as most of it's unheated.

Muddy Beach

Jubilee Wharf, Commercial Rd, Penryn TR10 8FG (01326 374424, www. muddybeach.com). Open 9.30am-3pm Tue-Sun; breakfast served 9.30-11.30am; lunch served noon-2.30pm.

This family-run cafe-restaurant-bar is about as welcoming as it gets, and offers fresh food and beach views all day long, with an emphasis on a big welcome: kids, dogs, solo customers and groups are all encouraged to come along for the smashed peas poached egg in the morning, a Cornish crab sandwich for lunch, or catch of the day for dinner.

Provedore♥

43 Trelawney Road, Falmouth, TR11 3LY (01326 314888, www.provedore. co.uk). Open 9am-3.30pm Tue, Wed; 9am-3.30pm, 6.30-10pm Thur, Fri; 9am-1pm, 6.30-10pm Sat. Breakfast served 9am-11.30am Tue-Fri; 9am-1pm Sat. Lunch served noon-3pm Tue-Fri. Dinner served 6.30-9pm Thur-Sat.

This minute neighbourhood restaurant used to be a deli specialising in the finest French and Mediterranean imports, with delicious soups, paellas and stews to take away. But the cooking was so good, and the welcome so warm, that everyone wanted to eat in and it morphed into a tapas bar and café. Saturday morning breakfasts (local sausages, foraged wild mushrooms, great coffee) have reached near-cult status, while the Cornish octopus, authentic bouillabaisse and paddle crab bisque have to be tasted to be believed (the seafood is delivered alive early evening). At time of writing, Provedore had reinvented itself as a deli and takeaway only due to the coronavirus pandemic. But the plan is to resume table service when possible.

Restaurant Four

33 High St, Falmouth TR11 2AD (01326 218138, www.restaurantfour.co.uk). Lunch served noon-2pm Wed-Sat and noon-4pm Sun; dinner served 6-9pm Tue-Sat.

Yet another great little seafood joint, the ultra cosy Restaurant Four has only been able to operate a takeaway service in spring 2021 due to its tiny number of covers, but by the time you read this it should have bounced back. Chef Matthew Unwin-Springett runs the gamut, from a relatively rustic lunch menu to a full-on, nine-course tasting menu with paired wines.

Star & Garter

52 High Street, Falmouth, TR11 2AF (01326 316663, www. starandgarterfalmouth.co.uk). Open 11am-midnight Mon-Sat; noon-11.30pm Sun. Lunch served noon-2.30pm, dinner served 6.30-9.30pm Mon-Sat. Food served 12.30-9.30pm Sun.

The prettily fronted Star & Garter pub, with original tiling and blue-painted windows, has always had fantastic, 180-degree views across the harbour and over to Flushing. But in recent years, it has also garnered a reputation for great food (particularly its Thursday sushi night) and music (jazz on Mondays, folk on Thursdays and blues on Sunday).

Wheelhouse

Upton Slip, Falmouth, TR11 3DQ (01326 318050).

The Wheelhouse has to be Falmouth's worst-kept secret. Despite shunning publicity, not having a website and occupying a side-street location, it is fully booked months in advance. The big deal? Some of the finest shellfish in these parts – always super-fresh and served with respect to the delicate flavours amid quirky, intimate surrounds. Ditch the cutlery at your earliest convenience, and dive in – fingers first – to whole crab, shell-on juicy prawns, lobster, oysters and mussels, all designed for sharing. Book well ahead, particularly for the excellent monthly paella night.

Where to stay

Greenbank Hotel

Harbourside, Falmouth, TR11 2SR (01326 312440, www.greenbank-hotel.co.uk). Rates £99-£319 double incl breakfast.

Dating from 1640, this is the oldest hotel in Falmouth, and it has a distinguised history to prove it, boasting Florence Nightingale and Kenneth Wind in the Willows Grahame as former guests. History is evident all around you, in the shape of high ceilings, sweeping staircases and tasteful but traditional decor. Situated on the Falmouth harbourfront with unrivalled views of Flushing – and its own 16th-century private quay to boot – the hotel is popular with the yachting crowd, but is also a great base for anyone wanting a touch of class within a stone's throw of the town centre. Modern British cuisine, with the emphasis on fish and seafood, and twinkling harbour views are the order of the day at the hotel's Harbourside restaurant.

St Michael's Hotel & Spa

Gyllyngvase Beach, TR11 4NB (01326 454246, www.stmichaelsresort.com). Rates around £130-£289 double incl breakfast (min 2-night stay).

Less prominent than the imposing Falmouth Beach Hotel, St Michael's has the advantage of being situated right opposite Gyllyngvase Beach (and ten minutes' walk from town). Set back from the main road behind subtropical gardens (which include a children's play area and an outdoor massage pagoda), it has a host of extra features to add to the business of bed and board – including an indoor pool, sauna, jacuzzi, steam rooms, gym and sundeck. The fresh, nautical-inspired interior is light and airy (where else would you find a boat for a reception desk and beach hut-style toilets?), the comfortable rooms are amply equipped, and there are a number of scenic lounges and outdoor terraces.

Sixteen

16 Western Terrace, Falmouth, TR11 4QW (01326 319920, www.sixteenfalmouth. co.uk). From £350 for the whole place.

The stylish rooms at Sixteen set themselves apart from average seaside digs with French antiques, flatscreen TVs and handmade Cornish soaps – and the all-round whiff of quality. All rooms are en-suite but shower only. It's a 15-minute walk into town, and about the same to the beach.

ROSELAND PENINSULA

Famously favoured by holidaying surrealist artists (Lee Miller, Roland Penrose, Max Ernst, Man Ray et al) in the 1930s, the glamorous yachting set in the 1950s and '60s, and a string of A-listers in recent years, the Roseland Peninsula could hardly be described as an insider secret. But even in the

Ten Cornish churches

St Anthony, Roseland
Architectural historian Nikolaus Pevsner described this as the 'best example in the county of what a parish church was like in the 12th and 13th centuries.' But it's also worth a visit for its roof, floor tiles and stained glass, added during a 19th-century restoration. See p111.

St Enodoc, Trebetherick
The church of St Enodoc, part of which dates from the 12th century, is the final resting place of Sir John Betjeman, who was particularly fond of the building, penning a verse to it: 'Sunday Afternoon Service at St Enodoc'. His grave is near the south side of the church. See p68.

St Germans
The site of the church at St Germans, in eastern Cornwall, served as the county's cathedral from 926, and is mentioned in the Domesday Book; it's still the largest parish in Cornwall. Much altered over the centuries, the church is a mix of styles; don't miss the magnificent Norman door on its west side. See p49.

St Ildierna, Lansallos
Dominating the tiny parish of Lansallos (see p48) in south-eastern Cornwall, this 14th-century granite church was damaged by fire in 2005, finally re-opening in 2009 after massive fundraising efforts. Happily, the church's medieval pews, carved from English oak, survived the blaze.

St Just-in-Roseland, Roseland
The beautiful 13th-century church of St Just-in-Roseland, north of St Mawes (see p111) stands by the water's edge, on the site of a fifth-century chapel. Its beautiful riverside gardens are filled with semi-tropical plants, while the path to the church is lined with granite blocks carved with biblical verses.

busy summer months, it somehow manages to feel like one. It's easy to escape the crowds, and the area offers a very peaceful brand of tourism: row your boat up a quiet creek, learn how to sail, or curl up with a book and a bucolic view.

A large part of the Roseland's charm lies in its deep seclusion. Attractive as its winding roads undoubtedly are, skirting open fields framed with leafy hedges and dipping down through wooded valleys, a couple of return trips by road to Truro or Falmouth are usually enough to make you swear to take the boat or the ferry next time. There are regular **boat crossings** from St Mawes to both Falmouth and Truro (Enterprise Boats, www.enterprise-boats.co.uk, 01326 313234, closed Oct-Apr), while the year-round King Harry Ferry (01872 862312, www.falriver.co.uk) is the only vehicular crossing of the Fal, and one of only five remaining chain ferries in the country. The *King Harry* takes just five scenic minutes to cross this section of the Fal, flanked on either side by thick woods.

An upmarket holiday resort since Edwardian times, **St Mawes** is the largest settlement on the peninsula. Neat white cottages and smart townhouses cling to the hillside above the small, sheltered harbour, with the dramatic shapes of dark Monterey pine trees framing the skyline on the brow of the hill behind – and **St Mawes Castle** (*see p106*) keeping watch on the headland. Across the sheltered mouth of the Percuil River, the views of **St Anthony lighthouse** have graced the covers of many a glossy holiday magazine citing comparisons with the South of France. The retreat was given further polish in 1999, when celebrated interior designer Olga Polizzi renovated the Hotel Tresanton (*see p113*).

From St Mawes, take the little **ferry**♥ (www.falriver.co.uk, closed Nov-Easter) across to **Place**; it's a short but very scenic excursion, and gives access to some superb walks on **St Anthony Head** and to the lovely church of **St Anthony** (*see p110*). There are no food and drink purchasing opportunities once there, so it's worth stocking up at the tiny **St Mawes bakery** (01326 270292) on the quay beforehand – their pasties are excellent.

The Roseland is awash with exquisite views, charming villages and untouched coves with clear waters, so you could strike out in almost any direction and encounter scenes of rare beauty. One soothing route is to head north of St Mawes and up St Just Creek to **St-Just-in-Roseland Church**♥ (*see p110*), set in steep subtropical gardens on the side of the creek, with its sandbar and moored yachts. It is a breathtaking spot – 'to many people the most beautiful churchyard on earth', according to John Betjeman.

Along the south coast, stop at the charming village of **Portscatho**, which has a tiny harbour, a scattering of shops and cafés and a tempting pint stop in the shape of the Plume of Feathers (*see p112*). Its nearest beaches are just around the curve of Gerrans Bay: secluded **Porthcurnick** (limited parking), and **Pendower** and **Carne**, which join at low tide to form a long, sandy stretch.

A few miles on, follow the narrow lane down to the tiny fishing village of **Portloe**, whose whitewashed and pastel-painted cottages are tightly packed around a steep rocky inlet and harbour. Although fishermen still sell the day's catch on its small, pebbly beach, the four-wheel drives and Mercedes parked up the hill tell a different story about the village's full- and part-time inhabitants. The coastal path heading westwards from here gives yet more stunning coastal views back towards the **Roseland** and nearby **Gul Rock**.

St Mary Magdalene, Launceston
One of Cornwall's most picturesque towns (*see page 20*) is also home to one of its most imposing churches. St Mary Magdalene's tower dates back to the 14th-century, but the rest of the structure was erected in the late 16th century. The church is best known for its ornately carved granite exterior – a tour de force of the highly skilled Cornish stonemasons.

St Morwenna & St John the Baptist, Morwenstow
Set near the cliffs on Cornwall's west coast, Morwenstow's church is a 13th-century Norman structure. A figurehead from a ship wrecked nearby lies in the graveyard, but the church is best known for its eccentric vicar, Reverend Hawker: he pioneered the notion of Harvest Festival as we know it, dressed in long sea boots and a pink hat, and wrote poetry in a driftwood hut on the cliffs (*see p72*), now run by the National Trust.

St Nonna, Altarnun
Known locally as the 'Cathedral in the Moor' (it's made from unquarried moorland granite), Altarnun's 15th-century church (*see p20*) is topped by one of the highest towers in Cornwall. Inside, carved 16th-century bench ends depict jesters, musicians and religious figures; at the entrance to the churchyard, a weathered, weighty Celtic cross is thought to date from the sixth century.

St Senara, Zennor
Extensively restored in the 19th century, this lovely 12th-century church is known for its carving of the Mermaid of Zennor. In the past, villagers came here to give thanks for the safe return of local fishermen, and a good day's catch. *See p151*.

St Winwaloe, The Lizard
A stone's throw from the sea at Church Cove, St Winwaloe is said to be one of the oldest churches in Cornwall. Its precarious position (it was once known as the 'church of the storms') has meant is has been reinforced several times since the main structure was built in the 15th century. The detached belltower dates from the 13th century. *See p127*.

Gul Rock *see p111*

Inland, the quaint village of **Veryan** is famous for its curious thatched and crucifix-topped roundhouses, built in the 19th century by a local minister for his five daughters. Constructed without any corners, these houses apparently ensured that the devil would have nowhere to hide.

Where to eat & drink

Outside of the hotels, the Roseland's sleepy villages are not the place for complicated food and fine wine. Nonetheless, they do have a pleasing selection of smart yet traditional pubs. The **Plume of Feathers** (The Square, 01872 580321) in Portscatho serves good, low-key food and Cornish ale; the **King's Head** (01872 501263, https://kings-head-ruan.co.uk, closed Nov-Easter Mon, Sun eve) is a popular gastropub in the hamlet of Ruan Lanihorne; and the **Roseland Inn** (01872 580254, www.roseland inn.co.uk) in Philleigh has its own microbrewery. In St Mawes, the **Victory Inn** (01326 270324, www.victory-inn.co.uk), formerly a fishermen's haunt, now sees more chinos and blazers than it does yellow fishing overalls.

Before catching the *King Harry Ferry*, you'll see the quirky **Smugglers' Cottage**, signposted right on the road to the ferry. Alas, this 15th-century riverside cottage – which served as the embarkation point for US troops for the D-Day landings –

seems not to have reopened as a café following a 'temporary' closure a few years back, but it's still an interesting spot and we can but hope.

The best restaurants for high dining are found in hotels. The dining room at the **Hotel Tresanton** (*see below*) is the standout choice, but the **Lugger** and the **Nare** (for both, *see p114*) are also accomplished.

Driftwood

Driftwood Hotel, Rosevine, Portscatho, TR2 5EW (01872 580644, www.driftwoodhotel. co.uk). Dinner served 7-9.30pm daily.

While the north coast gets most of the gastronomic glitter – Nathan Outlaw and Rick Stein are both on Cornwall's northern shores – the Driftwood boutique hotel, tucked away on the south coast near Portscatho, has been quietly making a name for itself in fine dining in recent years. Head chef Olly Pierrepont delivers an evening menu based around fresh Cornish seafood, plus afternoon tea, Sunday lunch, and even a picnic menu to take down to the beach.

Hotel Tresanton ♥

27 Lower Castle Road, St Mawes, TR2 5DR (01326 270055, www.tresanton.com). Lunch served 12.30-2.30pm, tea served 3.30-5.30pm, dinner served 7-9.30pm daily.

Dinner at the Tresanton exudes effortless quality: everything from the cut-above waiting staff to the thick, starched napkins, smart decor and elevated prices is a statement of serious gastronomic intent. The food delivers too: choose from a daily-changing Modern European menu of fresh fish dishes, classic meat selections or imaginative vegetarian fare (pappardelle with wild mushrooms and truffle oil, for example), all executed with flair and precision. Summer brings cocktails and dinner on the terrace, with views over the St Anthony lighthouse and Fal Estuary. For food and service of this quality in the area, the Tresanton has few peers. If your budget won't stretch to dinner, instead call by for a light lunch or a cream tea on the terrace.

108 Coffee House

108c Kenwyn Street, Truro, TR1 3DJ (07582 339636, www.108coffeehouse.co.uk). Open 7am-6pm Mon-Fri; 8am-6pm Sat.

Paul and Michelle opened this coffee shop on a shoestring in 2011 with the simple but thoroughly worthwhile aim of serving spectacular coffee, with home-made cakes on the side. The interior is spare, with only a few window stools and seats, but the coffee is worth a detour, served in glasses with milky foam art on top. Beans come care of Cornish coffee company, Origin. Free Wi-Fi.

Where to stay

The most distinguished self-catering accommodation on the Roseland is located on the romantic private estate of Rosteague (01326 555555. www. classic.co.uk), where there are two gorgeous old properties for rent.

Driftwood Hotel

See left. Rates £190-£315 double incl breakfast.

This privately owned beach house stands amid seven acres of gardens, with a path leading down to a private beach. Catering to families (there's a small games room for children) as well as couples, the Driftwood is all about carefully considered comfort. Design is crisp but informal, with lots of natural fabrics and stone. The smart white restaurant is another enticement, as are after-dinner drinks watching the moon on the water from the decking area. A beautiful but isolated location makes this one for willing escape artists rather than those on a whistle-stop tour of Cornwall.

Hotel Tresanton

See left. Rates £270-£365 double incl breakfast.

Renowned interior designer Olga Polizzi's Hotel Tresanton has become synonymous with waterside chic, having played host to a stellar cast of celebrities since it opened in 1999. Nevertheless, it still has an intimate and homely atmosphere that will make mere mortals feel welcome. Originally created in the 1940s as a yachtsmen's club, the hotel became a well-known haunt for yachties and tourists in the 1950s and '60s. Polizzi bought the place in 1997 and spent two years and a cool £2 million renovating and restoring it.

Occupying a cluster of houses built into the hillside on different levels, 27 of the Tresanton's 29 rooms have views out to sea and the St Anthony lighthouse on the headland beyond. Nautical patterns influence the design of some rooms, while others blend natural cream and beige hues with dark wood and richly coloured fabrics. Original works of art adorn the hallways and lounge areas, with pieces by Terry Frost, Barbara Hepworth and acclaimed St Mawes sculptor Julian Dyson in the collection. Unlike many seaside retreats, Tresanton is a hotel for all seasons: spend a day aboard the *Pinuccia* (a 48ft classic racing yacht built to represent Italy in the 1938 World Cup), followed by dinner on the terrace in summer; in winter, make the most of the bridge and treatment weekend packages, DVD library and cosy lounge. The upmarket restaurant is superb (*see p113*).

Lugger Hotel
Portloe, TR2 5RD (01872 501322, www. luggerhotel.com). Rates £200-£385 double incl breakfast.

The interior at the Lugger is elegantly simple with contemporary touches, but its unassailable asset is a remarkable setting. The 17th-century inn (ask about the landlord who was hanged for smuggling in the 1890s) and fishermen's cottages that now collectively form the 21-room hotel are built right into the cliffs above the tiny cove and fishing village of Portloe, mere yards from the water. Public areas include a lounge with a well-stoked log fire in winter and a terrace in summer, as well as a swanky British-European restaurant with sea views.

Nare Hotel
Carne Beach, TR2 5PF (01872 501111, www.narehotel.co.uk). Rates £328-£620 double incl breakfast & afternoon tea.

Standing proud above Carne Beach on Gerrans Bay, the four-star Nare is an elegant, wholeheartedly traditional retreat. First opened in 1925, the extended 37-room hotel still retains much of its original character, with winding corridors, log fires and rooms bursting with antiques. The bedrooms add to the sense of old-world charm, with carriage clocks, floral fabrics and high-backed armchairs. It's also worthy of note for its exceptional service, which is all about old-fashioned manners and attention to detail. Facilities include indoor and outdoor pools, subtropical gardens leading down to the beach, sauna, hot tub, gym, beauty salon and billiards room, plus two restaurants with views.

Rosevine
Portscatho, TR2 5EW (01872 580206, www.rosevine.co.uk). Rates from £169 for 2 people; from £244 family room.

This luxury family-oriented apart-hotel has some of the best-looking accommodation on the Roseland. Its 15 studios and mini apartments are equipped with compact kitchens and decorated in pastels, New England stripes and rejuvenated antiques. Other facilities include a children's play area, large gardens, a heated indoor pool and a games room – and, most usefully, the unspoilt beach of Porthcurnick at the end of the road. The Dining Room, serving rustic British food, looks out across the exotic gardens to the sea. Cots and baby monitors are provided at no extra cost, and babysitters can be called in from a local agency.

St Mawes Hotel
Marine Parade, St Mawes, TR2 5DW (01326 270266, www.stmaweshotel. co.uk). Rates £265-£415 double incl breakfast.

This waterfront establishment, in the centre of town, has nine simple but attractively decorated rooms for B&B (or dinner, bed and breakfast), along with four rooms in the newly converted fisherman's cottage out back. The sea-view brasserie and bar downstairs are popular, so be warned that this may not be the most serene of retreats in the summer months.

Truro Farmers' Market *see p117*

Place Ferry leaving St Mawes *see p110*

Five scenic branch lines

Back in the 1960s, the Beeching Axe saw the controversial closure of numerous branch lines, as the government attempted to cut the cost of maintaining the railways. Since then, many have reopened, with several now existing purely as heritage railways. Others are part of 'rail ale' trails (www.railaletrail.com) – routes that encourage rail travellers to sample the local brews at pubs near the lines. For more information on the following routes, visit www.greatscenicrailways.com.

Atlantic Coast Line

This 20-mile community railway runs from the village of Par to Newquay. En route, it passes through the steep-sided, densely wooded Luxulyan Valley, designated a World Heritage Site thanks to its early 19th-century industrial remains.

Looe Valley Line

Just under nine miles long, the Looe Valley Line offers access to some of Cornwall's finest walking and cycling terrain – not to mention some excellent country pubs. The route runs from the market town of Liskeard to Looe.

Maritime Line

Following the valley of the River Fal, the Maritime Line connects Truro and Falmouth, with stops at Perranwell, Penryn and Penmere. After Perranwell, the lines crosses a lofty viaduct, with views of the Carnon Valley – a former tin-mining area – below. Walking trails run from (and sometimes between) the various stations.

St Ives Bay Line

Taking just 12 minutes to make the journey from St Erth (where it connects with the mainline), along the birdlife-filled Hayle Estuary and Lelant Saltings, past the white sands of Carbis Bay and into the heart of St Ives, this has to be one of the most dazzlingly scenic branch lines in the country. There are also two or three direct services from Penzance to St Ives.

Tamar Valley Line

This glorious 14-mile stretch of track runs between Plymouth and Gunnislake, over the border in Cornwall. It follows the River Tamar and its estuary, before crossing the river on the mighty Calstock viaduct, completed in 1907.

TRURO

Located at the head of the **Carrick Roads estuary**, the 'capital' of Cornwall has an air of cultural and financial self-sufficiency that sets it apart from the rest of the county, with rows of pastel-painted Georgian townhouses and a triple-spired Gothic Revival **cathedral** (*see p107*). As a comforting microcosm of urban life, with boutiques, cocktail bars and fancy delis, Truro tends to attract big-city refugees wishing to live out the country dream without wanting to get their feet muddy.

There is hardly a trace now of the working quays that once ran along the river, but the **piazza**, on the old Lemon Quay, is a busy outdoor space with café tables, markets and a plethora of outdoor events year-round. **Truro Farmers' Market** (01637 830958, www.trurofarmers.co.uk) takes place here every Wednesday and Saturday, as does the Truro Food Festival in September (www.trurofood festival.com).

The well-heeled satellite villages of Truro – **Kea**, **Feock**, **Point** and **Devoran** – spread out south along the banks of the Carrick Roads.

Truro is linked to Falmouth by an attractive branch line (*see left*), which takes 20 minutes, and a ferry that leaves from Town Quay, near Tesco, or from Malpas just downriver if the tide is low; visit www.enterprise-boats.co.uk for details.

The **tourist office** (01872 274555, closed summer Sun; winter Sat, Sun) is next to the City Hall – now the Hall for Cornwall – on Boscawan Street.

Where to eat & drink

Café culture is thriving in Truro, with no shortage of lattes and posh paninis served in smart surrounds. Among the nicest spots are the **Duke Street Sandwich Deli** (10 Duke Street, 01872

Things to do

FALMOUTH

Cornish Diving Centre
Bar Rd, Falmouth, TR11 4BN (07885 771282, www.cornishdiving.co.uk). Open 9am-5.30pm Tue-Sat. Courses from £65.

The Cornish Diving Centre is a highly rated, family-friendly centre with taster dives – and parties! – for children over ten. There's a variety of courses, from an introduction to snorkelling or a 'safari' through the Cornish waters, to refresher courses aimed at those with prior experience looking to blow the cobwebs off.

Enterprise Boats
66 Trefusis Road, Flushing, TR11 5TY (01326 374241, www.enterprise-boats.co.uk). Open May-Sept; times vary, check website for details. Admission £10 return; £7.50 single.

Enterprise Boats links Falmouth, Truro and St Mawes, as well as Trelissick garden (see p107), with its small, charming ferries. The tranquil journey from Falmouth to Truro takes around an hour, and makes for a brilliant sightseeing trip. Boarding in Falmouth is from the Prince of Wales quay, and in Truro from Town Quay (tide-dependent). Check the website for timetables.

Orca Sea Safaris
Discovery Quay, Falmouth, TR11 3QY (01326 214928, www.orcaseasafaris.co.uk). Trips by arrangement only. Admission £24-£40; £16-£28 reductions.

Setting out from Falmouth, a 12-seater Rigid Inflatable Boat takes you out to sea to spot dolphins, seals and basking sharks (and even a whale, if you're lucky). The scheduled trips can be booked on the website year-round.

Sea Kayaking Cornwall
Swan Beach, Falmouth (07789 286080 www.seakayakingcornwall.com). Open by arrangement only. Courses from £195.

Based in Falmouth, SKC runs one- to five-day kayaking (and surf-kayaking) courses for all levels and abilities. Budding adventurers will be tempted by the multi-day expeditions, which might involve wild camping and foraging; destinations include the Isles of Scilly.

Ships & Castles Leisure Centre
Pendennis Headland, Falmouth, TR11 4NG (01326 212129, www.better.org.uk). Open times vary, check website for details. Admission £6.60; £5.50 reductions.

On days when the real sea is out of the question, families might try the wave machine and little 'beach' at this pool. In addition to areas for lengths, the fun pool has a flume, a rapid river ride, a ridewave machine and jacuzzis (with bubble pools for toddlers). Located on the Pendennis Headland, it's an attractive place to paddle, with a large glass ceiling making it feel much sunnier than your average leisure centre.

ROSELAND PENINSULA

Fish & Trips of St Mawes
01326 279204, www.fishandtripstmawes. co.uk. Open Apr-Oct. Trips from £25 per person; charters from £35 per person. No credit cards.

Skipper James Brown offers fishing trips (mackerel, live bait and trolling for bass) out of St Mawes, as well as private charters and day trips.

St Mawes Sit-on Kayaks
The Quay, St Mawes, TR2 5DG (07971 846786, www.stmaweskayaks.co.uk). Open Apr-Oct 9am-6pm daily. Hire from £15. No credit cards.

Hire out easy-to-paddle, family-friendly kayaks from St Mawes harbour and venture up the creek, around to St Anthony Head or all the way to St Just.

TRURO

Bike Chain Bissoe
Old Conns Works, Bissoe, TR4 8QZ (01872 870341, www.bikechainbissoe.co.uk). Open Summer 9am-6pm daily. Winter 9am-5pm Mon, Thur-Sun. Hire from £12 per day.

This place has a bike for eveyone, from tandems and tricycles to hybrids and mountain bikes. There's free parking for customers, so you can leave the car behind and pedal off along the Coast to Coast Trail on your new set of wheels.

Hall for Cornwall
Back Quay, Truro, TR1 2LL (01872 262466, www.hallforcornwall.co.uk). Open Box office by phone 9am-6pm daily. In person 9.30am-5pm daily.

Having worked with Sam Wanamaker on the rebuilding of the Globe Theatre in London, entrepreneur Chris Warner campaigned vigorously during the 1990s for the establishment of a venue west of Plymouth in which to stage commercial productions of any size. There is little in City Hall's grand Italianate façade to hint at its modern interior, but inside you'll find a slick 950-seat auditorium, as well as a coffee shop, bars and a restaurant. Entertainment here ranges from Abba cover bands to opera, world-acclaimed dance companies and big-budget musicals. It also hosts various fleamarkets and craft markets in the daytime.

Loe Beach Watersports
Feock, TR3 6SH (01872 300800, www.loebeach.co.uk). Open times vary, check website for details.

A wide range of watersports are on offer at this friendly Watersports Centre, including sailing, kayaking, rowing, windsurfing and motor boating. There's a compact pebbled beach here, and a small café just next door (see p120).

Skinners
Riverside, Newham, TR1 2DP (01872 245689, www.skinnersbrewery.com). Open Shop 9.30am-5.30pm Mon-Sat. Tours Apr-Oct 12.30-2.30pm, 7.30-10.30pm Mon-Sat. Admission £9.50 afternoon tour; £12.50 evening tour.

The names might be jocular – Betty Stogs, Ginger Tosser, Cornish Blond – but the Skinners are serious about ale. This family-run operation is one of Cornwall's leading brewhouses, and visitors are welcome for tastings and tours on the riverside Truro premises. We consider Skinner's Betty Stogs to be one of Cornwall's top five ales; see p74.

320025, www.dukestreetdeli.co.uk, closed Sun) for paninis, sandwiches and salad boxes; the **Gallery café** (01872 271733, closed Sun), within Lemon Street Market (*see below*); and veggie haven **Archie Browns** (105-106 Kenwyn Street, 01872 278622, www.archiebrowns.co.uk, closed Sun).

For picnic provisions, stop at **Lemon Street Market** (www.lemonstreetmarket.co.uk). There's bread by the much-lauded **Baker Tom** ♥ (08453 884389, www.bakertom.co.uk), including honey and lavender loaf, rock salt and rosemary foccacia, and 'beer bread' made with Betty Stogs Cornish ale. The **Old Cheese Shop** ♥ (29 Ferris Town, 01872 857130, www.theoldcheeseshop.co.uk, closed Sun) is also excellent, with a full range of Cornish specialities as well as European imports, plus some deli items.

A fledgling cocktail culture is apparent in a number of new venues in the centre of town, including the **Old Grammar School** (*see p120*), **Vertigo** (15 St Mary's Street, 01872 276555, www.vertigotruro.com). In Truro's move upmarket, only a handful of pubs seem to have escaped with their soul intact – the **Old Ale House** (7 Quay Street, 01872 271122) is one, a spit-and-sawdust sort of place that serves a range of real ale. Worth leaving town for is the pretty **Heron Inn** (Trenhaile Terrace, Malpas, 01872 272773, www.heroninnmalpas.co.uk), fronting the river.

Longstore Lemon Street
62 Lemon Street, Truro, TR1 2PN (01872 430000, www.thelongstore.co.uk). Open 4.30-10pm daily; 10am-3pm Sat; noon-3pm Sun.

Formerly the stalwart bistro Bustophers, the Longstore Lemon Street opens in 2021 as the sister restaurant the Longstore in Charlestown. The Truro branch was yet to open its doors at time of writing, but the original restaurant is rated locally for

its mix of hearty seafood and even heartier steaks.

Loe Beach Café

Feock, TR3 6SH (01872 870437, www. loebeachcafe.co.uk). Open times vary, phone for details.

It's little more than a shed with some benches and spotty bunting, but the Loe Beach Café serves better food than you might expect. There were three fish specials on our last visit, including very good whitebait, plus an all-day menu of freshly cooked family-friendly comfort food (ham, eggs and chips, and burgers). The cheery young staff happily sell mugs of tea and Twix bars to young kayakers from the watersports centre next door, and this place is popular with both locals and trippers.

Old Grammar School

19 St Mary's Street, Truro, TR1 2AF (01872 278559, www. theoldgrammarschool.com). Open 10am-midnight Mon-Sat. Lunch served noon-3pm; dinner served 6-9pm Mon-Sat.

Truro's hippest hangout is a neat, sleek space in the centre of town with the best cocktails around (from £7 each), each one attentively mixed with premium spirits, plus a DJ booth and a small repertoire of tapas. The posh glasses, prices and vibe tends to attract late twentysomethings and up, but this place still manages to be way too cool for school.

Old Quay Inn ♥

32-33 St John's Terrace, Devoran, TR3 6ND (01872 863142, www.theoldquayinn. co.uk). Open 11.30am-11pm daily. Lunch served noon-3pm; dinner served 6-9pm daily.

An old, white-painted village pub that's been brought up-to-date without being spoilt. An unfussy, spick-and-span interior is given warmth by a handsome fire; there's a friendly atmosphere, with no background music to hinder conversation. Real ales include Sharps' Doom Bar and Skinner's Betty Stogs and there's a guest ale at weekends. Fresh, local ingredients are transformed into hearty dishes such as slow-roasted pork belly or wild mushroom and spinach risotto – excellent stuff, and

Portloe see p111

much anticipated after a walk or cycle (Devoran is on the Mineral Tramways path, *see p39*). The setting, in a village on Restronguet Creek, is very pleasing, and a beer garden out back is a further plus.

Tabb's

85 Kenwyn St, Truro TR1 3BZ (01872 262110, www.tabbs.co.uk). Lunch served noon-2pm Tue-Fri; dinner served 5.30-9pm Tue-Sat.

Nigel Tabb's eponymous restaurant is so heroically low-key that it's often mistaken for a residential building. In fact, the modest ex-pub exterior houses Truro's fanciest restaurant: slaving away solo in the kitchen, Tabb creates a simple but powerful modern European menu that's netted him Truro's only mention in the Michelin guide.

Where to stay

Truro has a bizarre lack of desirable lodgings, possibly due to its inland location. Historically, the **Alverton Hotel** (Tregolls Road, 01872 276633, www.thealverton.co.uk) is considered to be the city's most luxurious – it benefitted from a substantial refurbishment a few years ago, which blew much of the chintz away.

If there are lots of you and you're happy to splash the cash (from £2,674 for up to 16 people) you can stay in the extremely fancy barn conversion at **Tregye Farm** (www.classic.co.uk) – it boast tennis courts, a pool table and a drum kit.

Mannings

Lemon Street, Truro, TR1 2QB (01872 270345, www.manningshotels.co.uk). Rates £150-£200 double incl breakfast.

The most up-to-date property in Truro, and the one with the best city-centre location (right on the piazza), Mannings has chic, business-like guest rooms, nine apart-rooms next to the hotel, and a smart bar-restaurant downstairs.

The Lizard Peninsula

In the rush for posh fish and chips in Padstow, surf shacks in Newquay and gallery-hopping in St Ives, visitors often overlook Cornwall's most remote corner. The Lizard Peninsula, the bulge of land south of the Helford River – south, in fact, of everywhere in mainland Britain – is on the way to nowhere. It is miles from anything you might class as a big town, barely served by public transport and almost completely surrounded by water. For all these reasons, it is one of the county's most rewarding areas, which has received a popular boost recently as the setting of the BBC's revamped *Poldark*.

For a relatively small expanse of land, the Lizard offers tremendous scenic diversity. The placid waters of the Helford River and the pulverising swell of Porthleven Sands are separated by just a few miles of countryside, and the colossal serpentine cliff-faces of the south coast are just a few snaking lanes away from creek-side beaches so small they look like scale models. Running down the centre of the peninsula are the eerily barren Goonhilly Downs, giving way at the edges to gently rolling countryside.

Keep an eye out for the chough, a jet-black bird with distinctive scarlet legs and bill. This rare member of the crow family, which takes pride of place on the Cornish coat of arms, disappeared from the Lizard in 1952 but returned to the area to breed in 2002, and now seems to be making a slow comeback.

HELSTON & AROUND

Helston

The only town of any size in the area is the pretty country town of Helston, famous for its annual **Flora Day celebrations** held on 8 May (unless it falls on a Sunday or Monday). During this ancient festival, the town is decorated with bluebells and gorse, and schoolchildren dress in white and wear garlands in their hair. Festivities include the play-like ritual known as the *Hal-an-Tow*, in which St Michael slays the devil and St George slays the dragon, and culminate with the processional 'Furry Dance', in which townsfolk dress up in their finery and dance in and out of the houses. Amid the springtime revelry, much Cornish ale is imbibed – in particular the

potent Spingo from the **Blue Anchor** pub (*see p126*).

Helston lost its role as a river port in the 13th century, due to the silting up of the Cober Estuary. However, it remained an important stannary (tin-mining district) and market town. Today, it's a delightfully old-fashioned sort of place, boasting a number of attractive buildings, many of them on Coinagehall Street. The neo-Gothic monumental gateway at the end of the street was built in 1834 in memory of Humphry Millet Grylls, a Helston banker and solicitor who had helped to keep the local tin mine open, thus safeguarding 1,200 jobs.

There's a **farmers' market** in the Cattle Market by the boating lake on the first Saturday morning of every month. South-west of Helston, pretty woodland paths take you through the National Trust's **Penrose Estate** to **Loe Pool**. The largest freshwater lake in Cornwall, it is cut off from the sea by a sand and shingle bank known as **Loe Bar**.

Porthleven

The prevailing winds whip straight into south-west-facing Porthleven, restricting its development into anything larger than a fishing village. Massive sea defences are testament to the village's vulnerability to gale-driven winter waves – and entry into the harbour remains a perennially hazardous undertaking. But the odd storm lashing doesn't stop Porthleven being perfect for an amble. In contrast to Cornwall's more cutesy fishing villages, its atmosphere is that of a bustling, year-round community.

Along the front, there's a scattering of shops, including a few galleries, a good fishmonger (**Quayside Fish**, Fore Street, 01326 562008) and **Kota** restaurant (*see p126*). The recent-ish arrival of the **Corner Deli** (*see p126*) and fruit and veg stalls on Wednesdays by the harbour reflects a burgeoning local food scene – as does the new annual **Porthleven Food Festival**, which takes place in April.

In bad weather, watching the breakers crash over the high sea wall is a stirring spectacle. If the wind happens to be blowing offshore, this is also a good place to watch advanced surfers in action – Porthleven offers some of England's best waves, surfed by a hardcore group of locals. Visiting surfers make pilgrimages here too, but this is a dangerous place for novices. Bathing off the long and attractive beach, especially near the Loe Bar, is also risky due to the strong currents and undertow.

Kynance Cove *see p129*

Where to eat & drink

For formal dining, you will need to travel beyond Helston now that the smart new restaurant at **Nansloe Manor**, on the outskirts of town, has closed. For picnicking purposes, stock up on pasties from the **Horse & Jockey** (41 Meneage Street, 01326 563534) or assemble a hamper of Cornish goodies from **Olivers deli** (65 Meneage Street, 01326 572420, www.oliverscornwall.com).

In Porthleven, the **Ship Inn** (Mount Pleasant Road, 01326 564204, www.theshipinncornwall.co.uk), above the entrance to the port, is an old smugglers' grotto and an excellent perch from which to survey the seascape.

Blue Anchor♥

50 Coinagehall Street, Helston, TR13 8EL (01326 562821, www.spingoales.com). Open 10am-midnight daily.

With more than 600 years of beer-making behind it, the Blue Anchor is reputedly the country's oldest continuously operating brew-pub. More importantly, it's still one of Cornwall's finest boozers, with a thatched roof, time-smoothed wooden tables and flagstone floors. Settle into one of the many nooks with a pint of its famous Spingo ale; there are few other places in Cornwall where you can get your hands on this locally revered liquid gold (*see p75*). You might be permitted a peek at the brewhouse at the end of the passage if you ask nicely. No food is served, but you can bring in your own.

Corner Deli

12 Fore Street, Porthleven, TR13 9HJ (01326 565554, www.thecornerdeliporthleven.co.uk). Open/food served Summer Deli 9am-6pm daily; pizzeria 6-9pm Mon-Sat. Winter Deli 9am-6pm Mon-Sat; pizzeria 6-9pm Wed-Sat.

This appealing deli is miniscule – one counter, a few shelves and two tables and chairs (for breakfast and lunch only) – but it packs a lot in: premium Cornish (and occasionally Italian) produce, including loaves by the esteemed Vicky's Bread, Camel Valley wine and Moomaid of Zennor ice-cream, as well as local duck eggs, organic carrots and muddied potatoes in baskets. It also serves superior sandwiches on organic flatbreads in the daytime, and pizzas from a wood-fired oven in the evenings. Seating is extremely limited, so you may find yourself eating outside on Porthleven harbour – no great hardship.

Kota♥

Harbour Head, Porthleven, TR13 9JA (01326 562407, www.kotarestaurant.co.uk). Lunch served noon-2pm Fri, Sat. Dinner served 5.30-9pm Tue-Sat.

Kota is Maori for shellfish and, taking full advantage of its fishing village location, chef Jude Kereama – half Maori, quarter Chinese, quarter Malaysian – oversees a menu of super-fresh Cornish seafood, crafted into Asian-accented cuisine. Monkfish green Thai curry is spicy and complex, and tempura Falmouth oyster appetisers with wasabi tartare (and a lettuce leaf for a spoon) are essential nibbling at £2 a pop. We'd be happy to declare this the best Asian food in Cornwall, but the distinct lack of competitors renders it a rather hollow statement; instead, we'll just say that Kota is quietly superb. This being an old mill, the decor is rustic and beamed, with big old wooden sideboards. Service is of rare efficiency, and prices where they should be for food of this quality. You can also pop down the street to its excellent sister bar and kitchen, **Kota Kai** (01326 727707, www.kotakai.co.uk).

Where to stay

Two unfussy B&B rooms are available at **Kota** (*see above*), one with harbour views. Another recommended B&B near Helston is the friendly **Black Swan** (TR12 6TU, 01326 221502, www.theblackswangweek.co.uk), in the tiny coastal village of Gweek, offering comfortable doubles at reasonable rates.

Beacon Crag

Porthleven, TR13 9LA (01326 573690, www.beaconcrag.com). Rates £100-£130 double incl breakfast. No credit cards.

It's not often that B&Bs bag the big views – but this handsome white house, on the edge of the cliff near Porthleven, is a notable exception. The setting really is in a league of its own, with far-reaching views along the coast in both directions; the remains of mine stacks can be seen on the cliffs. There are three chintz-free rooms to choose from, at mid-range prices.

THE LIZARD

South from Helston, the peninsula takes on an altogether more untamed character. The underlying serpentine rock, a greenish metamorphic stone, is covered by dour, dramatic sweeps of heathland (collectively named the **Lizard National Nature Reserve**), whose unusual geological make-up means it is home to some of Britain's rarest plants. The swathes of pink-flowering Cornish heath (*Erica vagans*), at its prettiest in summer, are particularly glorious.

On the coast, there are towering cliffs and rousing seas, preposterously pretty fishing villages and tempting sandy coves. Most visitors gravitate inexorably to Lizard Point, in order to spend a few moments as the most southerly person in mainland Britain.

Mullion & around

Just inland, Mullion is the largest village on the peninsula, with a good deli, a traditional pub – the **Old Inn** – a gallery and the pretty 16th-century church of **St Mellanus**, with its richly carved pews and a large Celtic stone cross outside. The village also has the virtue of being within easy striking distance of three beaches: tiny but dramatic **Mullion Cove**, with its small harbour beach and cluster of buildings; secluded **Polurrian**, accessible only by footpath and devoid of facilities; and popular

Poldhu Cove, a fine, sandy enclave with a little café and ice-cream shop. Poldhu's main claim to fame, however, is the **Poldhu Wireless Station**, from where Guglielmo Marconi sent the first transatlantic wireless signal in 1901. The remains can still be seen on the rugged cliffs above the beach – and the **Marconi Heritage Centre** (*see p138*) tells the story in brief.

Just to the north of Poldhu, but involving a considerable detour inland if travelling by car, **Church Cove** (*see p111*) is a peaceful, unspoilt family beach, with a precariously sited old church. Its idyllic sands belie its long history of smuggling and shipwreck. Nearby, the forbidding mass of the 200-foot **Halzephron Cliff** has claimed many ships. The bodies of sailors washed ashore along this unforgiving coastline were refused burial in hallowed ground, and until the early 18th century were unceremoniously dumped in a clifftop pit. Over the centuries, enduring tales of buried treasure have led numerous fortune-seekers to dive for the two tons of Spanish coins reputedly lying off this rocky coast.

Lizard Point & the coast

Like Land's End, Lizard Point – Britain's southernmost tip – is a tourist magnet. Other than stopping for one of Ann's legendary pasties (*see p131*), there's no cause to dally in Lizard village, whose charms are somewhat subsumed by dull cafés and tacky gift shops. But the blustery outcrop itself has escaped the worst of the tourist excesses, being marked only by the twin towers of the **Lizard Lighthouse** (*see p138*) and a few attendant cafés and shops selling carved and polished serpentine ornaments. All the same, it's the surrounding coastline that deserves attention: the jumble of cliffs, caves and coves oozes drama.

Things to do

HELSTON & AROUND

The Flambards Experience
Helston, TR13 0QA (01326 573404, www. flambards.co.uk). Open Mar-Oct times vary; check website for details. Admission £19.95; £14.95 reductions.

Flambards was an aviation museum when it first opened. Now it's a far more broad-based family day out. There are thrill rides (Thunderbolt, Hornet Coaster and Canyon River Log Flume are among the white-ish knuckle ones), an animal section and Hands-On Science Experience, a Victorian village with cobbled streets, an exhibition on Britain in the Blitz, an indoor theatre and, hanging on in there, the exhibition of aircraft relics and models. The school holidays also bring weekly firework displays.

THE LIZARD

Coverack Windsurfing Centre
Cliff Cottage, Sunny Corner, Coverack, TR12 6SY (01326 280939, www.coverack.co.uk). Rates Windsurfing from £75; surf skis from £5. No credit cards.

Based in the secluded Coverack Bay and open from April to November, this centre offers tuition for all levels, as well as residential holidays and courses.

Mullion Golf Course
Cury, TR12 7BP (01326 240276, www. mulliongolfclub.co.uk). Open all year.

England's most southerly golf club has 18 holes and magnificent clifftop views.

Porthkerris Divers
Porthkerris Cove, St Keverne, TR12 6QJ (01326 280620, www.porthkerris.com). Open all year. Rates vary. Phone for details.

This family-run dive centre offers great shore dives to the sunken shipwrecks off the notoriously treacherous Manacles.

Roskilly's ♥
Roskilly's Ice Cream & Organic Farm, Tregellast Barton, St Keverne, TR12 6NX (01326 280479, www.roskillys.co.uk). Open Summer 9am-6pm daily. Winter 11am-3pm Mon-Fri; 11am-5pm Sat, Sun. Admission free.

At this idyllic organic dairy farm you can feed the ducks, watch the cows being milked or just stroll around the meadows and ponds in the grounds. Entrance is free, but you won't be able to hold on to your money when you see the farm shop and

Roskilly's

From Lizard Point, the coastal path leads north-east towards Cadgwith, passing the **Devil's Frying Pan** – a 200-foot-deep collapsed blowhole that makes for a memorable sight, especially when the 'pan' is spitting. The mood changes as you reach idyllic **Cadgwith Cove**, where fishing boats line up on the pebble beach and pretty thatched cottages cling to the steep terrain. There's a wonderful 300-year-old pub, the **Cadgwith Cove Inn** (*see p130*), a few small shops and a hatch selling crab and lobster sandwiches by the beach. Park at the top to avoid becoming entangled in the village's narrow lanes.

On the east side of the Lizard, **Kennack Sands** is easily accessible and offers good bathing and a little surf. It's one of the area's most generous stretches of sand, backed up by crag and rock pools. There's a car park, and a small café/shop.

Kynance Cove 💜

It may not be the place to hire pedaloes, surfboards and deckchairs, and getting there involves something of a walk, but Kynance Cove is undoubtedly the jewel in the Lizard's crown. 'Kynans' means gorge in the Cornish language, and this particular gorge is backed by vast cliffs and scattered with striking green-blue stacks, pinnacles, arches, caves and rock pools, all set against turquoise waters. In the right light, the combination of brilliant seas, pinkish sands and rocks calls to mind Bermuda, *The Tempest* and any number of treasure islands. Its beauty has lured creatives down the ages, including, most famously, Tennyson and the artist William Holman Hunt. One of the original Pre-Raphaelites, the colour-obsessed Hunt was naturally taken with the cove, whose hues feature in his work of 1860, *Asparagus Island*.

Helford River Boats

the Bull Pen Gallery, selling sweet wooden toys, furniture and the work of local artists. There's also the cosy restaurant (Croust House; see p130), and, of course, 24 scrumptious flavours of Roskilly's ice-cream on sale.

THE HELFORD RIVER

Helford River Boats 💜
Helford Passage, TR11 5LB (01326 250770, www.helford-river-boats.co.uk). Open Ferry Easter-Oct 9.30am-5.30pm daily; July, Aug 9.30am-9.30pm. Tickets £7 return; £5 single.

There is no better way to take in the quiet beauty of the Helford River than from the water. This boating company, which operates a kiosk at Helford Passage (on the north bank), hires out self-drive motor boats by the hour, day and week (from £40 for one hour, maximum six people), for which no experience is required. Kayaks are also available for £15 an hour. The same company runs the ferry service between the north bank and the south from April till the end of October.

At low tide, Kynance's azure waters and countless sandy nooks, caves, rock pools and crannies are the stuff of fantasy. On a calm day, having a splash or a body surf in these sparkling waters is a joy. If, however, there is mild to moderate swell, and the tide is high, swimmers – especially children – should take care, as it is easy to be lulled into a false sense of security by the peaceful scene. And be careful not to be cut off by the tide if you stroll over to nearby **Asparagus Island**, accessible on foot via the Bellows, a stretch of white sand that emerges at low tide. Wild asparagus, a spiky flowering plant that grows only in a handful of places, flourishes on this hump of rock.

It's a steepish climb down from the National Trust car park at the top of the cliffs to the seasonal café and shop on the edge of the sand.

St Keverne & around

The B3293 heads south-east through Goonhilly Downs to the village hub of St Keverne, a mile or so inland. Arranged attractively around a main square are its two pubs, shop and distinctively steepled church. Within easy striking distance are **Porthallow Cove** and **Porthoustock**, quiet fishing villages with uncompromising grey shingle beaches. Between them, **Porthkerris** has become something of a diving hotspot (*see p128*) thanks to its proximity to the notorious **Manacles** – a jagged, mostly submerged two-mile offshore reef, upon which many ships and men have come to grief.

More conventionally appealing is the fishing village of **Coverack**, with its tidal beach. Once a centre of smuggling, it is now favoured for its quiet coastal setting, with traditional granite cottages and a few cafés and galleries lining up along an arc of sand and shingle. There's a working harbour at the southern end of the

bay, a pub (incongruously named the **Paris Hotel**, after a French liner that was wrecked on the headland on which it stands), the old lifeboat station (now housing a restaurant and fish and chip shop) and glorious views out to sea.

Where to eat & drink

In addition to the Halzephron Inn (*see below*), we're partial to a pint in the cosy **Cadgwith Cove Inn** (01326 290513, www.cadgwithcoveinn.com), which is particularly lively on Friday evenings. **Jumunjy Thai Cusine** (01326 241321, www.jumunjy.com) was founded in Koh Phangan in 2003 then upped sticks to the Lizard a few years later, and has a good local rep.

Croust House ♥

Roskilly's Ice-Cream & Organic Farm, Tregellast Barton, St Keverne, TR12 6NX (01326 281924, www.roskillys.co.uk). Open Summer 9am-9pm daily. Winter 11am-3pm Mon-Fri; 11am-5pm Sat, Sun.

The excellent restaurant at Roskilly's (*see p128*), converted from the old milking parlour, is all about homely, comforting fare (pasty and salad, jackets, baguettes, quiche and soup) at sensible prices. The atmosphere here is refreshingly low-key – you order from the counter, and are welcome to hang out on the farm for the rest of the day. With ample bench seating in the large courtyard, a dedicated kids' menu and farm activities on site, families are in their element.

Halzephron Inn

Gunwalloe, Helston, TR12 7QB (01326 240406, www.halzephron-inn.co.uk). Open 11am-2pm, 6.30-11pm daily. Food served 11am-2.30pm, 6.30-9pm daily.

Ruling the roost on top of a particularly formidable stretch of cliff ('halzephron' derives from the Cornish for 'cliffs of hell'), this famous old inn has a long-standing – and deserved – reputation for good pub food. Expect solid renditions of standards such as ploughman's, burgers, steak and chips and scampi, and more adventurous

Vicky's Bread

A rising sensation in these parts, Helston-based Vicky's Bread – the brainchild of Vicky Harford – produces a small range of superb handmade bread, and delivers daily to dozens of small independent shops and delis across west Cornwall. The process, and the results, could not be more different to mass-produced loaves. The ingredients are all organic, and no artificial preservatives or enhancers are added – the sourdough culture (inspired by the French *pain au levain*) used in the loaves naturally gives the bread a longer shelf life, as well as lending the finished product a beautifully springy, moist texture. The loaves are shaped by hand and then allowed to rise slowly – for maximum taste – in willow baskets, with the divinely crunchy, brittle crust created by steam baking.

Vicky's everyday range consists of five breads – the classic baguette, multigrain, sourdough, spelt sourdough and, our favourite, the rustic bordelais – with speciality loaves often available at weekends. Look out for the small baskets with a hand-written 'Vicky's Bread' sign sitting modestly on the counters of delis and grocer's throughout west Cornwall – great things lie within.

Vicky's Bread (www.vickysbread.co.uk). See website for a list of stockists.

THE LIZARD PENINSULA

specials. With the pick of the Cornish ales on tap, including Doom, Betty Stoggs and the local Chough Brewery ale, this is one of the most popular stops along the south coast of the Lizard. Choose from the old-school bar, a smarter restaurant, the family room or the bracing front terrace – the same menu applies to all.

The Lizard Pasty Shop

Beacon Terrace, Helston, TR12 7PB (01326 290889, www.annspasties.co.uk). Open Jan-Mar 9.30am-2.30pm Tue-Sat. Apr-Dec 9.30am-2.30pm Mon-Sat.

Ann's bright yellow pasty shop is justly famous for its first-rate rendering of the Cornish classic – and even more so now that a certain super-chef from Padstow has given it his stamp of approval. Despite the touristy setting, this is the real deal. Note that the shop closes early if the pasties have sold out, and occasionally shuts on Mondays.

Where to stay

This being probably as far as you can go off the tourist trail in Cornwall, there isn't a lot of accommodation on the Lizard – and what there is tends to predate the boutique hotel boom. Still, a number of the big hotels on the coast make up for what they lack in design nous with jaw-dropping clifftop settings and impressive old buildings. The **Mullion Cove Hotel** (01326 240328, www.mullion-cove. co.uk) and the **Housel Bay Hotel**

Mullion Cove harbour see p127

Cornish heath (Erica vagans)

Cadgwith Cove see p129

PZ601

FH,

Lizard Lighthouse Heritage Centre *see p138*

National seal sanctuary *see p139*

Cormorant colony, Lizard Point *see p127*

FH 529

FH706

(01326 290417, www.houselbay.com) are two such traditional hotels with panaromic vistas.

Roskilly's (*see p128*) farm has self-catering cottages for rent and, at Lizard village, the endearingly eccentric **Henry's Campsite** (01326 290596, www.henryscampsite.co.uk) is the most southerly campsite in Britain. Cider is served by the jug, most pitches have sea views, and pigs, ducks and guinea pigs roam at will.

In the tiny village of **Kuggar**, **Namparra** (01326 290040, www.namparracampsite.co.uk, closed Nov-Easter) is another delightful campsite, 20 minutes' walk from Kennack Sands. Campfires are allowed – or you can rent a freestanding clay chimenea.

The Bay
Coverack, TR12 6TF (01326 280464, www.thebayhotel.co.uk). Rates £120-£270 double incl breakfast & dinner.

An independently owned hotel on the waterfront at Coverack, the Bay is a good-value hideaway on the Lizard. The decor, while not in the business of chasing trends, is modern, attractive and soothingly toned – and rooms at the front have knockout sea views, as does the conservatory restaurant.

Coverack Youth Hostel
Parc Behan, School Hill, Coverack, TR12 6SA (0345 371 9014, www.yha.org.uk). Rates from £15.95 per person; £11.95 reductions. At time of going to press dorm rooms were closed due to coronavirus restrictions.

This small, simple youth hostel, set in a Victorian house with spectacular views over the cliffs and coves of the eastern coast of the Lizard, is much loved. Of the nine bedrooms, six have double beds and five are en-suite. Breakfast, picnic lunches and evening meals are all available.

Lizard Point Youth Hostel
Lizard Point, TR12 7NT (0345 371 9550, www.yha.org.uk). Rates from £15.95 per person; £11.95 reductions. At time of going to press dorms rooms were closed due to coronavirus restrictions.

From the driveway and manicured gardens, you'd think you were about to check into a luxury clifftop hotel. Instead, this smartly painted old Victorian hotel is now a first-rate YHA hostel, offering fresh, homely rooms (including some doubles and triples) – most of which have sea views.

The Polurrian
Mullion, TR12 7EN (01326 240421, www.polurrianhotel.com). Rates £119-£359 double incl breakfast.

Taken over by the owners of the elegant Budock Vean hotel (*see p141*) on the Helford River, this stately old Edwardian building has undergone a much-needed facelift. The style is still strait-laced, but the rooms are fresh and comfortable. More excitingly, the hotel is set in 12 acres of rugged coastal moorland – there are notices in the rooms reminding guests to shut the windows during gales, and in the sea-view rooms you drift off to sleep to the sound of waves crashing outside. There are tennis courts, a family putting green, children's climbing frames, a football area, indoor and outdoor pools and a jacuzzi; the hotel's own sandy beach is a quick abseil below. Indoor facilities include a squash court, a toddlers' play area and a games room that includes PlayStations, a pool table, table football and table tennis.

THE HELFORD RIVER
In *Frenchman's Creek*, Daphne Du Maurier's tale of passion and piracy, she paints the Helford River as a 'symbol of escape', a place paused in time. And the effect on today's visitors is remarkably similar. The Helford, whose spidery creeks intersect the sheltered northern shores of the Lizard Peninsula, is one of few places in Britain to which time has been so gentle – thanks to its profound geographical isolation, lack of fast roads and the commitment of various interested parties to preserving its peace and natural beauty.

Du Maurier fans will still find plenty to feed their imagination in and around the Helford's hidden waterways and in the dense woodland that grips its shores – some of the last pockets of wild woodland in the country. From the choppy waters of the open sea at the mouth of the 'river' (technically it's a ria, or drowned river valley) to the small port of Gweek at its head, the scale gradually diminishes: the creeks, coves and inlets become calmer and more hidden, and the tiny shingle beaches are perfect miniatures.

Plenty of footpaths (consult an OS map) weave through the thickets, leading walkers deep into the woodlands and down to the water's edge. Our favourite walks are the short **circular trail** from Helford to Frenchman's Creek, via lovely **Penarvon Cove**, and a longer excursion through **Trelowarren Estate**'s tall, echoey woods down to National Trust-managed **Tremayne Quay** (open Feb-Sept; ask at the estate's reception for a leaflet with a map) – a tranquil spot, only accessible on foot or by water.

Heading inland, sinuous lanes lead to the heart-meltingly pretty villages and hamlets – **Manaccan**, **St Anthony**, **Gweek** and **Mawgan** on the south side, and **Helford Passage**, **Port Navas**, **Mawnan Smith** and **Constantine** on the northern banks – dotted with thatched white cottages, village shops, pubs and church steeples reminiscent of slower times.

The affluent north bank of the river, home to two stunning gardens (see p139), is most easily accessed by road from Falmouth. Alternatively, a foot **ferry** makes the very short crossing from Helford village on the south side to the cluster of houses and the pub at **Helford Passage** to the north (£5.50; 9.30am-5.30pm Apr-Oct, until 9.30pm July, Aug).

Where to eat & drink

The **Boatyard Cafe** (Gweek, 01326 221404, www.theboatyardcafe.co.uk) is a pleasant spot, well worth a look for its range of responsibly sourced comfort food; further upriver, the **Port Navas Yacht Club** (Port Navas, 01326 340065, www.pnyc.co.uk) offers an idyllic waterside location with a restaurant open to the public.

Ferryboat Inn
Helford Passage, TR11 5LB (01326 250625, www.ferryboatcornwall.co.uk). Open Summer 11am-10pm Mon-Thur, Sun; 11am-11pm Fri, Sat. Winter 11am-10pm Tue-Thur; 11am-11pm Fri, Sat; 11am-6pm Sun. Lunch served Summer noon-2.30pm Mon-Sat; noon-3pm Sun. Winter noon-2.30pm Tue-Sat; noon-3pm Sun. Dinner served Summer 6-8.30pm Mon-Thur, Sun; 6-9pm Fri, Sat. Winter 6-8.30pm Tue-Thur; 6-9pm Fri.

This old riverside pub – with dreamy views of the water from the terrace at the front – has been transformed into a thoroughly upmarket affair. It is now run by Zander and Sarah Towill. The design, menu and prices now place the Ferryboat on a posher plane than your average gastropub, and there's even a seafood counter serving local oysters and champagne. It's an incongruously urbane set-up for such a remote locale, but there can be no doubting the quality of the produce: with the Wright Bros running the Duchy Oyster Farm at Port Navas, less than a mile away, these could well be the freshest oysters in the land.

Gear Farm Pasty Company
St Martin, TR12 6DE (01326 221150, www.gearfarm.co.uk). Open Summer 9.30am-4.30pm Mon-Sat. Winter 9.30am-4.30pm Tue-Sat.

Gear Farm, just outside the small village of St Martin, sells its superior own-baked pasties out of a small farm shop, alongside a range of organic veg from its fields (the same that goes into the pasties). If you're looking to stock up, they sell frozen pasties too.

Helford River see p134

THE LIZARD PENINSULA

Places to visit

HELSTON & AROUND

Godolphin House ♥
Godolphin Cross, TR13 9RE (01736 763194, www.nationaltrust.org.uk). Open House varies; check website for details. Open Garden Feb-mid Dec 10am-4pm daily. Admission House and Garden £7; £3.50 reductions; £17.50 family. Admission Garden only £5; £2.50 reductions; £12.50 family.

This wildly romantic National Trust country house looks a bit like an Oxbridge college dropped deep in the west Cornish countryside. Hugely advanced for the 17th century, the architecture is impressive despite its state of disrepair, and the historically significant formal gardens are thought to be the oldest in the country. The Grade I-listed house is a stunning evocation of the period, with mullioned windows, original Elizabethan stables and a glorious colonnade leading through the screen wall into a courtyard. The overgrown gardens – little changed in centuries – and work-in-progress feel won't be to everyone's tastes, but we couldn't help but fall for the untamed beauty of it all, and the tangible sense of history.

Museum of Cornish Life
Market Place, Helston, TR13 8TH (01326 564027, www.museumofcornishlife.co.uk). Open 10am-1pm Mon-Sat; extended opening times during school hols. Admission free.

Behind the Guildhall, in the old market building, the Museum of Cornish Life displays an intriguing miscellany of local domestic, industrial and agricultural artefacts of the 19th and 20th centuries, plus Helston man Henry Trengrouse's original Rocket Apparatus and Bosun's Chair. Although his invention was ignored by successive British governments during his lifetime, it later evolved into the Breeches Buoy, a winch now used all over the world for sea rescues.

Poldark Mine
Wendron, TR13 0ES (01326 573173, www.poldarkmine.org.uk). Open Apr-June, Sept, Oct 10.30am-5.30pm Mon-Fri, Sun. July, Aug 10.30am-5.30pm daily. Admission £7; £4-£6 reductions. Tours £20-£27; £12-£26 reductions; £60-£90 family.

North of Helston, Wheal Roots tin mine, as it was originally known, dates from 1725, making it probably the oldest complete mine workings open to the public in Europe. Subterranean guided tours (not for the claustrophobic) detail the life and work of the miners, while the surrounding buildings house pieces of old mining equipment and attendant amusements – very much of the old school – for younger visitors (candle-dipping, panning for gold, remote-controlled boats). And yes, scenes from both the classic 1970s BBC series *Poldark* and the sexier 2010s revival were filmed here.

THE LIZARD

Lizard Lighthouse Heritage Centre
Lizard Point, TR12 7NT (01326 290202, www.trinityhouse.co.uk). Open Apr-June, Sept, times vary Mon-Wed, Sat, Sun. July 11am-6pm daily. Aug 11am-7pm daily. Oct-Dec, Feb, Mar times vary Mon-Wed, Sun. (Closed Jan). Admission £4; £2-£3.50 reductions.

Warning ships off this perilous headland since the 18th century, Lizard Lighthouse, a striking white hexagonal structure, opened to the public in 2009, along with a smart visitor centre. The lottery-funded exhibition is full of interesting snippets about lighthouse life through the ages – you can sound a foghorn, listen to lighthouse keepers' tales and tap out dots and dashes by morse code. But by far the most exciting part is the enthusiastically narrated lighthouse tour, during which you climb 62 feet up into the hothouse at the top. Here you gain sweeping sea panoramas, and an up-close encounter with the equipment that emits one powerful white flash every three seconds – visible for up to 26 nautical miles.

Marconi Heritage Centre
Poldhu, Mullion, TR12 7JB (01326 241656, www.marconi-centre-poldhu.org.uk). Open July, Aug 7-9pm Tue, Fri; 1.30-4.30pm Wed, Thur, Sun. May, June, Sept 7-9pm Tue, Fri; 1.30-4.30pm Wed, Sun. Jan-Apr, Oct-Dec 7-9pm Tue, Fri; 1.30-4.30pm Sun. Admission free.

This tiny but informative multimedia exhibition is a tribute to Italian radio inventor Guglielmo Marconi. It marks the location on the headland above Poldhu Cove where Marconi built his wireless station in 1901, later using his vast antenna on the cliff to transmit a message – albeit a weak one – over 2,000 miles to Newfoundland (now Canada).

THE HELFORD RIVER

Glendurgan Garden

Mawnan Smith, TR11 5JZ (01326 252020, www.nationaltrust.org.uk). Open Aug 10.30am-5.30pm Mon-Sat. Mid Feb-late July, Sept, Oct 10.30am-5.30pm Tue-Sat. Admission £5; £2.50 reductions; £12.50 family.

Planted by devout Quaker Alfred Fox in the 1820s, Glendurgan is one of Cornwall's most exotic gardens. Its theatrical subtropical planting includes tall, swaying palms and tree ferns with vast fronds, and greenery cascading all the way down the steep, wooded valley to a sandy beach on the Helford at the bottom. The jungle-like setting – roped-off flowerbeds are pleasingly absent – will appeal to families, with the 19th-century laurel maze and Giant's Stride rope swing providing added entertainment. A covered outdoor café serves good, solid lunches and snacks.

National Seal Sanctuary

Gweek, TR12 6UG (01326 221361, www.seal sanctuary.co.uk). Open Summer 10am-5pm daily. Winter 10am-3pm daily. Admission £15.50; £12.50 reductions; £48 family.

Opened in Gweek in 1975, this sanctuary for rescued seals is now a popular family attraction. The seals are brought here to convalesce, before being released back into the wild. There are nursery pools, a hospital, and a pool for the centre's permanent residents – rescue seals that wouldn't survive in the wild. There's also a nature trail with other animals to see, and a children's play area.

Trebah ♥

Mawnan Smith, TR11 5JZ (01326 252200, www.trebah-garden.co.uk). Open 10am-5.30pm daily, times may vary. Admission £12; free-£6 reductions.

Originally laid out by the outrageously creative Charles Fox – brother of Alfred, who owned Glendurgan next door – Trebah

has 26 acres of lush, subtropical vegetation tumbling down a wooded ravine. Legend has it that Fox was a stickler for detail, even asking that the head gardener put up scaffolding towers to indicate the eventual height of each tree. The garden design cleverly saves the best till last: the view from the bottom leads the eye up past a pond, reflecting a pretty white bridge, beyond the vast bed of pastel-hued hydrangeas, the gunnera (or 'giant rhubarb') and flanks of mature trees, all the way up to the white house at the top. Children can whoop it up on the climbing frames, swings and paraglide (over-fives only) in the Tarzan's Camp play area; there's also a conservatory selling plants, a shop and the Planter's Café, with its appealing seasonal menu.

Trelowarren

Mawgan, TR12 6AF (01326 221224, www. trelowarren.com). Open to public Apr-Sept. Admission free.

Occupying 1,000 acres between the Helford River and Goonhilly Downs, the beautiful Trelowarren Estate has been passed down through the Vyvyan family for some 600 years. Visitors are welcome, and it would be easy to fill the best part of a day exploring the exquisite parkland and on-site microbusinesses. The converted outbuildings house the superb New Yard restaurant (*see p140*), a plant nursery and an excellent gallery run by the Cornwall Crafts Association (open Mar-Oct). You can even venture into a well-preserved Iron Age fogou (underground chamber), the purpose of which is lost in the mists of time. But the most magical part of any visit is a ramble along the woodland tracks leading down to the secluded riverbank (open to non-guests Feb-Sept; ask a member of staff for a map). Daphne Du Maurier described the estate as a 'a shock of surprise and delight, lying indeed like a jewel in the hollow of the hand', and it provided the inspiration for *Frenchman's Creek*.

Trebah *see p139*

New Inn

Manaccan, TR12 6HA (01326 231323, www.newinnmanaccan.co.uk). Open noon-3pm, 6-11pm Mon-Sat; noon-3pm, 7-10pm Sun. Lunch served noon-2.30pm Mon-Sat; noon-2pm Sun. Dinner served 6.30-9pm Mon-Sat; 7-9pm Sun.

There's nothing new about this picture-perfect, cream-and-thatch inn. In fact, it has barely changed for decades and, from the outside, probably centuries. A fine specimen of a country pub, it has just one room, with a log fire, real ale and the quiet, cosy feel of another era.

New Yard ♥

Trelowarren, TR12 6AF (01326 221595, www.newyardrestaurant.co.uk). Breakfast served 8.30-10.30am Tue-Sat. Lunch served noon-2pm Tue-Sat; noon-2.30pm Sun. Dinner served 7-9pm Tue-Sat.

Such is the beauty of this riverside country estate, we'd settle for any excuse to visit Trelowarren – so the fact that its chic, airy restaurant is also the best place to dine on the Lizard is a happy bonus. In the evening, prices dictate that New Yard, converted from the old carriage house, is somewhere for a Nice Meal Out rather than a casual bite, but thankfully it's not a tense, cutlery-scraping kind of place – the warm, friendly service and deep country setting keep things relaxed. There are half a dozen outdoor tables in the pretty courtyard.

Shipwright Arms

Helford Village, TR12 6JX (01326 231235, www.shipwrightshelford.co.uk). Open/ food served 11am-2.30pm, 6-10.30pm Tue-Sat. Winter opening hours vary.

The absurdly picturesque Shipwright Arms, right on the water in Helford Village, was a smugglers' hangout back in the days when these winding creeks provided a bounty of hiding places for smugglers, pirates and fugitives. These days, it's a pleasant spot in which to smuggle yourself away for a pint and a spot of lunch (crab sandwiches, a pint of prawns or a ploughman's) overlooking the creek, watching birds duck in and out of the water, and the sailing boats quietly come and go. There is no parking on these narrow streets – leave the car at the car park at the entrance of the village.

Where to stay

Budock Vean

Helford Passage, Mawnan Smith, TR11 5LG (01326 252100, www.budockvean. co.uk). Rates £252-£376 double incl breakfast in high season.

Sitting proudly on the prosperous north bank of the Helford River, this lavish four-star resort presides over its own golf course, tennis courts, pool and spa, and vast, organically managed gardens (the latter lead down to a private foreshore on the river, complete with private sun lounge). The emphasis here is on the traditional values of service and comfort – and the decor is more old guard than avant-garde. As you might expect, afternoon tea is a hallowed institution. Hotel guests can enjoy a four-course dinner for £29. Ask for a room in the original hotel building, rather than the modern extension.

Trelowarren

Trelowarren, TR12 6AF (01326 221224, www.trelowarren.com). Rates from £595 per week for 4 people-£2,075 per week for 10 people.

Since its inception, the UK's first 'eco timeshare' – in the green and peaceful grounds of the Trelowarren Estate – has been stacking up awards, thanks to its exacting environmental agenda and green technology (coppice-fired heat and power system, rainwater harvesting, low-energy appliances). Owner Sir Ferrers Vyvyan, who has ambitions for an entirely self-sufficient estate in his lifetime, considers the timeshare concept, despite its unfashionable ring, to be a potentially low-impact form of tourism, avoiding the 'empty second home' syndrome afflicting many Cornish towns and villages. When not booked by their part-owners, the high-spec houses – located next to whispering woodland, and a short walk from the Helford River – are available to everyone for rent. Tennis courts and a swimming pool occupy the old walled gardens.

PRAA SANDS & AROUND

Praa Sands

A mile-long stretch of golden sand, backed by dunes, Praa Sands (pronounced 'pray') may be one of West Cornwall's most popular beaches, but it suffers from something of an identity crisis. Geographically, some people consider it part of the Lizard, others part of the Penwith Peninsula. Although it lacks the star quality of some of its Cornish brethren (Kynance Cove, say, or St

New Yard see p140

Ives), being backed by some weathered beachfront shops and cafés and a bevy of old-fashioned bungalows, it is an excellent family beach, with clean water, good swimming and plenty of space.

It's surfing that really put Praa Sands on the map, though. The summer boarding hordes may flock to Cornwall's north coast, but, on the right swell and especially in winter, this is the place to be. To lose the crowds, head to the eastern side. From here, there's great walking to be had around **Rinsey Head**, where a grand old mansion, often used as a filming location, stands in total isolation on the edge of the cliff.

Perranuthnoe

The tidal beach of Perranuthnoe, just a few miles along the coast towards Penzance, offers less crowded conditions than Praa and a more secluded setting. Like Praa, Perranuthnoe has beachbreak surf, working on big south-westerly swells held up by a north-easterly wind. It also boasts a reef break, known as the 'cabbage patch', at the eastern end of the bay. However, high tide is not the time to come for a surf, a walk or anything else for that matter, as the beach all but disappears. The pretty village is home to the **Cowhouse Gallery** (www.cowhousegallery.org. uk, closed Jan), a pink-painted gastropub (the **Victoria Inn**; *(see p143)*) and the beachside **Cabin Café** (*01736 711733, www.thecabinbeachcafe. co.uk*).

A walk along the coast path to **Prussia Cove** – actually a group of isolated coves – is a must. The romance of the landscape is enhanced by its history: the cove was named after a notorious smuggler, John Carter – alias the King of Prussia.

Praa Sands *see p141*

Carter got his nickname as a boy, when he played soldiers on the beach and pretended to be the Prussian monarch. As an adult, his rich pickings were stashed away in Piskies and Bessy's Coves. Between the two coves, an iron post and chains are relics of the HMS *Warspite*, which ran aground here in 1947 and was the largest wreck ever to occur on the Cornish coast. There are no ice-cream kiosks or cafés in these parts, and access is via footpaths; leave your car in the car park.

Where to eat & drink

Peppercorn Café

Lynfield Yard, Perranuthnoe, TR20 9NE (07907 691639, www.thepeppercorncafe. co.uk). Open Apr-Sept 10am-5pm daily. Oct-Mar 10am-4pm daily. No credit cards.

Improbable as it might seem on arrival, this modest outdoor café – essentially a shack and a handful of open-air tables near to Perranuthnoe beach – serves praiseworthy food. Stop by for a slice of cake and a glass of own-made cordial, a hefty bacon butty, or one of the tempting daily specials. Vegan, vegetarian and gluten-free meals are also available.

Sandbar

Praa Sands, TR20 9TQ (01736 763516, www.sandbarpraasands.co.uk). Open 11am-11pm Mon-Fri; 10am-11pm Sat, Sun. Food served 11am-9pm Mon-Fri; 10am-9pm Sat, Sun.

This beachside hangout – a 1970s disco reborn – has a nicely low-key, sand-worn feel and a large terrace overlooking the sand. Flip-flops and soggy hair are perfectly acceptable attire for a hot chocolate stop, post-surf pub food (locally sourced fillet steaks, Sunday carvery, fish pie) or a round of pool or table football.

Victoria Inn

Perranuthnoe, TR20 9NP (01736 710309, www.victoriainn-penzance.co.uk). Summer Lunch served noon-2pm Mon-

Sat; noon-2.30pm Sun. Dinner served 6.30-9pm Mon-Sat. Winter Lunch served noon-2pm Tue-Sat; noon-2.30pm Sun. Dinner served 6.30-9pm Tue-Sat.

Furrowed away in sleepy Perranuthnoe, this lovely old thatched inn has been quietly making a name for itself as a culinary hotspot over the last decade or so. Current head chef Matthew Rowe offers a menu heavy on the local ingredients: lots of seafood by night, and some impressively hearty sandwiches at lunchtime.

Where to stay

In keeping with its understated appeal, Praa Sands doesn't have a single hotel – just a few old-fashioned B&Bs.

Ednovean Farm

Perranuthnoe, TR20 9LZ (01736 711883, www.ednoveanfarm.co.uk). Rates £100-£140 double incl breakfast.

Technically we must call this a B&B, although its three exquisite rooms – Pink, Blue and Apricot – feel more like a luxurious country hotel, with the bonus of being within walking distance of the lovely Victoria Inn (*see left*). The rooms are romantically furnished with sumptuous antiques and fabrics (toile de Jouy, vintage Liberty), as well as roll-top baths, fluffy towels, DVD players and private terraces. Best of all, you are free to roam the huge, impeccably landscaped gardens, which afford changing coastal panoramas and are dotted with hidden seats and benches. Note that check-in isn't until 4pm.

Prussia Cove

Prussia Cove, Rosudgeon, TR20 9BA (01736 762014, www.prussiacove.co.uk). Get in touch for rates.

The family-owned Porth-en-Alls Estate, comprising numerous cottages and houses for rent around Prussia Cove, offers get-away-from-it-all properties amid untamed scenery. A world away from beach bars, celebrity chefs and surf shops, this is Cornwall at its best: wild and untouched.

The Penwith Peninsula

There is something infinitely head-clearing about pushing on in the direction of the setting sun, all the way to the end of the line, the end of the 'motorway' (as the A30 is locally known), and eventually, of course, the end of the land. In this remote corner of the country, the cliffs drop dramatically into the relentless swell of the Atlantic and you can, should you feel so inclined, find a blustery perch, gaze out to sea and ponder the nothingness in front of you stretching all the way to North America.

Also known as Land's End Peninsula, the Penwith Peninsula could be another country: it's wild, distant and bounded by so much sea it's almost an island in itself. The primitive landscape – a granite wilderness of open moorland, sea-ravaged cliffs and prehistoric remains – and the area's famous clarity of light continue to exert a magnetic pull on artists, hundreds of whom call it home. If you think our prose excessive, consider instead the words of DH Lawrence, who, on arrival at the pretty village of Zennor in 1916, attempting to escape the hostilities of war, felt like 'a Columbus who can see a shadowy America before him... a new continent of the soul'. Or turn to the Cornish poet John Harris, for whom Land's End's 'granite arches mock the rage of Time'.

Inspirational landscapes aside, the peninsula also has dozens of unspoilt sandy beaches and coves, a quietly flourishing food scene and, of course, galleries galore.

ST IVES BAY & AROUND

St Ives

The approach to St Ives by train – a journey holidaymakers have been making since the line was built in the 1870s – is a veritable sight for sore eyes. The single-carriage train chugs along the curve of St Ives Bay, opening up glorious vistas of golden sands and treating you to a bird's-eye view of the UK's most perfect seaside town: a pretty old granite harbour scooped out of the bay, filled with water the colour of lime cordial, and a tangle of cottages and lanes nudging each other for space.

Long a magnet for artists, on account of the extraordinary quality of light, St Ives still has a wonderfully exotic feel. The vivid colours rebel against the restrained English palette, and its island-like setting means there are soft, white-sand beaches and glimpses of the sea at every turn. A scattering of Cornish palms – not to mention the more recent arrival of frothy cappuccinos, fancy restaurants and fluffy white towels – combine to make it all feel considerably more French

145

St Ives harbour see p145

Porthminster Café see p153

St Ives see p145

Things to do

ST IVES BAY & AROUND

Gwithian Academy of Surfing
Godrevy House, Prosper Hill, Gwithian, TR27 5BW (01736 757579, www.surfacademy. co.uk). Open phone for details.

The British Surf Association-approved Gwithian Academy teaches surfers of all levels in the beautiful setting of St Ives Bay.

Paradise Park
Trelissick Road, Hayle, TR27 4HB (01736 751020, www.paradisepark.org.uk). Open Mar, Apr, Oct 10am-4pm daily. May-Sept 10am-5pm daily. Nov-Feb 10am-3pm daily. Admission £14.45; free-£13 reductions; £47.50 family.

In the event of beach overload, you might consider seeking distraction in this family-oriented wildlife sanctuary. It contains parrots and tropical birds galore, many of them rare and endangered species (among them the Cornish chough, the symbol of Cornwall, now making a comeback on the Lizard). There are regular free-flying bird shows and flamingos roam in the gardens. There's also an indoor playground, a mini railway and, of course, a shop stacked to the rafters with brightly coloured parrot toys and paraphernalia.

MOUNT'S BAY

Atlantic Coasters
0845 600 1420, www.firstgroup.com. Tickets £13; £26 family.

Set aside any prejudice about bus tours – if you book via the First Group app this open-top double decker does a good-value circuit of the Penwith Peninsula for just £13 (hop-on, hop-off). It's a round trip from Penzance, stopping at Newlyn, Porthcurno, Land's End, Sennen Cove, St Just, Geevor Tin Mine, St Ives and Marazion. There are usually five services a day from mid April to October.

Cornish Way Cycle Path
www.sustrans.org.uk

Following the sea all the way from Penzance to Marazion (with access to St Michael's Mount), this very manageable, flat section of the Cornish Way cycle track takes you around the sweep of Mount's Bay. It is traffic-free most of the way, apart from a short stint at Marazion, and the views are fantastic. Bikes can be rented from the Cycle Centre Penzance (1 New Street, 01736 351671, www.cornwallcycle centre.co.uk, closed Sun) for £12.50 per day. For a longer ride, set off from Mousehole, which is part of the same designated national cycle route.

Jubilee Pool ♥
The Promenade, Penzance (www.jubileepool. co.uk). Open early 10am-4pm Tue-Sun. Admission £4.25; free-£3 reductions.

Penzance's stunning art deco lido, which points gracefully into the waters of Mount's Bay, was built to mark George V's silver jubilee in 1935. Saved from destruction a few years back, the triangular pool, which is fed by sea water with the flowing of the tide, is now a listed building. The curving white edges, lines of changing cubicles and Cubist pale blue tiers and steps, set against the background of the open sea, are a photographer's dream (several books of images are for sale around town). Its beauty is no protection against the often limb-numbing water temperatures, though, and savvy locals often wear a wetsuit. The new geothermal pool, with natural salt

Gwithian Academy of Surfing

Minack Theatre

water 30-35°C opened in 2020. There are deckchairs for hire, and the lichen-coloured Jubilee Pool Cafe is the perfect spot for a light lunch or a late afternoon tipple with views out to sea and across to Newlyn. Needless to say, the pool closes in winter.

LAND'S END & AROUND

Fat Hen 💜
Gwenmenhir, Boscawen-noon Farm, St Buryan, TR19 6EH (01736 810156, www. fathen.org).

With the help of two specialist chefs, ecologist Caroline Davey runs gourmet Wild Food Weekends and foraging outings deep in the West Cornwall countryside.

Minack Theatre 💜
Porthcurno, TR19 6JU (01736 810181, www. minack.com). Visitor Centre Open Summer 9.30am-5.30pm Mon, Tue, Thur, Sat, Sun; 9.30am-noon Wed, Fri. Winter 10am-4pm daily. Admission £7.50; £3.75 reductions.

There can be few more memorable theatre trips for children (or adults, for

that matter) than a performance at the open-air Minack Theatre, a Greek-inspired amphitheatre carved out of a granite cliff 200 feet above Porthcurno Beach, with the ocean as the backdrop. The theatre was founded by the quite extraordinary Rowena Cade, and its first production in 1932 was, aptly given the wild surrounds, *The Tempest*; the visitor centre tells the story. Performances take place from May to the autumn: book early and bear in mind that performances go ahead in all but the most extreme weather conditions – bring jumpers, anoraks, a picnic and cushions (the Minack also hires them out, for a charge).

Sennen Surfing Centre
Churchtown House, Sennen, TR19 4AD (01736 871227, 01736 871561, www. sennensurfingcentre.com). Open Easter-Sept; call in advance to book. Lessons from £20.

There can be few greater settings for a surf lesson than Sennen in the far west, where long-haired, youthful instructors take group and private lessons.

Riviera than Cornish Riviera.

In the 1850s, St Ives was a thriving centre of the fishing industry, but by the 1900s pilchard stocks had declined and the town was attracting schools of artists instead. Abstract painters and sculptors such as Barbara Hepworth, Ben Nicholson and Naum Gabo put St Ives firmly on the creative map. This small seaside town still has a big reputation when it comes to art, cemented by the construction of the third branch of the **Tate** (*see p158*) in 1993, right on the beach, and the reopening of the **Leach Pottery** (*see p158*) in 2008.

St Ives is best explored on foot; its narrow, winding streets are no place for a car, and parking can be problematic. Besides, one of its great pleasures is to take an aimless stroll through the twisting 'downalong' alleys and lanes behind the harbour, where the fishermen used to live. These endlessly picturesque streets, forming an 'old town' of sorts, are lined with pint-sized white and granite cottages, decorated with bursting window boxes and pastel-coloured paintwork. The town's main shopping street, pedestrianised **Fore Street** – now as much home to bijou boutiques, delis and galleries as to old-fashioned fudge shops – is a good place to dive in, with the subtropical **Trewyn Gardens** close by.

Alongside the inevitable tourist tat of a seaside town, St Ives has some characteristically creative small enterprises, such as **I Should Coco** (39 Fore Street, 01736 798756, www. ishouldcoco.co.uk), for fresh, hand-crafted chocolates and truffles of Cornish inspiration (try the Cornish sea-salted caramel); and **Seasalt** (4 Fore Street, 01736 799684, www. seasaltcornwall.co.uk), a Cornish mini chain with outlets all over the country. On Fore Street, **St Ives Bookseller** (no.2, 01736 796676, www.stives-bookseller.co.uk) is a dapper little

establishment, and a rewarding place for a browse.

At the entrance to **Smeaton's Pier**, you can stick your nose into the miniature stone-built **St Leonard's Chapel**, where fishermen prayed before they went to sea. On the opposite side of the harbour stands the **Lifeboat Station**, open to visitors in summer. Between the two is the atmospheric **Sloop Inn** (01736 796584, www.sloop-inn.co.uk), one of the oldest pubs in Cornwall, and with tables right on the harbour. Stretching out north of the harbour like a big toe is the area known as 'the Island', an outcrop whose grassy footpath takes you on a short walk around the headland to **Porthmeor Beach**, and the Tate, on the other side.

Town beaches

It is hard to imagine a town of these diminutive dimensions with more (or better) beaches: if you count the harbour, which also transforms into a soft, sandy beach at low tide, St Ives has four beaches, all with clear waters and bright, clean sand. There's little **Porthgwidden**, hidden away in a nick on the Island, which is great for kids; Atlantic-facing **Porthmeor**, St Ives' surf star and home to the Tate gallery; and palm-trimmed **Porthminster**💙, whose waters and sands have been awarded Blue Flag status. Barely a mile out of town (and an exquisite walk along the coastal footpath) is another fine, Blue Flag beach at **Carbis Bay**.

Hayle

Gently curving round the north-eastern reaches of St Ives Bay are Hayle's impressive (and much-touted) 'three miles of golden sand', reaching from the mouth of the Hayle estuary all the way around the bay to **Godrevy Point**, an epic spot guarded by the Godrevy Lighthouse (thought to have been the inspiration for

Zennor

Virginia Woolf's novel *To the Lighthouse*). A world away from the cuteness and crowds of St Ives across the bay, the beaches of **Gwithian** and **Godrevy**, joined at low tide, are altogether more elemental scenes, pounded by some of Cornwall's best surf and with big open skies and sunsets.

The surf peters out as you walk south and, in the bay's sheltered south-western elbow, at **Hayle Towans**, fishing boats putter along the glassy estuary. Behind the harbour, the long, thin town of Hayle is slowly shedding its dated skin. It has a smattering of boutiques, including a good surf shop (**Down the Line**, Market Square Arcade, 01736 757025, www.downthelinesurf.co.uk), **Mr B's ice-cream parlour** (24 Penpol Terrace, 01736 758580, www.mrbsicecream.co.uk, closed Mon-Wed), and a contemporary art gallery. Up on the dunes, however, Hayle Towans, with its holiday parks and chalets, still has an air of Butlins about it.

Zennor

In the opposite direction, the scenic B3306 road heads west towards St Just, taking in some heart-stopping moor-meets-sea scenery along the way – as well as the famously pretty village of Zennor. DH Lawrence and his German wife Frieda spent two years living here during World War I, first staying at the Tinner's Arms, then renting a cottage for the sum of £5 per year, until their eventual expulsion from Cornwall amid allegations of spying; their story is evocatively told, and the scenery painted, in Helen Dunmore's 1994 novel *Zennor in Darkness*. Little has changed in this tiny hamlet, and there is a timeless quality to the old buildings, the surrounding remains of ancient field systems and the wilderness of the granite moors.

Stop for a pint in the delightful one-room **Tinners Arms** (*see p153*), and wander around the pretty **St Senara church** (*see p111*) which has a famous carving of the mermaid of Zennor that is thought to be over 600 years old.

Stunning coastal walks stretch out to either side of Zennor, and it's well worth taking in the windy drama of the **Gurnard's Head**, which pushes out into the Atlantic a mile or so to the west, before eating at the superb inn of the same name (*see p152*).

Where to eat & drink

The best harbourside spot for an honest pint in St Ives is the 14th-century **Sloop Inn** (see p150), with benches by the water. Good café stops include the simple but chic **Tate café**, looking out to sea; and the classy **Source Kitchen** (6 The Digey, 01736 799487, www.sourcekitchen.co.uk) and its fine array of evening sharing plates. At the risk of being glib, if you like rum and crustacea you'll almost certainly dig the rustic joys of the **Rum & Crab Shack** (Wharf Road, 01736 796353, www.rumand crabshack.com).

Over at Gwithian, the **Sunset Surf Shop & Café** (10 Gwithian Towans, 01736 752575, www.sunset-surf.com, closed Nov-Feb Tue, Wed) lives up to its name, with views out to sea and to Godrevy Lighthouse – ideal for when the sun melts into the sea. It's a busy, post-surf refill station (with surf school attached), its tables usually packed with groups wolfing down chunky burgers and spicy wedges. A few doors down, the **Jam Pot** is a cosy caff serving mugs of tea and monster breakfasts.

A short drive out of Hayle, near Conner Downs, is one of Cornwall's most successful farm shops, **Trevaskis Farm** (Gwinear, 01209 713931, www.trevaskisfarm.co.uk) – renowned for its sausages, but stocking a huge variety of local produce. Meanwhile, its rustic **Farmhouse Kitchen Restaurant** serves solid bistro fare in generous portions.

Blas Burgerworks♥

The Warren, St Ives, TR26 2EA (01736 797272, www.blasburgerworks.co.uk). Food served July, Aug noon-2pm, 5-10pm daily. Sept-June 6-10pm Tue-Sun. Closed Nov-mid Feb.

St Ives' very own gourmet burger company occupies a pint-sized space secreted down a pretty, narrow lane. Seating is on stools at communal tables and elbow room is scarce, but once you've sunk your teeth into one of Blas's chargrilled burgers, comfort seems a secondary consideration. In the absence of an available seat, grab a burger and walk a few yards to the seafront (keeping a watchful eye on the circling seagulls, renowned for their barefaced swoop-and-steal operations). Cornish meat is used in all the beefburgers, and Blas has a committed green agenda: all organic waste is composted, the furniture is made from reclaimed timber and local produce is king. Service is exemplary. Note that opening times do vary – and that sometimes (spring half-terms, for example) lunch is served out of season.

Gurnard's Head♥

Treen, nr Zennor, TR26 3DE (01736 796928, www.gurnardshead.co.uk). Open 11am-11pm daily. Lunch served 12.30-2.30pm, dinner served 6.30-9pm daily.

With the desolate Penwith moorland on one side and the foaming sea on the other, this coastal inn – named after the rocky outcrop a few fields away, shaped like a gurnard's head – boasts a splendidly isolated setting. Although the gastronomically astute menu, confident service and rustic chic decor place the Gurnard's well out of the pub grub bracket, the atmosphere is buoyant and informal, the prices fair and the food fuss-free. This is hearty British comfort food of the highest order: pork belly with mash, cabbage, cider and thyme or rabbit and partridge terrine. Also the owners of the celebrated Felin Fach Griffin in Wales, the Inkins are firm believers in 'the simple things in life done well'. And so now are hundreds of hungry hikers, urban refugees and locals getting together for a family roast – so bookings are essential in high season. One of Cornwall's best eats. There are also seven rooms available, if you want to stay over.

Moomaid in the Village

Zennor, St Ives, TR26 3BT (www.moomaidofzennor.co.uk). Open 9.30am-5pm daily.

Made in the hip village of Zennor, Moomaid is a contender for the Cornish ice-cream crown – and the competition is fiercer than ever (*see right*). Its boutique St Ives ice-cream parlour has recently relocated from bustling St Ives to Zennor itself, where it serves drinks, snack and 24 delicious varieties of ice-cream. In the summer there's a pop-up (Moomaid in the Field) off the road between St Ives and Zennor.

Porthgwidden Beach Café
Porthgwidden Beach, St Ives, TR26 1PL (01736 796791, www.porthgwiddencafe. co.uk). Food served Summer 8-11am, noon-3pm, 6-9.30pm daily. Winter 9-11am, noon-3pm Tue, Wed, Sun; 9-11am, noon-3pm, 6-9pm Thur-Sat.

The Porthminster Café's (*see below*) more easy-going sister restaurant is a delightful spot for a full English, a light lunch or just a good Lavazza coffee overlooking St Ives' most secluded beach. The white-walled and wooden-floored interior is beachside breezy but in summer it's all about the terrace, with its blue gingham tablecloths and fabulous views out into the bay. Prices are very fair given the prime location – and it's open year-round.

Porthmeor Cafe Bar
Porthmeor Beach, St Ives, TR26 1JZ (www.porthmeor-beach.co.uk, 01736 793366). Open 9am-10pm Mon-Sat; 10am-4.30pm Sun.

Rock up on the terrace or grab one of the heated pods, enjoy the lovely beach views, and – depending upon the time of day – fill up with a 'build your own' breakfast, tuck into Mediterranean-style small plates or go to town on more substantial seafood mains (like boned whole seabass stuffed with potted shrimp) at this popular spot. A new fish bar is due to open on its middle level in summer 2021.

Porthminster Café ♥
Porthminster Beach, St Ives, TR26 2EB (01736 795352, www.porthminstercafe. co.uk). Food served Summer noon-4pm, 6-10pm daily. Winter noon-3pm Tue, Wed, Sun; noon-3pm, 6-9pm Thur-Sat.

The name rather understates its case: far from being your average beach-side caff, the Porthminster Café is a serious restaurant in

Five Cornish ice-creams

Jelberts Ices
A splendid scoop of ice-cream nostalgia, Jelberts (New Road, Newlyn, no phone) has been selling vanilla, and vanilla alone, out of these tiny Newlyn premises since time began... Or since the 1950s, at any rate. Measured against the wacky flavours doing battle across the county, its adherence to own-made vanilla might seem old-fashioned, but with clotted cream and a flake, it's ice-cream heaven. Small, fresh batches of unadulterated ice-cream are made daily, and the slightly grainy texture tastes wonderfully home-made. Closed out of season.

Kelly's of Cornwall
Available in supermarkets nationwide, and at almost every beach in Cornwall, Kelly's (www.kellysofbodmin.co.uk) is hardly an artisinal operation. Nonetheless, it does sterling service in producing just under ten million litres a year of very commendable (and affordable) clotted cream vanilla ice-cream. Its 'whip' cones are the smoothest around.

Moomaid of Zennor
The new kid on the ice block, Moomaid (www.moomaidofzennor.co.uk) has speedily made inroads into the very competitive Cornish ice-cream market with its fantastic range of 'creams and fruity sorbets, and some inspired flavours (peach bellini, anyone?).

Roskilly's
Producing high-grade artisan ice-cream on its dairy farm on the Lizard, Roskilly's (www.roskillys.co.uk) stands out by dint of its texture; there's no stinting on chunk size either. It's available all over west Cornwall, although true devotees head for the farm where it's made on the Lizard (see *p128*).

Treleavens
South-east Cornwall's finest parlour produces a tasty, all-natural product that can be found in the Treleavens shop in Looe (www.treleavens.co.uk) and various other outlets all over east Cornwall. Award-winning flavours include panna cotta with summer fruits and orange and mascarpone.

the body of a laid-back beach house – albeit a very classy one. Australian chef Michael Smith's sun-kissed menu sets the perfect tone for holiday dining, with the emphasis on Mediterranean flavours and fresh seafood, as well as posh fish and chips (with white balsamic vinegar, naturally). Friendly, slick service, fresh decor and dreamy views over the white sands of Porthminster Beach make this the ideal perch from which to contemplate the light dancing in the bay with a glass of local bubbly (try the Polgoon Aval or Camel Valley Bacchus). Porthminster is not only one of St Ives' best kitchens, but is quickly making inroads into the upper echelons of Cornwall's burgeoning restaurant scene. Booking recommended.

Porthminster Kitchen

Wharf Rd, St Ives, TR26 1LG (01736 799874, www.porthminster.kitchen). Breakfast served 9.30-11am daily; lunch served noon-3pm daily; dinner served 5.30pm-late daily.

Billing itself as offering a 'refreshing, playful take on Cornish cuisine', this restaurant on popular Porthminster beach would be pretty much worth it for the panoramic views of St Ives and its harbour. Sister to the much-loved Porthminster Café and Porthgwidden Beach Café, dishes on the menu include catch of the day with herb gnocchi, or a tandoori monkfish starter with onion seed flatbread.

Tinners Arms

Zennor, TR26 3BY (01736 796927, www.tinnersarms.com). Open 11.30am-11pm Mon-Sat; noon-10.30pm Sun. Lunch served noon-2.30pm, dinner served 6-9pm daily.

A peaceful little pub in Penwith's prettiest village, the Tinners feels like it probably hasn't changed a great deal since it was built in the 13th century. And we mean that in a good way: flagstone floors, a log fire, good beer, no musak, no TV and no fruit machines. In short, just the sort of place you daydream about stumbling across after a windy walk on the moors. The White House next door (*see p157*) has simple but tasteful white rooms.

Where to stay

Blue Hayes Private Hotel

Trelyon Avenue, St Ives, TR26 2AD (01736 797129, www.bluehayes.co.uk). Rates £160-£315 double incl breakfast. Closed from Nov-Feb.

The 'private' tag is fitting: tucked discreetly away above Porthminster Beach (a mere ten minutes from the harbour), Blue Hayes has just five luxuriously appointed suites and a guests-only restaurant. Owner Malcolm Herring spent two years overhauling an old 1920s guesthouse, halving the number of rooms and creating a clean, classic interior design with the odd touch of glamour. The rooms have spacious terraces, dazzling sea views and immaculate bathrooms – but the icing on the cake is the balustraded white terrace. Here, you can take breakfast (or a cocktail at sunset) overlooking the harbour. More St Tropez than St Ives.

Boskerris

Boskerris Road, Carbis Bay, St Ives, TR26 2NQ (01736 795295, www.boskerrishotel.co.uk). Rates £220-£310 double incl breakfast.

This 1930s hotel – on the southern edge of St Ives in Carbis Bay – has been transformed by the Bassett family into a haven of contemporary coastal chic. It's furnished with unerring good taste (Osborne & Little outsized floral wallpaper, perspex coffee tables, pristine white rugs) and run with admirable attention to detail (perfectly placed mirrors to reflect the sea, fresh milk for tea). The panoramic terrace is in pole position to take in the sweep of the whole bay, with St Ives on one side and the white horses crashing into the Godrevy Lighthouse on the other, and nearly all rooms have ocean views. Breakfast is sure to satisfy the fussiest of foodies – a named-local-source menu includes ricotta hot cakes with berry compote and French toast with pan-fried bananas and maple syrup. The centre of St Ives can be accessed via a 20-minute walk along the coastal path, or a three-minute train journey on the charming branch line train (*see p117*).

Eleven Sea View Terrace

11 Sea View Terrace, St Ives, TR26 2DH
(01736 798440, www.11stives.co.uk).
Rates £90-£135 double incl breakfast.

Technically it's a B&B, but aesthetically this Edwardian townhouse is breaking well out of its bracket. The three rooms are stylish and understated, with white walls, navy blue accents and spotless modern bathrooms. In terms of views, the address says it all: located at the top of town, it has two rooms with views over the old town below; the other has a private south-facing terrace by way of compensation.

Gwithian Farm Campsite ♥

1 Church Town Road, Gwithian, TR27 5BX (01736 753127, www.gwithianfarm. co.uk). Rates £18-£35 for 2 people.

Despite boasting the kind of coastal setting that leads many a campsite to nonchalance, Gwithian Farm shows an unwavering commitment to high standards, providing the sort of cut-above facilities that usually involve braving a large, expensive holiday park. Campsite luxuries include a state-of-the-art shower block, a plethora of child-friendly features, large pitches and an incredibly well-stocked campsite shop (miniature bottles of Felippo Berio olive oil, locally picked strawberries, a visiting fishmonger, OS maps, national newspapers). There is a solid village pub just across the road, and the beach is a 15-minute walk away. Advance booking is essential in high season.

Primrose Valley Hotel

Porthminster Beach, St Ives, TR26 2ED
(01736 794939, www.primroseonline. co.uk). Rates £180-£235 double incl breakfast.

This lovingly run hotel is one of St Ives' best boutique options, with a quiet but central beachside location, contemporary styling and keen attention to guests' needs. Just metres from the soft sands of Porthminster Beach (ask for directions, as the location is decidedly discreet), white-fronted Primrose Valley has the feel of a seaside villa; request a front-facing room with sea views for the full effect. Despite hip hotel accents, this is an unpretentious

Boutique Retreats *see p165*

Mayon Cliff Old Coastguard Lookout *see p168*

THE PENWITH PENINSULA

place, where substance is as important as style. Expect a superb breakfast, personal service, and a commitment to reducing its ecological impact.

Salt House 🧡

Venton Road, St Ives, TR26 2AQ (01736 791857, www.salthousestives.co.uk). Rates £1,600-£5,460 per week (sleeps up to 10).

When it comes to modern high design, Salt House is unrivalled in these parts. Owned by graphic designers Alan and Sharon Spencer, this large rental occupies a modernist wood-clad cube of a house in Carbis Bay, with two pristine white rooms of very generous proportions and with serious design credentials. Bathrooms are five-star hotel standard, with waterfall showers, vast, tablet-shaped sinks, and engulfing, egg-shaped mosaic baths. There's beauty in the detail too: Alessi bottle openers, Orla Kiely mugs, coconut-flecked home-made cookies, fresh coffee, complimentary mini bar and Molten Brown smellies. Flatscreen tellies, DVD library, free Wi-Fi and Sky Plus are also present and correct, but they could have got away with much less given the fantasy views. Bedrooms have not so much windows as a wall of glass, affording vast views over the golden sands of St Ives Bay. Technically, Salt House isn't in St Ives – it is in the quiet residential village of Carbis Bay, but St Ives is just a 15-minute walk

along the (unlit) coastal footpath from the bottom of the garden.

Treliska Apartments

3 Bedford Road, St Ives, TR26 1SP (01736 797678, www.treliska.com). Rates £130-£160 per night in high season.

A few minutes' walk from the harbour and just off the high street (there's no dedicated parking area, though staff can arrange a private space nearby at £8 per day), Treliska has two of St Ive's best-value apartments – modern, clean and tastefully decorated. The two-bedroom apartment is sunny and south-facing and spread over three floors. The one-bedroom apartment has a sofa bed in the lounge and a patio with gas barbecue.

White House

Tinners Arms, Zennor, TR26 3BY (01736 796927, www.tinnersarms.com). Rates £150 double incl breakfast.

Attached to the lovely old Tinners Arms in Zennor, this tiny guesthouse is one of those rare places where you can find simple good taste and a beautiful setting and still get change from £100 (if you book an £85 single). The four rooms (two doubles, two singles) are decorated in fresh whites, with rustic wooden furniture and fresh flowers.

Places to visit

ST IVES BAY & AROUND

Barbara Hepworth Museum & Sculpture Garden 💜

Barnoon Hill, St Ives, TR26 1AD (01736 796226, www.tate.org.uk/stives/hepworth). Open Mar-Oct 10am-5pm daily. Nov-Feb 10am-4pm Tue-Sun. Admission £7; free-£6 reductions.

Owned and managed by the Tate, this small museum is an engaging tribute to one of the 20th century's most important artistic figures. Sculptor Barbara Hepworth made

Barbara Hepworth Museum & Sculpture Garden

this her home and studio from 1949 until her death in 1975. It offers a fascinating insight into Hepworth's life, with her studio and garden preserved as she left it. Her curving sculptures, including *Fallen Images* (which was completed only a few months before her death), are complemented by biographical material, while the garden, which she helped to design, displays her larger pieces in a peaceful subtropical setting.

Leach Pottery 💜

Higher Stennack, St Ives, TR26 2HE (01736 799703, www.leachpottery.com). Open Mar-Oct 10am-5pm Mon-Sat; 11am-4pm Sun. Nov-Feb 10am-5pm Mon-Sat. Admission £5.50; free-£4.50 reductions.

Among the modernist heavyweights of the 1930s St Ives art colony (which included the likes of Barbara Hepworth, Ben Nicholson and Naum Gabo) was the pioneering potter Bernard Leach, widely hailed as the 'father of studio pottery'. After long years of neglect, his internationally renowned Leach Pottery, founded in 1920 with Japanese potter Shoji Hamada, reopened in 2008 after a £1.7 million restoration and redevelopment programme – furnishing St Ives its third major artistic attraction, alongside the Tate and the Barbara Hepworth Museum. Born in Hong Kong, Leach spent his formative years mingling with the artists of the Japanese Shirakaba folk craft movement; when it opened, the Leach Pottery was the first in the Western world to install a Japanese wood-burning kiln. Now a scheduled monument, the kiln stands – as it did the 1970s – in the most evocative part of the museum: the old pottery, which has been left respectfully unpolished. The Leach Tableware collection, produced on site and sold in the shop, makes a classy souvenir.

Tate St Ives 💜

Porthmeor Beach, St Ives, TR26 1TG (01736 796226, www.tate.org.uk/stives). Open Mar-Oct 10am-5pm daily. Nov-Feb 10am-4pm Tue-Sun. Admission £10.50; free-£9.50 reductions.

The undisputed flagship of Cornwall's art scene, the UK's smallest Tate occupies a striking, curving building in an even more striking location: Porthmeor Beach. At the heart of the building is an open-air rotunda (representing the gas-holder that once occupied the site at the old gasworks); the brightly coloured glass display is the work of late Cornish artist Patrick Heron. The museum's changing exhibitions (there is no permanent collection) showcase the work of 20th-century painters and sculptors, particularly those associated with St Ives (the naive art of Alfred Wallis, say, the geometrical paintings of Ben Nicholson or the studio pottery of Bernard Leach), as well as exhibiting contemporary artists as part of its artist-in-residence programme. Take a breather in the top-floor café, which has great views.

St Michael's Mount see p160

MOUNT'S BAY

Chysauster Ancient Village

TR20 8XA (07831 757934, www.english-heritage.org.uk). Open July, Aug 10am-6pm daily. Apr-June, Sept 10am-5pm daily. Oct 10am-4pm daily. Admission £6.50; £3.90-£5.90 reductions reductions.

This wild, exposed site dates from the first century BC and features the best-preserved hut circles in the UK – not to mention some awesome views over the granite-strewn moors. More ancient village remains and a fogou (an Iron Age underground structure) can be seen at Carn Euny, near Sancree, further west.

The Exchange

Princes Street, Penzance, TR18 2NL (01736 363715, www.newlynartgallery.co.uk). Open Mar-Oct 10am-5pm Mon-Sat. Nov-Feb 10am-5pm Tue-Sat. Admission free.

The wave-like exterior of the old phone exchange building – after dark, pulsing with the sea blues and greens of Peter Freeman's light installation – announces your arrival at west Cornwall's major contemporary art gallery, an offshoot of the Newlyn Art Gallery. The look is sleek and modern and the curating ambitious – you are more likely to find a boundary-pushing installation than a pretty seascape. There is no permanent collection, but four or so exhibitions a year spotlight local and national artists. The airy café/shop is good for a light lunch of smoked mackerel with salad, or soup and crusty bread.

Newlyn Art Gallery

New Road, Newlyn, TR18 5PZ (01736 363715, www.newlynartgallery.co.uk). Open Mar-Oct 10am-5pm Mon-Sat. Nov-Feb 10am-5pm Tue-Sat. Admission free.

Home to the Newlyn School of artists from the late 19th century, Newlyn continues to support a thriving art scene, with this long-standing gallery at its heart. It has occupied this site just back from the promenade for over 100 years, but underwent a much-needed redevelopment and expansion in 2007 (which included the addition of the affiliated Exchange gallery in the centre of Penzance, *see left*), and holds exhibitions of national and international contemporary art. There is a small shop, and a café serving light lunches.

Penlee House Gallery & Museum

Morrab Road, Penzance, TR18 4HE (01736 363625, www.penleehouse.org.uk). Open Easter-Sept 10am-5pm Mon-Sat. Oct-Easter 10.30am-4.30pm Mon-Sat. £6; free-£3 reductions; all admission free Sat.

Places to visit

A smart Italianate Victorian villa, Penlee House holds the largest collection of paintings by the Newlyn School. Look out for Norman Garstin's *The Rain it Raineth Every Day*, painted in 1889, and the earliest work in the collection – *Mount's Bay* (1794) by William Brooks, as well as key works by Stanhope Forbes and Walter Langley. Note that there is no permanent display and only a selection of paintings is hung at any one time. A small museum covers Cornish history in brief, with exhibits ranging from Stone Age tools to the mining safety lamp invented by Penzance's famous son Humphrey Davy (1778-1829). The Orangery Café is an idyllic spot for an open-air lunch, amid exotic gardens.

St Michael's Mount ♥

Marazion (01736 710507, www. stmichaelsmount.co.uk). Open Castle Apr-Oct 10.30am-5pm Mon-Fri, Sun. Tours Nov-Mar 11am, 2pm Tue, Fri (weather permitting; call to check). Gardens May, June 10.30am-5pm Mon-Fri. July-Oct 10.30am-5pm Thur, Fri. Admission £14 castle; £24 castle & gardens; free-£13 reductions.

Just off the coast of Marazion, St Michael's Mount – bearing an uncanny resemblance to its namesake across the channel – is the stuff of fairytale; an iconic island castle holding court in the bay. Legend claims the mount was once the lair of the giant Cormoran, who tyrannised the local population but was defeated in true David and Goliath fashion by a little Cornish boy. Early records, however, show that the mount began life as a bustling port for the fishermen of Marazion. Its religious status was conferred when a church was added and, by the eighth century, a monastery had been founded. It was used as a store for Royalist arms during the Civil War, before becoming the residence of the St Aubyn family. St Michael's Mount was donated to the National Trust in 1954 by Lord St Levan, although his son, the fourth baron, still lives on the island.

For visitors, it's a rousing walk across the granite causeway at low tide (there's also a ferry), followed by a steep climb from the harbour up the Pilgrim's Steps to the castle entrance; pause to admire the giant's stone heart in the cobbles on the way. Inside, the castle is disarmingly cosy and compact, with paintings, weapons and military trophies dominating the displays.

Trengwainton Garden

Madron, TR20 8RZ (01736 363148, www. nationaltrust.org.uk). Open Feb-Oct 10.30am-5pm Mon-Thur, Sun. Admission £5; £2.50 reductions.

The handsome pile at the end of the sweeping drive isn't open to visitors, but there is plenty to admire in the extensive gardens. At its best in springtime, the sheltered estate incorporates magnificent wooded walks through a stream-fed valley, gorgeous kitchen gardens with unusual sloped beds, and all manner of exotic plants. On a sunny day, the lawn terrace and summerhouses at the top, with views to Mount's Bay, invite a picnic break or even a siesta.

LAND'S END & AROUND

Geevor Tin Mine ♥

Pendeen, TR19 7EW (01736 788662, www. geevor.com). Open Apr-Oct 9am-5pm Mon-Fri, Sun. Nov-Mar 9am-4pm Mon-Fri, Sun. Admission £16.10; free-£13.75 reductions; £49.75 family.

Geevor was a working mine for over 80 years, employing some 400 at its peak, before its closure in 1990 after the crash in tin prices had rendered the huge clifftop operation economically unfeasible. Following a multi-million-pound preservation programme, which included the addition of the interactive Hard Rock Museum, the mine was brought back to life as a visitor attraction. The site has been sensitively adapted, leaving the workings of the mine wonderfully intact – everything from the hulking machines of the compressor house and the ore processing mill down to the helmets and paperwork of the employees remains in place. Visits culminate with an underground tour of the tunnels, conducted by ex-miners – an experience that is as emotive as it is claustrophobic.

Geevor offers a captivating insight into the scale of the mining operation in the area, and Cornwall's preeminence in the industrial world before it became better known for cream teas, beach holidays and surfing. With even a passing curiosity you could spend hours here, and with any sort of specialist interest you could be absorbed for days. One of Cornwall's great unsung sights – and serving a fine home-made pasty in the café to boot.

Levant Mine & Beam Engine
Trwellard, TR19 7SX (01736 786156, www. nationaltrust.org.uk). Open mid Feb-Oct 10.30am-4.30pm Mon-Thur, Sun. Admission £10; £5 reductions; £25 family.

With a panoramic cliffside location, just around the coast from Geevor Tin Mine, Levant offers visitors the chance to see an original steam-powered Cornish beam engine in action. Originally used to winch men and materials up from the shaft, this one was restored after lying dormant for 60 years. Check the website for the times and days before setting out; underground tours are also conducted.

Merry Maidens
Off B3315, nr Lamorna (www.cornishsites. com).

One of the country's best-preserved stone circles, the Merry Maidens comprises 19 standing stones set in a tidy circle, next to the road from Newlyn to Land's End. There's no fanfare on arrival, just the occasional curious onlooker, but that makes the scene all the more bewitching. Legend has it that the stones are a group of women who were petrified for dancing on a Sunday.

Levant Mine

PK Porthcurno

PK Porthcurno
Porthcurno, TR19 6JX (01736 810966, www. pkporthcurno.com). Open Apr-Oct 10am-5pm daily. Nov-Mar 10am-5pm Mon, Sun. Admission £9; free-£5.50 reductions; £26 family.

Now more talked about for its tropically coloured waters and white sands – and, of course, the Minack Theatre (see p149) – the remote cove of Porthcurno was also once a pioneering communications station, and the landing point for the first long-distance underwater telegraph cable connecting Britain with India. The Eastern Telegraph Company grew through the 19th century and into the early 20th (and eventually merged with Marconi's Wireless Telegraph Company, later to become Cable & Wireless), making Porthcurno a target during World War II. To this end, a bomb-proof underground tunnel, bored by local miners, was built: the bunker now houses part of the museum. Overhauled and opened in 1998 as a visitor attraction, this is an absorbing museum, with interactive exhibits, an engaging talk (during which you get to hold sections of underwater cable) and clear explanations of what are – even for internet agers – tricky concepts.

MOUNT'S BAY

Penzance

The best way to arrive in Penzance is by train (*see p169*) – partly for the feeling of having escaped to the end of the line, but also because when the track emerges from the Cornish countryside on to the curve of Mount's Bay, it reveals a perfect view of the town on the hill above. The commercial centre for the western district of Penwith, Penzance was once a fashionable seaside resort – the trappings of which can still be seen in the fading but elegant architecture along Cornwall's only seaside promenade, notably the art deco **Jubilee Pool** (*see p148*).

These days, compared to Cornwall's more prettified seaside towns – Fowey, Padstow, St Ives – Penzance is rather frayed around the edges. But it is an atmospheric place, with plenty of bohemian charm, a smattering of seaside irreverence and a newly prospering art scene, consolidated by the opening of the **Exchange**, a major modern art centre, in 2008. Leading commercial galleries include **Cornwall Contemporary** (1 Parade Street, Queens Square, 01736 874749, www.cornwallcontemporary.com), closed on Sundays. On Market Jew Street, **Books Plus** (no.23, 01736 365607, www.booksplusuk.com) stocks books on the local art scene amid its enjoyably eclectic stock.

Traditionally, Penzance is renowned for its mild climate and sun-trap feel. On a windy February weekend you may not be convinced, but subtropical plants genuinely thrive in havens such as **Morrab Gardens** and **Penlee Park** in the centre of town – and don't be surprised if you see banana trees and palms poking out of front gardens. Further evidence of clement climes comes in the shape of the **Polgoon vineyard** (Rosehill, 01736 333946, www.polgoon.com) on the outskirts of town, which is open for tours (£10-£15). The first year's rosé garnered praise, and the Aval, a refined, French-style sparkling cider, is now served in Rick Stein outposts and the **Porthminster Café** (*see p153*), among others.

For many, Penzance is the jumping-off point for the **Scilly Isles**, 28 miles west – the *Scillonian III* leaves from the harbour and the heliport is on the outskirts of town. For the Isles of Scilly, *see p171*.

Marazion

Although it is now hard to believe, Marazion, not Penzance, was the major port and commercial centre in Mount's Bay until the 17th century, and it is one of Cornwall's oldest chartered towns. These days, its winding, narrow main street gets tourist-logged in summer, with visitors flocking to see the area's star attraction, **St Michael's Mount** (*see p160*). You can walk across to the island via a causeway that reveals itself at low tide, but ferries also run.

Even if you're not visiting the Mount, it's well worth walking or cycling the coastal trail (*see p148*) that hugs the bay from Penzance all the way to Marazion; in the right conditions, you'll see kite- and wind-surfers in action against the backdrop of the Mount. At the end, repair to the large terrace of the **Godolphin Arms** (West End, 01736 710202, www. godolphinarms.co.uk), a pint of ale in hand, to admire the bay twinkling in the foreground and Penzance in the distance.

Newlyn

Almost joined to Penzance to the south, Newlyn nevertheless retains its own identity, with a history that is strongly linked to both art and fishing. Despite the decline in the fishing industry, this is still the county's biggest fishing port and the site of **Newlyn Fish Festival**, held over the August bank holiday. In contrast to Mousehole, a few miles round the coast, Newlyn has the look and feel of a working port, and anyone with an interest in fishing should take a closer look at the harbour – or at the very least, invest in some gleaming fish or fresh Newlyn crab from **W Stevenson and Sons** (01736 362982, closed Sun) on the main street.

The town's importance as a centre of art in the late 19th and early 20th century, when the **Newlyn School** nurtured such names as Stanhope Forbes, Henry Scott Tuke and Walter Langley, is represented in the long-standing but recently revamped **Newlyn Gallery** (*see p159*), just off the promenade. There is little else to detain you, bar a couple of good commercial galleries along the main street and traditional ice-cream maker **Jelberts** (*see p153*), on New Road.

Mousehole

On a sunny morning, before the summer crowds throng the harbour walls and car-owners make misguided attempts to navigate its minuscule streets, Mousehole (pronounced Mowzel) seems too perfect to be true. Its tiny harbour is fringed with soft, yellow sand, while the granite cottages huddling together behind are made all the more irresistible by carefully tended window boxes and the odd cat peeking out. But even if Mousehole has, by dint of its beauty, become a tourist magnet, with cramped fisherman's cottages attracting mind-boggling offers, the village has retained plenty of character, and has a strong sense of community year-round. The village's colourful Christmas lights, draped across the boats in the harbour and the quayside, are a sight to be seen. The best date for a visit is 23 December,

when the village makes *Starry Gazey pie* in honour of Tom Bawcock's Eve; its namesake is said to have saved the village from starvation in the early 20th century, setting sail in stormy seas to land a bountiful catch of fish.

Where to eat & drink

Penzance has no shortage of pleasant cafés and small, laid-back eateries. Among the most appealing are **Archie Brown's** (Bread Street, 01736 362828, www.archiebrowns.co.uk, closed Sun), perennially popular for its healthy veggie food; the **Cornish Hen Deli** (27 Market Place, 01736 350223, closed Sun), selling Cornish goodies and good coffee; the **Honey Pot** (5 Parade Street, 01736 368686, www.thehoneypotpz.com, closed Sun), a cosy nook that has at least three types of chocolate cake on the go at any one time; and, in season, the alfresco **Jubilee Pool Cafe** (Wharf Road, 01736 369224, www.jubileepool. co.uk), next to Jubilee Pool, which has views out into the bay.

The best pasties in town can be found at **Lavender's** (6A Alverton Street, 01736 362800, www.lavenders cornishpasties.co.uk, closed Sun) or county-wide stalwart **WC Rowe** (73 Causewayhead, 01736 333193, www. rowesbakers.co.uk, closed Sun).

On the way into Mousehole is the casually chic café-restaurant at the **Old Coastguard Hotel** (01736 731222, www.oldcoastguardhotel.co.uk), with palm-fronted sea views. If you'd prefer a boozer, we recommend the **Ship Inn** (South Cliff, 01736 731234, www. shipinnmousehole.co.uk), an archetypal Cornish pub that's right on the harbour.

The Garden

Hotel Penzance, Britons Hill, Penzance, TR18 3AE (01736 366890, www. hotelpenzance.com). Food served 7.30am-6.30pm, dinner served 6.30-

9.30pm daily. Rates £199-£219 double incl breakfast.

The restaurant at the Penzance Hotel has a superb view, out to St Michael's Mount, and a fine veranda with stylish rattan furniture from which to survey it. Dinner ventures into pricey terrain, but the daily menu is good value, offering two courses for £14.95. The menu is a modern Cornish affair (smoked mackerel, goat's cheese and rocket, local catch of the day...), taking few risks – but the results, combined with the view, merit a stop.

Turks Head

Chapel Street, Penzance, TR18 4AF (01736 363093, www.turksheadpenzance. co.uk). Open 11am-11pm Mon-Sat; 11am-10.30pm Sun. Lunch served noon-2.30pm, dinner served 6-9.30pm Mon-Sat. Food served noon-9.30pm Sun.

On historic Chapel Street, Penzance's oldest pub is a nicely worn nook dating back to the 13th century, which cries out for a cosy pint by the log fire. This place was originally a smugglers' hangout; ask about the underground tunnel that once led from the harbour. With Doom and Betty Stoggs on tap, a quiet atmosphere and resolutely traditional furnishings, the Turk's is a fine antidote to Cornwall's new wave of blue and white bistros. There's a palm-shaded beer garden at the back. A few doors down, the **Admiral Benbow** (01736 363448), surreally decorated with objects retrieved from shipwrecked vessels, is another historic inn.

The Shore

13-14 Alverton St, Penzance, TR18 2QP (01736 362444, www.theshorerestaurant. uk). Dinner Tue-Sat 7pm (only one sitting).

Don't expect sea views from chef Bruce Rennie's tiny restaurant – but do expect a supperclub-like vibe with the menu created from whatever he picked up from Newlyn fish market that day, plus locally sourced herbs and veg, and organic bread made on the premises. The menu costs £59 a head, and may not be able to accommodate the fish averse (it is literally just Rennie in the kitchen).

Tolcarne Inn

9 Tolcarne Terrace, Newlyn, TR18 5PS (01736 363074, www.tolcarneinn.co.uk). Open 11.30am-late daily. Lunch noon-2.15pm Mon-Sat, noon-3pm Sun; dinner 6.30pm-9.30pm daily.

The Tolcarne is a 300-year-old maritime inn run by Ben Tunnicliffe. Formerly of swish eco-hotel Scarlet, he's moved away from the world of fine dining for something a little bit more hale and hearty, albeit still based on the freshest seafood he can get his hands on. Lunch is super-affordable, with nothing more than a £10; there are still light options at dinner (ray fillet, trout tartare) or you can splash out something a little fancier like red mullet or whole plaice.

2 Fore Street

2 Fore Street, Mousehole, TR19 6QU (01736 731164, www.2forestreet.co.uk). Lunch served noon-3pm, dinner served 6-9pm daily. Closed Mon Nov-Mar.

This bright bistro on Mousehole harbour is as dinky and perfectly formed as the village itself. The kitchen isn't in the business of statement cooking, sticking instead to a short but sweet menu of favourites, prepared to a very high standard: shell-roasted Newlyn scallops with lemon butter, crab and chilli linguine or whole baked sea bream, and the likes of chocolate and orange torte for dessert. Own-made bread, cheerful service and locally sourced ingredients add to the appeal. There's not a huge amount of space but there's also a pretty, sheltered garden with a few tables at the back.

Where to stay

Artist Residence

20 Chapel St, Penzance, TR18 4AW (01736 365664, www.artistresidence. co.uk). Rates £175-£390 double incl breakfast.

Formerly the much-missed Penzance Arts Club, the Artist Residence aims to retain some of its predecessor's boho bustle, albeit in a rather more boutiquey style. The rooms are plush and comfortable with a sprinkle of tasteful eccentricity, while the former Georgian coach house's lovely walled-garden remains its highlight. Its ramshackle Clubhouse restaurant offers food and beers all day, with light bites from the Seafood Shack and fancier stuff from the kitchen.

Boutique Retreats 💚
Mousehole (01872 553491, www.boutique-retreats.co.uk). Rates £466-£1,213 Fri-Sun.

This crossover concept falls somewhere between a swanky boutique hotel and a cute holiday cottage. You get all the perks of a high-end hotel – roll-top bath, king-size bed, goose-down duvet, freshly cut flowers, soft white towels, mini toiletries, Wi-Fi – all the while being in possession of your own key, and therefore total privacy. So no small talk with the receptionist, and no need to surface in time for the dregs of the breakfast buffet. Choose between 13 romantic boltholes in the pretty village of Mousehole, available for short breaks and week-long sojourns.

The Summer House
Cornwall Terrace, Penzance, TR18 4HL (01736 363744, www.thesummerhousepenzance.com). Rates £198-£233 double incl breakfast. Closed Nov-Feb.

Squeezed into a little mews in Penzance, this blue-painted boutique B&B is just a few paces from the promenade. The rooms are invitingly fresh and stylish (and 100% chintz-free). Breakfast can be consumed in the pretty patio garden, complete with Cornish palms, and guests can also take advantage of the Summer House's 12-table 'dinner club', serving superb Mediterranean cuisine. Book ahead as there are only five rooms, and they are much coveted.

Venton Vean 💚
Trewithen Road, Penzance, TR18 4LS (01736 351294, www.ventonvean.co.uk). Rates £92-£145 double incl breakfast.

Penzance tends to come up short on chic accommodation but this immaculate B&B is helping turn the tide. Located on a leafy street in a spacious granite-fronted period property, Venton Vean has been newly and stylishly renovated by its friendly owners,

with design accents, a sprinkling of modern art, chic bathrooms and an extraordinary breakfast menu that includes Mexican and Spanish options, as well as home-made muffins and jam, and the full range of fried and toasted British and Continental fare. A rare luxury option in this price range and an ideal base for exploring west Cornwall.

LAND'S END & AROUND

Land's End
By all means go and get your photo taken at Land's End, the most westerly point on the mainland, with the sign pointing to New York, 3,147 miles away (for which you will be duly charged), but we recommend avoiding the **Land's End Experience** theme park. This sorry development, built in the late 1980s on the country's most remote headland, could only ever seem naff when compared to the unprocessed drama of the scenery, just metres away – and many locals continue to smart at the fact that planning permission was granted.

For the most atmospheric approach to Land's End, walk the short stretch of coastal footpath from Sennen, just over a mile away.

St Just
St Just in Penwith (not to be confused with St Just in Roseland), once the centre of the mining industry in the area, is the only significant town in the far west of Cornwall. It's a stark-looking, no-fuss sort of place, with granite terraces and old miners' cottages radiating out from a busy market square. It has a lively, arty community, a deli, several galleries, pasty shops, a few good traditional pubs and a grassy amphitheatre, the focal point during the town's Lafrowda Festival in July.

Stop for a pint of well-kept ale at the **Star Inn** (1 Fore Street, 01736 788767, www.staustellbrewery.co.uk), a 17th-century pub with a terrific 'no musak, no mobiles' policy – if your

Porthgwarra Cove

Five Poldark filming locations

Poldark Mine *See p138.*
Brooding hero Ross Poldark was, of course, a completely fictional character, but in the mid-1970s this then recently rediscovered tin mine adopted the Poldark name with creator Winston Graham's blessing. It proved to be self-fulfilling: underground scenes from both the 1970s and 2010s *Poldark* series were shot here.

Charlestown *See p38.*
This perfectly preserved, Grade II-listed Georgian port stood in for Truro and Falmouth in both versions of *Poldark* and is a popular stand-in for historic ports generally, having appeared in the likes of *Mansfield Park* and *Hornblower*. Adding to the ambiance is the fleet of sailing ships harboured there.

St Breward *See p18 and p21.*
This little village on Bodmin Moor is made up of a series of neat granite cottages, one of which stood in for the Poldark family home, Nampara, in the new series. The miners' cottages in the nearby village of Minions also featured heavily in series one, while the bleak, rugged moor itself makes regular appearances.

Bodmin Jail *See p14.*
The South-West's most infamous house of correction is looking decidedly gentrified these days thanks to a multi-million pound makeover that has turned part of it into a boutique hotel. Still the museum experience has been massively upgraded too – all the better for you to see where light-fingered farmhand Jim Carter died miserably in series one.

Porthgwarra Cove *See p168.*
This hitherto obscure little cove in the Porthcurno vicinity became an overnight sensation after it was chosen as the scene for Ross's now legendary skinny-dipping sesh at the end of series one of the new version. There's not a lot going on here, but it's pretty, there's a café, and there's the opportunity to strip off in the same waters as Aiden Turner.

St Just *see p165*

Newlyn *see p162*

St Michael's Mount *see p160*

phone rings you'll have to pay a donation to the lifeboat fund. The pub doesn't serve food, but you can bring your own pasties.

For an unspoilt end-of-the-land experience, consider swapping Land's End for a walk at gusty **Cape Cornwall**, two miles west of the town. Topped by a 19th-century mine chimney, England's only 'cape' is but one degree east of Land's End proper – and was, before the arrival of cartographers, taken to be Britain's most westerly point.

North from St Just along the B3306 are the silent ruins of what was once hardcore mining territory. One of the most spectacularly sited mines is **Botallack**, right on the edge of the cliff, which can be seen from the coastal footpath. Around the coast at **Pendeen**, **Geevor Tin Mine**, the last operating mine in Penwith, is now a superb heritage centre and museum (*see p160*).

Sennen Cove

Shored up on the banks of Whitesand Bay, the stunningly scenic village of Sennen Cove perches on the very edge of mainland Britain, its weathered houses hatched into the hillside and a sweep of golden sand stretching into an arc below.

Britain's surfing cognoscenti have long flocked to Sennen, and there is a saying among locals: 'If there's no swell here, there's none anywhere.' They have a point. Even in summer, there's usually a wave to be had, as the beach takes the brunt of any swells driven by bands of low pressure in the Atlantic.

To walk the coast path the length of the bay and on to Land's End – just over a mile away – is to experience one of the most exquisite seascapes in the British Isles. On a clear summer's day, the Isles of Scilly can be seen, the sea looks wonderfully limpid, and gulls, shearwater, puffins, kingfishers

and Arctic skua are the local aviators. If the weather is rough, walk up from Sennen Cove's lifeboat station to **Mayon Cliff Old Coastguard lookout** and admire the power of the sea smashing into the cliffs.

There's a surf boutique and restaurant next to the beach (The Beach; *see right*), the Old Success Inn (*see below*), a fish and chip shop, and an arts and crafts gallery in the **Round House** (01736 871859, www.round-house.co.uk, closed Mon-Wed).

Porthcurno & around

Porthcurno, three miles from Sennen Cove, regularly appears in 'top ten' beach lists. From the stone balustrades of the open-air **Minack Theatre** (*see p149*), carved into the cliffs above, you can gaze upon a scene that seems to have landed by some trickery from more exotic climes: creamy white sands and a shock of vivid turquoise sea. At low tide, an expanse of sand enables access to the secluded nudist beach of **Pedn Vounder**.

Moving east around the coast, you'll come across a series of picturesque settlements: the sweet village of Treen, clinging to the clifftop; and the delightfully hidden-away fishing coves of **Penberth** and **Lamorna**. The latter was a muse for Newlyn School painters, with its steep, weather-sculpted granite stones creating striking geometric shapes, and is still popular with artists and craftmakers.

Where to eat & drink

As you might expect, this remote corner of the country is not about fine dining or wild nightlife, but that's not to say you can't get a good square meal and a nice pint of Cornish ale.

Cosy old pubs include the 17th-century **Old Success Inn** (01736 871232, www.oldsuccess.com) at Sennen; the **Logan Rock Inn** (01736

810495) in the idyllic coastal hamlet of Treen; and the sublimely old-fashioned **Star Inn** (*see p165*) in St Just. Less log fire and more white-hot is the über-chic **Cove** (*see below*) in Lamorna, whose restaurant-bar is pricey but first-rate, and open to non-guests.

The Beach

Sennen Cove, TR19 7BT (01736 871191, www.thebeachrestaurant.com). Open varies; check website for details. Closed Nov-mid Feb.

Just when the market for chic beachside restaurants with jaw-dropping views seemed thoroughly saturated, along came this aptly named hangout. Overhanging the sands at Sennen, it offers far-reaching views out into Whitesand Bay. It is family-run and friendly, with an easy-eating menu (sirloin steak, pork fillets, sea bass).

Where to stay

If you're looking for some wow factor, the **Shark Fin** (www.cottages.com) is an architect-designed house near Sennen with 270-degree views from which you can glimpse the Scilly Isles and Land's End Lighthouse. It's chock-a-block with hi-tech eco features and starts at £1,775 a week, sleeping up to seven.

The Cove

Lamorna, TR19 6XH (01736 731411, www. thecovecornwall.co.uk). Rates £100-£130 for 2-4 people.

One of west Cornwall's hottest hotels, the Cove – set into the steep hill above quiet Lamorna Cove – brings a sprinkling of glitz to Britain's furthest reaches. Its 16 luxury self-catering apart-rooms have slick kitchens, and guests enjoy all the conveniences of an exclusive hotel, including a sauna, terraced gardens, a chic bar-restaurant and a curvy outdoor pool. Decor is decidedly cosmopolitan, with mirrored bedside tables, perspex chairs and turquoise accents. The bar-restaurant is superb, with ultra-fresh fish and immaculate service.

The sleeper

There is no getting around the fact that Cornwall is a long way away from London: six hours by car, nine hours by bus and only minimally served by plane. Even by 'express' train, a series of geographical obstacles – moors, hills and spindly creeks – add up to a five-hour jaunt. When a journey's that long, you might as well make an adventure of it.

The sleeper train from London to Penzance, a service locals fought successfully to save in 2005, is a vital connection for the Cornish, being the only way to reach the capital for a morning meeting. It's also one of only two remaining sleeper services in the country.

The Night Riviera, as it is romantically called, is a very comfortable way to travel, thanks to a £2 million renovation, care of Eurostar's interior designer Michael Rodber. Berths feel almost like pod hotel rooms (albeit very small ones), with soft cotton sheets and towels, TV, a kit of mini toiletries, a sink with piping hot water, and breakfast (with filter coffee) brought in the morning half an hour before your destination.

Book yourself a solo berth, repair to the bar for a nightcap, and let the rocking motion lull you all the way to the end of the line. Top tip: sleeper berths count as first-class tickets, so you are granted access to the sleek first-class lounge at London Paddington, where you can help yourself to drinks and nibbles before boarding at around 11pm, or smarten yourself up on arrival. How thoroughly civilised...

From £98 return in advance (www. firstgreatwestern.co.uk).

Isles of Scilly

Small, quiet and extraordinarily beautiful, the Isles of Scilly are a low-lying archipelago strung out across the Atlantic, some 28 miles off Land's End – the last dots of land before North America. Basking in the warmth of the Gulf Stream, in summer the islands paint an exotic scene: softly curving, silver-sand beaches are splashed by clear, shallow waters, and a shock of weird and wonderful flowers and plants, many of which would struggle to survive in any other part of the country, run riot. Fiery red-hot pokers and purple-headed agapanthus, both natives of Africa, make themselves at home, and the waxy 'cactus roses' of aeoniums, originally from the Canaries, crawl over garden walls.

Only five of the islands are inhabited; St Mary's, which is the largest, and the 'off-islands' of St Martin's, St Agnes, Tresco and Bryher. Around them there are more than 100 unoccupied islets, rock formations, reefs, outcrops and ledges, which provide a sanctuary for grey seals, puffins, shearwater, migratory birds and passing dolphins. Come winter, the islands show another face: when an Atlantic gale comes roaring in, the memory of more than 700 local shipwrecks is brought forcefully to mind.

INTRODUCING THE ISLANDS

Dotted with prehistoric burial chambers, standing stones and settlements, the Scillies have been occupied for at least 4,000 years, with even the Romans recognising them as 'Sun Isles' (the translation of their Latin name, *Sillinae Insulae*). In legend, this is the Lost Land of Lyonesse, to which King Arthur's men retreated after their leader's last fatal battle.

With a total population of around 3,000, these are small communities. Thanks to an almost complete absence of cars, the pace of life is slowed to an enjoyable stroll, and there's a pleasing pragmatism to even the most deluxe accommodation. Don't expect theme parks, nightlife or a cutting edge on anything except a fisherman's knife – just the unflashy excitement of stunning views and the chance to hide away. Happily stranded, visitors find themselves shifting swiftly down through the gears and entertaining themselves with nothing more complicated than shell collecting (the lovely cowrie shell is particularly prized), birdwatching, reading, walking or chatting over a pint of Ales of Scilly.

Tourism is carefully managed, which means there is a relatively small range of accommodation, especially on the off-islands and for short stays in peak season. As a result, occupancy levels and prices stay high, and advance booking is essential. B&Bs, self-catering accommodation and camping (there is a campsite on each of the islands, save Tresco) are the best ways to save money.

Thanks to the combination of a remote location and a cornered market, transport costs also stack up. The inter-island boats cost around £10

Tresco *see p177*

Scillonian III **docked at St Mary's** *see p174*

return per person, and the boat from Penzance starts at £85 return; the breathtakingly scenic helicopter ride, meanwhile, reaches well into triple figures. Still, at least when you make it back to the mainland (via the Skybus, helicopter or the notoriously rough *Scillonian III* crossing), you're guaranteed to feel that you have come back from somewhere much further away, and a long way from England.

ST MARY'S

Although it measures just two and a half miles across at its widest point, St Mary's is the largest of the Isles of Scilly, as well as the most populous – it even has a recognisable road system. Its centre, **Hugh Town**, seems bustling if you've already spent time on the other islands, laid-back if you've come here first. Set on a narrow isthmus on the island's south-western side, the town is flanked to the south by pretty, sheltered **Porthcressa Beach**, and to the north by the less appealing **Town Beach**, where the Penzance ferry and inter-island passenger boats come and go.

Itineraries of tours and boats to the off-islands are chalked up on boards on the quay, and the **Isles of Scilly Wildlife Trust** (01720 422153, www.ios-wildlifetrust.org.uk) has an information centre in the harbour waiting room, with details of nature walks and tours. From May to September, the harbour also hosts the islands' famous pilot gig races. The gigs – 32 feet of brightly painted wooden rowing boat, some of them more than 100 years old – are raced on Wednesday and Friday evenings.

Above the harbour, west of Hugh Town, **Garrison Hill** offers brilliant views. It is dominated by the 16th-century, eight-pointed **Star Castle**, built as a defence against the Spanish Armada and now a hotel (*see p176*). In the other direction,

Telegraph Road leads from Hugh Town towards the island's interior, and a pleasant trail around a dozen galleries, open studios and craft shops, making a comfortable circuit south to Old Town. En route take a look at **Carreg Dhu**, pronounced 'Crake Dew' (01720 422404) – a small, volunteer-run community garden in a disused quarry.

Heading east from Porthcressa Beach, a path loops south around jagged **Peninnis Head**, passing some intriguing geological formations, such as the 'Kettle and Pans', near the lighthouse. Beyond is sheltered **Old Town Bay**, whose straggling settlement was, until the 17th century, the island's main port.

Near the airport, the small bay at **Porth Hellick** is overlooked by a monument to naval hero Sir Cloudesley Shovell, whose fleet ran into the rocks off the island during a storm in 1707, with the loss of 2,000 men. A mile north, **Pelistry Bay** is one of the most secluded and picturesque beaches on St Mary's, with the small **Carn Vean Café** (Pelistry, 01720 423458, closed Oct-Apr) providing sustenance. At low tide, a sand bar enables visitors to cross to the idyllic **Toll's Island** (don't attempt to swim across at high tide, as the sand bar causes vicious rip tides). Head north-west around the coast and you'll come to the most impressive prehistoric remains on the archipelago: **Halangy Down** has stone huts, a burial chamber and a standing stone that is thought to date from 2000 BC.

Where to eat & drink

Also worth trying – though check opening times before making a special trip – is **Dibble & Grub** (01720 423719), right on Porthcressa Beach. Brunch and light lunches are served from 10am.

Places to visit

ST MARY'S

Isles of Scilly Museum

Church Street, St Mary's, TR21 0JT (01720 422337, www.iosmuseum.org). Open Easter-Sept 10am-4.30pm Mon-Fri; 10am-noon Sat. Oct-Easter 10am-noon Mon-Sat. Admission £3.50; £1-£3 reductions. No credit cards.

There's no escaping the thread of disaster and loss, primarily from shipwrecks, at the endearingly low-tech Isles of Scilly Museum. Alongside the cases of flotsam and jetsam you'll find curiosities such as a Scilly shrew's nest in a discarded can, stuffed birds, shells, Iron Age axeheads and, fascinatingly, a Bronze Age sword found by a Bryher potato farmer in the 1990s. Downstairs are stuffed birds and fish, including 6lb 2oz of broad-nosed eel. Another exhibition is devoted to former prime minster Harold Wilson (including his famous Gannex mac), who is buried nearby at St Mary's Old Church.

TRESCO & BRYHER

Abbey Garden💜

Tresco, TR24 0PQ (01720 424105, www.tresco.co.uk/see/abbey-garden). Open 10am-4pm daily. Admission £15; free-£14 reductions.

Even those not usually drawn to horticulture find this exotic garden exciting, so confirmed garden geeks can safely expect to be catapulted into horticultural heaven. The Abbey Garden is without doubt Scilly's biggest attraction, but that rather understates its significance: for many, this is one of the most extraordinary gardens in the world, a singular experiment in horticulture – or, as author Walter Besant famously described it, 'Kew with the roof off'.

When Augustus Smith arrived in 1834 to take on the lease of the islands, Tresco was exposed to vicious winds and far from sympathetic to the kind of tropical vegetation now thriving here. A man of supreme vision and drive, Smith had tall windbreaks built around the remains of the 12th-century Benedictine priory to shelter sloping terraces, and the magnificent gardens now have over 20,000 plants from 80 countries, including succulents, palms, cacti and eucalyptus. It is a surreal sight to see such intense colour in Britain; red-hot pokers, birds of paradise, pink proteas and lobster claws all invite the attention of your zoom lens. These plants flourish thanks to the Scillies' mild climate, and many would not survive in mainland Cornwall. Thoughtful Italianate landscaping adds perspective and ensures that, even in high season, it's easy to forget your fellow visitors. Valhalla is the on-site collection of salvaged ships' figureheads, now colourfully restored. There's also a small shop, and the Garden Café for refreshments.

Abbey Garden

Hugh Street Cafe

Hugh Street, St Mary's, TR21 0LL (01720 422734, www.hughstreetcafe.co.uk). Open/food served Summer 8.30am-8pm Mon-Sat. Winter 8.45am-2pm Mon-Wed; 8.45am-5pm Thur-Sat.

A great place to put together a picnic, the Hugh Street Cafe is housed in a delightfully converted butcher's shop – with some of the fixtures and fittings retained – and sells hams, cheeses and olives, and an array of Scillonian delicacies. There are half a dozen wooden tables for light lunches (quiches, pasties, salads) and drinks, with Wi-Fi available, or you could take out a mini tub of Troytown Farm ice-cream from St Agnes.

Juliet's Garden Restaurant

Seaways Flower Farm, St Mary's, TR21 0NF (01720 422228, www. julietsgardenrestaurant.co.uk). Food served Easter-Oct 10am-5pm daily; 6pm-late Mon, Wed-Sun.

A 20-minute amble along the coast from Hugh Town, Juliet's is a picturesque spot for lunch, with bird's-eye views of Hugh Town harbour and plenty of seating in the garden. Service is quick and upbeat, and the menu comprises simple café classics – cakes, sandwiches, quiche, soup, mackerel pâté with chunky granary bread – prepared with care. In the evening, with the lights dimmed and candles lit, there's a more formal menu.

Mermaid Inn

The Bank, St Mary's, TR21 0HY (01720 422701, www.mermaidscilly.co.uk). Open 10am-midnight Mon-Sat; noon-11.30pm Sun. Lunch served noon-2pm Mon-Sat; noon-2.30pm Sun. Dinner served 6-9pm Mon-Sat.

The Mermaid is a traditional local on the quay, greeting visitors as they come off the boat from the mainland. Hugh Town's social hub, it dispenses real ales downstairs (including Scuppered, from the Ales of Scilly brewery), while the upstairs bar-restaurant is a more modern-looking affair, serving light meals in the daytime and more substantial fare after 6pm.

Where to stay

Apart from the Star Castle Hotel, the only high-end accommodation on St Mary's is the **St Mary's Hall Hotel** (Church Street, 01720 422316, www. stmaryshallhotel.co.uk, closed Nov-Mar), whose imposing old building, Italianate accents and wood-panelled hall combine to create a sense of occasion.

More affordable options on the island include the six B&B rooms at the handsome **Belmont** (Church Road, 01720 423154, www.the-belmont.co.uk, closed Nov-Easter), on the outskirts of Hugh Town, and the long-standing, friendly **Mincarlo** (Carn Thomas, 01720 422513, www. mincarloscilly.com, closed mid Dec-Mar). The latter has big windows and sea views; outside, steps descend to the beach.

Star Castle Hotel

St Mary's, TR21 0JA (01720 422317, www.star-castle.co.uk). Closed Jan. Rates £153-£490 double incl breakfast & dinner.

This star-shaped granite Elizabethan castle above Hugh Town is an atmospheric place to stay. Despite steady refurbishment, the prevailing style remains traditional; stay in one of the four rooms on the first floor to be in a point of the star, or the second floor for even better views through mullioned windows. Most of the accommodation is in the modern, more spacious 'garden' rooms out back, which are simply furnished, light and airy. The rooms on the western side look over the cliff path to the ocean; those to the east on to a lawn and green fields. There's a fantastically eccentric bar in the dungeon, and two restaurants, whose menus feature produce from the kitchen garden. One is a fairly formal affair, set in the castle's original, stone-walled officers' mess room; the other (summer only) occupies a bright conservatory, serving mostly seafood under the vines. There is an indoor pool and the grounds are lovely.

TRESCO & BRYHER

Tresco

For some, a visit to the Scillies' privately run and closely managed island estate (still leased from the Duchy of Cornwall by descendants of 19th-century reforming landlord Augustus Smith), Tresco, is altogether too cosseted. For others, it represents a life of delicious simplicity: one pub, one hotel, one café and no cars. The scene is set by the toy town jollity of the tractor ride between the heliport and your accommodation.

Two miles long and a mile wide, Tresco is the largest of the off-islands. The unassailable highlight – and the most impressive sight of the entire archipelago – is **Abbey Garden** (*see p175*). A walk around the island also takes in exquisite beaches, two peaceful lakes, tranquil woods and a solitary, heather-clad headland with two defensive fortifications – the 17th-century Cromwell's Castle and, above it, the earlier King Charles's Castle.

Most settlement on Tresco runs across the island between Old and New Grimsby. **New Grimsby** is home to **Gallery Tresco** (New Grimbsy Harbour, closed Nov-mid Feb), a single room of local art and souvenirs overlooking the sleepy jetty, the **New Inn** and the **Flying Boat Club**.

Bryher

Just opposite New Grimsby, separated by a quarter of a mile of water, tiny Bryher feels like a place apart – even in Scilly. It takes its name from the Celtic for 'place of hills' and is a beautifully wild island looking out on stunning rock fortresses such as Scilly Rock, Castle Bryher and Maiden Bower.

On the western shore, **Hell Bay** lives up to its name when a storm's up; the **Hell Bay Hotel** (*see p178*), one of the most dramatically positioned hotels in

England, is just to the south. Nearby, artist **Richard Pearce** (01720 423665, www.rpearce.net) has a similarly awesome outlook from a studio barely the size of a rowing boat (it is, in fact, a converted gig shed). The considerably more sheltered east shore has **Green Bay**, a fine sandy beach, along with boats and kayaks for hire from long-time islanders the **Bennetts** (07979 393206, www.bennettboatyard.com).

A circuit of Bryher takes little more than an hour on foot but is incredibly invigorating, with bees and birds around you as you walk and truly superb views. **Gweal Hill** offers the loveliest sunset in the Scillies, while Samson Hill opens up the whole archipelago.

Where to eat & drink

Fraggle Rock Bar-Café
Bryher, TR23 0PR (01720 422222, www. bryher.co). Open 10.30am-4.30pm, 7-11pm daily. Lunch served noon-2pm, dinner served 7-8.30pm.

Based in a small granite house with a beer garden at the front, this relaxed spot serves lunches (double-decker crab sarnies, soup, burgers) and evening meals (pizza, risotto, and fish and chips on Friday), as well as pints of Doom Bar. The first floor has sea views, internet access and stripped pine decor – comfortable enough, but less cosy and pub-like than the downstairs. They also run Harbourview, which has self-catering cottages and cabins to rent.

New Inn
Tresco, TR24 0QE (01720 422844, www. tresco.co.uk). Open Apr-Oct 10am-11pm daily. Lunch served noon-2.15pm, dinner served 6.30-9pm. Nov-Mar 10am-2.30pm, 6-11pm daily. Lunch served noon-2pm, dinner served 7-9pm.

Tresco is at its liveliest in the New Inn's snug Driftwood Bar, lined with dark reclaimed wood. Sunny days seem to draw the entire population of the island to its shady outdoor terrace, where they are joined by cheekily well-fed sparrows and chaffinches. There's a fine selection of ales (including Ales of Scilly and Skinners) and wines (25 in total, about ten of which are available by the glass), as well as good pub food. Local produce is used as much as possible, on a simple but satisfying menu that might include bangers and mash and fish and chips with a choice of Cornish fish. An additional conservatory-style space serves Roskilly's ice-cream and cakes. The adjoining hotel has 16 bright, comfortable rooms (£110-£240 double incl breakfast).

Where to stay

Tresco's only hotel, the Island, was turned into self-catering chalets in 2011. The **New Inn** (*see above*), is decent enough for shortstay accommodation. Bryher has a pretty **campsite** (01720 422559, www. bryhercampsite.co.uk, closed Oct-Mar) with basic facilities as well as cottages and cabins rented out by Harbour View (01720 422222, www. bryher.co).

Flying Boat Cottages

Tresco, TR24 0QQ (01720 422849, www.tresco.co.uk/staying/flying-boat-cottages). Rates from £2,275 per week for 6 people.

The Flying Boat Club comprises a string of 12 luxurious, modern houses, built on the beachfront at New Grimsby. The curious name is a reference to the Royal Naval Air Station that stood on this site and sent out seaplanes during World War I to counter German submarines. FBC's beach-chic houses combine the freedom of a holiday home (proper kitchen, breakfast when you want it, privacy) with the luxuries of a high-end hotel – flatscreen TVs, thick bathrobes and sleek bathrooms. Guests also get access to the Flying Boat across the road, with its restaurant and bar, as well as the Tresco Island Spa, tennis courts and leisure club. As with everything on Tresco, and the Scillies in general, the prices sting. But tariffs do at least include entrance to the Abbey Garden – and where else in Britain can you climb down half a dozen steps from your holiday home,

directly on to the soft sand of a deserted white-sand beach?

Hell Bay Hotel

Bryher, TR23 0PR (01720 422947, www. hellbay.co.uk). Rates £145-£325 double incl breakfast.

In an unbeatable position on the edge of the Atlantic, Hell Bay Hotel was a pioneer of contemporary – if not quite cutting-edge – style on the Scillies. Its relaxed, spacious suites sport a jaunty colour scheme of light greens and blues, and have portholes in the doors; most of the rooms open on to private balconies or patios, and all but two have sea views. Details are carefully attended to (fresh milk in the fridge, a personal cafetière) and there's some striking modern art in the expansive bar area, and sculptures dotted throughout – thanks to its art-collecting owners, the Dorrien-Smiths (who also own Tresco). Food can be served on the patio, as well as in the restaurant; expect the likes of seared Cornish scallops with cauliflower purée and pancetta, pan-roasted fillet of West Country beef, or burgers and superior sarnies from the bar menu. Facilities include a heated outdoor pool, a seven-hole golf course and a mini gym and spa.

Flying Boat Cottages

ST MARTIN'S

Trimmed with sugary, silver-flecked beaches and translucent waters, St Martin's shores could, in the right light, pass for St Kitts – an illusion that tends to shatter the moment your toes touch the sea, which is rarely anything other than glacial. Entirely free from man-made construction (bar the grey hotel built on the westerly beach) and deserted by default, St Martin's sands are a special sight – even by the Scillies' high standards.

Flower-growing is the main industry, which accounts for the colourful fields, but St Martin's has attracted a number of sensitive entrepreneurial operations, from the organic smallholding and café at **Little Arthur Farm** to the Island Bakery. **Higher Town**, the main hub, has few other attractions, so head instead for the stunning beaches and views – in particular from **St Martin's Head** on the north-east coast. Sparsely inhabited and virtually pollution-free, St Martin's is also fantastic for diving (*see p181*).

The main quay is on the magnificent **Par Beach**, a pure white curve of sand; the **St Martin's Vineyard & Winery** (01720 423418, www. stmartinsvineyard. co.uk, closed winter) is close by. On the southern coast, **Lawrence's Bay** is long, sandy and perfect for shell-collecting. To the west, **Lower Town** has views across to the uninhabited islands of Teän and St Helen's, and on the north-east coast, **Great Bay** ★ and **Little Bay** offer sweeping, isolated stretches of sand; the former is a strong contender for Britain's best beach. At low tide, climb across the boulders from Little Bay to wild **White Island** (pronounced 'Wit') to explore **Underland Girt**, a huge sea cave.

Where to eat & drink

Tiny St Martin's has a surprising number of eating options. The pretty **Polreath Tearoom** (Higher Town, 01720 422046, www.polreath.com, closed Sat & Nov-Easter) serves tea and light lunches in the café and courtyard or, best of all, under the vines in the greenhouse.

The Island Bakery

St Martin's, TR25 0QL (01720 422111, www.theislandbakery-stmartins.com). Open Mar-Oct 9am-6pm Mon-Sat; 9am-2pm Sun. Nov-Feb bakery courses only. No credit cards.

As well as organic bread, baker Barney McLachlan makes homity pie, pasties with Scilly beef, quiches and pizza slices. Sip own-made lemonade and tuck in at the outdoor trestle tables, leaving a few crumbs for the chicken pecking about your ankles. The bakery uses local ingredients, including eggs produced on its farm, and own-smoked ham and fish, and provides gluten-free options. There's takeaway pizza in the evenings, and baking holidays take place off-season.

Little Arthur Farm

Higher Town, St Martin's, TR25 0QL (01720 422457, www.littlearthur.co.uk). Lunch served Apr-Sept 10.30am-4pm daily. Dinner served 6.30-8.30pm Mon-Fri. No credit cards.

Looking down the slope to Par Beach, this wholefood café offers excellent salads and rolls filled with own-grown organic ingredients, soups, shellfish salad, ploughman's lunches and own-baked cakes and scones, served in a small conservatory. **Adam's Fish & Chips** (01720 423082, www.adamsfishandchips. co.uk) used to operate on the farm but now has its own premises just down the road.

Seven Stones

Lower Town, St Martin's, TR25 0QW (01720 423560, www.sevenstonesinn. com). Open Mar-Oct 10.30am-4pm, 6-11.30pm daily. Lunch served noon-2.30pm, dinner served 7-9pm daily. Nov-Feb 6-11.30pm Fri; noon-2.30pm Sun.

Things to do

The Scillies may not have much in the way of organised attractions, but those interested in simpler pleasures will be in their element. Rockpooling, birdwatching, butterfly spotting, shell collecting and walking are all pastimes that demand neither guide nor equipment. For others – boating, sailing, fishing, snorkelling, kayaking, diving, golf – the islands are well equipped.

ST MARY'S

Island Wildlife Tours
01720 422212, www.islandwildlifetours. co.uk. Open Apr-Oct. Tours £10 per half day.

Wildlife expert Will Wagstaff leads these

Island Wildlife Tours

walking tours of the islands. Tours tend to leave at 9.45am from St Mary's quay on weekday mornings, but times and itineraries vary. Call for further details, or check the board on St Mary's quay.

Isles of Scilly golf course
St Mary's, TR21 0NF (01720 422692, www. islesofscillygolfclub.co.uk). Open 8am-dusk Mon-Wed, Fri-Sun. Green fee from £10. No credit cards.

Opened in 1904, after much bracken-clearing, this gently sloping nine-hole course has great views.

Sailing Centre
Porthmellon Beach, St Mary's, TR21 0NE (01720 422060, www.sailingscilly.com).

A variety of watersports taster sessions, courses and equipment hire is offered here, including windsurfing, snorkelling, dinghies and kayaks. All ages and abilities are catered for.

St Mary's Boatmen's Association
Rose Cottage, The Strand, St Mary's, TR21 0PT (01720 423999, www.scillyboating. co.uk). Tickets £12-£14 return; £6-£7 reductions. No credit cards.

Information about the day's boat excursions can be found written up on the quay, outside the Atlantic Hotel and Tourist Information Centre in Hugh Town. The Association has a fleet of large boats and runs direct journeys daily to the off-islands, but also arranges wildlife spotting jaunts, fishing trips (mackerel or pollock for beginners, shark fishing for the more advanced) and birdwatching forays on Annet.

St Mary's Cycle Hire
The Strand, St Mary's, TR21 0PT (07796 638506). Cycle hire from £6 per half-day (around £10 for a whole day); £50 per week.

Tandems and child seats are available too.

Scilly Walks
www.scillywalks.co.uk.

Katharine Sawyer offers guided walks with a historical angle on St Mary's and the off-islands.

TRESCO & BRYHER

Bennett Boatyard

Bryher, TR23 0PR (07979 393206, www.bennettboatyard.com). Open Apr-Sept 9am-6pm daily. Boat hire from £55-£115 per day. No credit cards.

The boatyard hires out kayaks, small dinghies, rigged sailing boats and even a glass-bottomed rowing boat – all available by the hour, half-day, day or week. You can also hire a fishing line to tow along behind.

Tresco Boat Services

Bryher, TR23 0PR (01720 422886, www.bryherboats.co.uk). Tickets from £2.50 single. No credit cards.

The company runs scheduled boats from Bryher and Tresco to the other islands, plus private charter jet boats to Penzance, when the *Scillonian* sailing is fogged off.

Tresco Cycle Hire

Tresco Estate, Tresco, TR24 0QQ (01720 422849). Cycle hire from £6 per half-day.

Cycling is not only the best way to get around Tresco, it is also pretty much the only way. Hire mountain bikes from next to the Tresco Stores by the half-day, day or week.

ST MARTIN'S

St Martin's Diving Services

Higher Town, St Martin's, TR25 0QL (01720 22848, www.scillydiving.com). Open Apr-Oct. Diving/snorkelling from £48, min 2 people. No credit cards.

Thanks in part to the islands' ocean-edge location, the waters around Scilly are some of the most biodiverse in the country, populated by exotic species, ornate corals and colourful sponges. This, combined with the clarity of the waters and the numerous shipwrecks, makes it one of the best places to dive in the UK. The dive school offers diving courses, scuba outings and safaris snorkelling.

ST AGNES

St Agnes Boating

The Barn, St Agnes, TR22 0PL (01720 422704, www.st-agnes-boating.co.uk). Tickets £8 return. No credit cards.

As well as daily passenger trips to St Mary's and the off-islands year-round, St Agnes Boating offers private charters (charged by the hour), two-hour fishing trips (gear hired at £15 a rod) and trips out to the Western Rocks and Bishop Rock Lighthouse.

Scilly Walks

Inter-island ferry at St Agnes

St Martin's Campsite

It may look more like someone's front room than a pub, but the Seven Stones is nonetheless a welcoming hideout, serving Ales of Scilly and sturdy pub food, as well as seafood hotpot with catch of the day. The views from the beer terrace are sublime – and in wet weather you'll find the toasty interior busy with de-anoraked campers from the nearby campsite. Note that the pub was up for sale when this guide went to print; visit the website to keep abreast of any changes.

Where to stay
Polreath Guesthouse & Tearoom (Higher Town, 01720 422046, www. polreath.com, closed Nov-Easter) has three sea-view rooms, and **Little Arthur Farm** (*see p179*) also has a cute eco-cabin for rent.

Karma St Martin's
St Martin's, TR25 0QW (01720 422090, www.stmartins hotel.co.uk). Rates £357-£592 double incl breakfast.

The only hotel on St Martin's is a somewhat angular affair, built in stern grey stone, but its setting is beautiful: the hotel overlooks gardens dotted with incongruous Caribbean rush parasols and, beyond them, the quay and a beautiful white-sand beach. Many of the 30 rooms have enviable sea views, but are otherwise rather lacking in character. Teän, the acclaimed main restaurant, is on the first floor and has several prized tables perched right in the angled window, looking over the channel to its namesake island. The menu draws on a wealth of local ingredients, particularly seafood – something of a necessity, one might imagine, when running Britain's most remote fine dining restaurant. A swimming pool is tucked away indoors.

St Martin's Campsite
Oaklands Farm, Middletown, St Martin's, TR25 0QN (01720 422888, www.stmartinscampsite.co.uk). Open mid Mar-Oct. Pitch £11.50-£13 per night for 2 people.

There can be few more effective ways of switching off than pitching your tent on a tiny off-island of the Isles of Scilly. One of the more sheltered campsites in these parts – protected, to a degree, by the dunes and the high hedges that divide the site into cosy strips – St Martin's also has the best facilities. The toilet and shower block is modern, and the showers are reliably hot. No electric hook-ups means minimal light and noise pollution, and the lack of cars, caravans or motorhomes is a rare treat.

ST AGNES

Craggy St Agnes, set apart from the cluster of islands, is the most south-westerly community in the British Isles – with a wild, windswept setting to match. What the island might lack in sandy beaches, it more than makes up for with edge-of-the-world scenery and weirdly weathered granite rock formations. The only inhabited island without a hotel, St Agnes has more of a community feel than the others – and the simple, outdoor life is fully embraced here.

Boats land at and leave from **Porth Conger**, under the watchful eyes of the Turk's Head pub. There you'll also find St Agnes's most attractive beach, **Covean**. When the tide is right you can walk across the sand bar to the tiny island of **Gugh** (pronounced 'Goo'), where there are rocky outcrops, a Bronze Age burial chamber and a standing stone – or rather a crazily leaning stone – called the Old Man of Gugh. In **Higher Town**, stop by the **Pot Buoys** (Higher Town Farm, 01720 423002, closed Sat; Oct-Mar) for locally made quaility local art and crafts.

Inland, St Agnes is dominated by the squat, white form of the **Old Lighthouse**, which dates from 1680, making it one of the oldest in England. Near to **Periglis Cove**, on the western side of the island, is Troy Town Maze – laid out in large pebbles in 1729 by, it

is said, the lighthouse keeper's bored son.

The wild heathland of the wonderfully named **Wingletang Down** takes up much of the south of St Agnes, edged on its western side by impressive coastal scenery and on its eastern side by **Beady Pool**. This inlet takes its name from a haul of beads from a wrecked 17th-century Venetian trader that was washed up on the shores. Above the cove, two enormous boulders indented with a three-foot-deep basin form the **Giant's Punchbowl**, the most impressive rock formation on Scilly.

Where to eat & drink

Coastguards Café/High Tide

St Agnes, TR22 0PL (Coastguards Café 01720 422197, High Tide 01720 423869, http://hightide-seafood.com). Food served Apr-Oct 10.30am-4.30pm, 6.30pm-late Mon-Sat.

It's effectively just a tiny – and we really do mean tiny – stone outhouse, but there's something special about this place. Perhaps it's the wild views out to the Bishop Rock Lighthouse, the smart decor or the contemporary art (pop art takes on the cairns and crags of Scilly) on the walls. In true multi-tasking islander fashion, this place pulls off a great double act: by day, it's the Coastguards Café, serving toasties, rolls (including an inspired pastrami and rock samphire combination), cakes and St Agnes ice-cream. Come the evening, Emma and Mark Eberlein take over as High Tide, a licensed, globally inspired seafood restaurant that concentrates, quite rightly, on a short menu prepared with local produce (St Martin's microgreens are a highlight).

Turk's Head 💙

St Agnes, TR22 0PL (01720 422434). Open Apr-Oct 10.30am-11.30pm daily. Lunch served noon-2.30pm, dinner served 6-9.30pm.

Our favourite Scilly pub has a superb location, looking out over the lucent waters of the island's mini harbour. It's perfect for tucking into one of the legendary pasties (get your order in quick) while taking in the view – or keeping an eye out for your boat home. Inside, it's all model boats, maps and flagstone floors. Sup on a pint of the pub's own Turk's Head ale, or a comforting hot chocolate braced with a nip of something stronger.

Where to stay

There is no hotel on St Agnes, just a handful of B&Bs and the dramatically sited **Troytown Campsite** (01720 422360, www.troytown.co.uk, closed Oct-Mar), occupying a spectacular if exposed position facing the Atlantic. At the sweet **Covean Cottage guesthouse and café** (St Agnes, 01720 422620, www.coveancottage. com), all rooms have sea views; picnic lunches are available.

UNINHABITED ISLANDS & BISHOP ROCK LIGHTHOUSE

Samson, the largest uninhabited island, was populated until the 1850s, when poverty and the threat of eviction by Augustus Smith forced the islanders to resettle. A beautiful beach lies at the foot of North Hill, while significant prehistoric remains dot the slopes above. At low tide look out for the Samson Flats, the remains of ancient field systems that show up in the sands between Samson and Tresco.

Just off St Martin's, **Teän** has large, crescent-shaped sandy beaches; on St Helen's, just behind it, stands an interesting ruined church. On the other side of St Martin's, the milder **Eastern Isles** have fantastic beaches on Great Arthur and Great Ganilly, also home to puffins and grey seals. However, the best place to spot these captivating creatures is the storm-harried **Western Rocks** beyond St Agnes, the site of numerous shipwrecks.

Several miles further out west is the remarkable **Bishop Rock Lighthouse**, a miracle of Victorian construction that perches on a rock base little wider than its own circumference; it has been automatically operated since 1991.

For visits to Scilly's uninhabited islands, ask at your hotel or at the quay for details of boat trips.

Turk's Head *see page 183*

Further reference

USEFUL ADDRESSES

www.bbc.co.uk/cornwall
Local news, weather and events.
www.cornwall-beaches.
co.uk Cornwall Beach Guide.
www.cornwall.gov.
uk Cornwall County Council.
www.cornwall.gov.uk/
buses Cornwall Public Transport
www.english-heritage.org.uk
www.heritageopendays.
org.uk
www.metoffice.gov.uk
www.nationalrail.co.uk
www.nationaltrust.org.uk
http://newlynfish.jimdo.
com Get freshly caught Newlyn
fish delivered to your door.
www.ordnancesurvey.co.uk
www.sustrans.org.uk
www.thegoodpubguide.
co.uk
www.thetrainline.com
www.visitbritain.com
www.visitcornwall.
com Official tourist information
site.
www.visitengland.com

COAST & COUNTRYSIDE

www.bcusurf.org.uk BCU
Surf.
www.camping.uk-directory.
com UK Camping and
Caravanning Directory.
www.classic-sailing.
co.uk Classic Sailing.
www.commercialballooning.
org.uk British Association of
Balloon Operators.
www.cpre.org.uk Campaign
for the Protection of Rural
England.
www.gov.uk/government/
organisations/natural-
england Natural England.
www.gov.uk/right-of-way-
open-access-land Countryside
Access.

www.nationalparks.
uk National Parks.
www.nationaltrail.
co.uk National Trails.
www.ngs.org.uk National
Gardens Scheme.
www.outdoorswimming
society.com Lidos in the UK.
www.paddleandsail.
com Cornwall Sailing School.
www.ramblers.org.
uk Ramblers Association.
www.river-swimming.
co.uk River & Lake Swimming
Association.
www.rya.org.uk Royal Yachting
Association.
www.sas.org.uk Surfers
Against Sewage.
www.surfingengland.
org Surfing England.
www.thebeachguide.
co.uk UK Beach Guide.
www.ukclimbing.com UK
Climbing.
www.uk-golfguide.com UK
Golf.
www.walkingbritain.
co.uk Walking Britain.
www.walking-routes.
co.uk Walking Routes.
www.wildaboutthe
britishisles.uk Wild About
Britain.
www.wildswimming.
com Wild Swimming.
www.woodlandtrust.org.
uk The Woodland Trust.

HOLIDAY HOME COMPANIES

The Big Domain *www.*
thebigdomain.com.
Cottages.com *www.cottages.*
com.
Duchy of Cornwall Holiday
Cottages *01579 346473,*
www.duchyofcornwallholiday
cottages.co.uk.
Landmark Trust *01628*

825925, www.landmarktrust.
org.uk.
The Little Domain *www.*
thelittledomain.com.
Superior Cottages *www.*
superiorcottages.co.uk.
Toad Hall Cottages *01548*
202020, www.toadhall cottages.
co.uk.
Unique Home Stays *01637*
881183, www.uniquehomestays.
com.

TOURIST INFORMATION CENTRES

More details can be found at
www.visitcornwall.com. The
main tourist offices are listed
below.
Bodmin *01208 76616, www.*
bodminlive.com
Falmouth *01326 741194,*
www.falriver.co.uk
Fowey *www.fowey.co.uk*
Isles of Scilly *www.simplyscilly.*
co.uk
Newquay *01637 838516,*
www.visitnewquay.org
St Ives *01736 796297, www.*
stives-cornwall.co.uk.

FICTION

Nicola Barker *Five Miles from*
Outer Hope Quirky, appealing
novel about a 16-year-old misfit
growing up in the Burgh Island
Hotel.

WJ Burley *The Wycliffe Novels*
This series of Cornwall-based
detective novels were later made
into an enormously popular
television series.

Sir Arthur Conan Doyle *The*
Adventure of the Devil's Foot
Holmes and Watson's holiday,
in a cottage near Poldhu Bay, is
interrupted by a grisly mystery
that only the great detective can
unravel.

Daphne du Maurier *The*

Loving Spirit; Jamaica Inn; The Birds; Rebecca; The King's General; The House on the Strand Du Maurier made superb use of the Cornish landscape's drama in many of her novels.

Patrick Gale *Notes from an Exhibition, Rough Music* Two excellent, Cornish-set novels by the acclaimed contempary novelist, who lives near Land's End.

Winston Graham *The Poldark Novels* A series of 12 historical novels, set around Perranporth and St Agnes and later made into a television series (twice!).

Thomas Hardy *A Pair of Blue Eyes* A tragic tale of love and class conflict, partly based on Hardy's Cornish courtship of his first wife.

Rosamund Pilcher *The Shell Seekers* This hugely popular novel tells the story of three generations of the Keeling family, with much of the action set in Cornwall.

Arthur Quiller-Couch *The Delectable Duchy* Short stories set in Fowey (loosely disguised as Troy Town), at the end of the 19th century.

JK Rowling *Harry Potter and the Deathly Hallows* Two chapters of the boy wizard's adventures take place in Cornwall, just outside the fictional village of Tinworth.

Mary Wesley *The Camomile Lawn* Set on the Roseland Peninsula, Wesley's novel charts the lives and romantic intrigues of Richard and Helena Cuthbertson's five nieces and nephews.

Virginia Woolf *To The Lighthouse* Despite being set on the Isle of Skye, Woolf's masterpiece was inspired by Godrevy Lighthouse. St Ives, meanwhile, helped inspire *Jacob's Room* and *The Waves*.

NON-FICTION

John Betjeman *Betjeman's Cornwall* Prose and poetic musings on the life, landscape

and architecture of the poet laureate's favourite county.

Tom Cross *Catching the Wave: Art & Artists in Contemporary Cornwall* A fine introduction to the Cornish art scene.

Daphne Du Maurier *Vanishing Cornwall* An eloquent evocation of Cornish life and culture.

Henry Jenner *Handbook of the Cornish Language* Jenner is seen as the man who led the revival of the Cornish language.

AL Rowse *A Cornish Childhood* This autobiographical work describes the eminent historian's childhood in Cornwall in the early 1900s.

POETRY

Robert Laurence Binyon *For the Fallen* Binyon penned his famous poem, honouring the dead of World War I, while sitting on the cliffs between Pentire Point and the Rumps in North Cornwall; in 2001, a plaque was erected there.

Charles Causley *Collected Poems* Born in Launceston in 1917, Causley is one of the county's most beloved poets – best known, perhaps, for his children's poems.

Thomas Hardy *Poems 1912-1913* An ageing Hardy reflects on youth and love in Cornwall.

John Harris *A Story of Carn Brea 1863* Harris's most important work describes this mining area of Cornwall.

RS Hawker *Song of the Western Men, A Cornish Folk Song, The Cornish Emigrants 1803-1875* The eccentric Reverend Hawker was a gifted poet as well as a Cornish clergyman; indeed, his Song of the Western Men is now the Cornish national anthem.

FILM

Blue Juice (Carl Prechezer, 1995) Sean Pertwee, Catherine Zeta Jones and Ewan McGregor live the surfing life in North Cornwall.

Ladies in Lavender (Charles Dance, 2004) Dames Judi Dench and Maggie Smith star in this period tale, set in a Cornish fishing village in the 1930s.

The Manxman (Alfred Hitchcock, 1929) Although Hitchcock's last silent film was set on the Isle of Man, much of it was shot in North Cornwall and Polperro.

Rebecca (Alfred Hitchcock, 1940) Daphne du Maurier's classic tale became a masterly Hitchcock movie, starring Laurence Olivier and Joan Fontaine.

Saving Grace (Nigel Cole, 2000) Gently humourous film set in Cornwall, about a widow who tries to clear her debts by growing marijuana.

Straw Dogs (Sam Peckinpah, 1971) Re-released in 2011, this controversial film tells the story of a mild American university researcher who erupts into violence in a Cornish village.

Swept from the Sea (Beeban Kidron, 1997) Based on a Joseph Conrad short story, the film tells the tale of a Russian vessel shipwrecked near an isolated Cornish village in the 19th century.

TV

Doc Martin *ITV, 2004-present* Set in a fictional Cornish hamlet, this mild-mannered comedy drama – all 70 episodes and counting – is actually filmed in the fishing village of Port Isaac.

Frenchman's Creek *BBC 1998* This television dramatisation of the Daphne du Maurier novel was set and filmed around Charlestown.

Poldark *BBC, 1975-1977 and 2015-2019.* A 1970s classic, the original Poldark closely followed the novels of the same name by Winston Graham. Forty years later, a new, slicker, sexier version was an equally massive hit. For five of the many Poldark filming locations, *see p166.*

Wycliffe *ITV, 1993-1998* This long-running detective series, based on the novels by WJ Burley, was set and shot in various locations around Cornwall.

MUSIC

Eric Ball *The Fowey River Suite (1964)* Ball wrote a number of brass band compositions inspired by the West Country; this one was dedicated to the Cornwall Youth Brass Band.

Dalla *Rooz (2007)* Singing in both Cornish and English, this Cornish group are known for producing music for traditional Cornish Noze Looan ('happy night') dances.

Richard D James *Surfing on Sine Waves (1993)* Also known as Aphex Twin, James grew up in Cornwall. The cover of *Surfing on Sine Waves* which he released under the pseudonym Polygon Window, was shot on Porthtowan Beach.

Brenda Wooton *The Voice of Cornwall (1996).* The late Cornish folk singer, who performed both in English and Cornish, was seen as an ambassador for Cornish culture.

WALKS & CYCLE TRAILS

For more, see www.cornwall.gov.uk.

South West Coast Path
www.southwestcoastpath.com
see p36.

Camel Trail, Clay Trails, Mineral Tramways *see p39.*

Picture credits

Pages 2, 56 Adrian Baker/shutterstock.com; 2 Junk Culture/shutterstock.com; 3 4 season backpacking/shutterstock.com; 3 Keith 316/shutterstock.com; 5 Alan Foster/shutterstock.com; 6 LANStudios/shutterstock.com; 7 padstow.com/Stuart Higgins; 9 Glenmore/shutterstock.com; 9 Paolo Paradiso/shutterstock.com; 12 www.cornwalls.co.uk; 13, 36, 69, 136 Helen Hotson/shutterstock.com; 13, 96 PJ photography/shutterstock.com; 15 ,16 Ismay Atkins; 15, 28, 29, 32, 33 Bill Bradshaw; 18 Tony Mills/shutterstock.com; 19 David Ambler/shutterstock.com; 23 Tim Knight/shutterstock.com; 25 Chrisatpps/shutterstock.com; 25, 120, 132 Mick Blakey/shutterstock.com; 26 Nicole Kwiathowski/shutterstock.com; 28 James Pearce/shutterstock.com; 32 Patra Hatrikova/shutterstock.com; 34, 35, 59, 61, 62, 63, 71, 105, 115, 116, 146, 151 Aleida Strowger; 37 Tom Gowanlock/shutterstock.com; 42 Kamil Malinowski/shutterstock.com; 44 Michelle Grant; 47 Phillip Bird/shutterstock.com; 43, 48, 102, 156 Ian Woolcock/shutterstock.com; 46, 172 English Heritage; 49 Mike Charles/shutterstock.com; 56 Hannah Stanbury/shutterstock.com; 58 Gary Perkin/shutterstock.com; 59 Paolo Trovo/shutterstock.com; 60 sergioboccardo/shutterstock.com; 61 Marc Eade; 61, 90, 142 Charlesy/shutterstock.com; 73 travellight/shutterstock.com; 80 Matt Gibson/shutterstock.com; 81 Paul Nash/shutterstock.com; 82 David Rustell/shutterstock.com; 88 Vanessal.123/shutterstock.com; 103 Chris Pierre; 106 Ron Ellis/shutterstock.com; 107 from museum; 112 Aaron Trevena/shutterstock.com; 121 Wirestock Creators/shutterstock.com; 124, 156 Britta Jaschinski; 124, 125 Clare Louise Jackson/shutterstock.com; 128 The Longest Day/shutterstock.com; 129, 140 Andrew Ray; 132 islavicek/shutterstock.com; 133 David Hughes; 133 JLRphotography/shutterstock.com; 133 stasia naumova/shutterstock.com; 133 Tony Skeri/shutterstock.com; 141 Ben Rowe; 146 Derek Adams; 146 jaroslava V/shutterstock.com; 146 Stephen Gibson/shutterstock.com; 147 Gareth McKillop/shutterstock.com; 149 Ant Clausen; 155 Sam Morgan Moore; 156 Gillian Parr/shutterstock.com; 157 Holly Auchincloss/shutterstock.com; 158, 161 Scott Moore; 159 Richard Bowden/shutterstock.com; 161, 166 chrisdorney/shutterstock.com; 166 Clare McEwen/shutterstock.com; 167 Boris Stroujko/shutterstock.com; 167 Chris Lawrence Travel/shutterstock.com; 167 Peter Turner Photography/shutterstock.com; 167 Scott Garfitt/shutterstock.com; 172 Neil Duggan/shutterstock.com; 172 Stephen Butler/shutterstock.com; 173, 178, 180, 181 Council of the Isles of Scilly; 175 Gardens by Design/shutterstock.com; 181, 185 Stephen Rees/shutterstock.com; 184 Jeremy Pearson.

The following images were supplied by the featured establishments: pages 16, 19, 33, 45, 71, 81, 84, 86, 88, 89, 95, 103, 131, 136, 137, 148, 169, 182.

Index

Credits

Crimson credits
Editor Andrzej Łukowski
Proofreader Felicity Laughton
Picture research Ben Rowe and Mihaela Botezatu

Maps Contains OS data © Crown copyright and database right (2021) Licence number:100049681.

Production Designer Patrick Dawson

Design Mytton Williams

Managing Director Andy Riddle

Sales & Marketing Diane McEntee and Tania Rosss

Acknowledgements
This edition of *Time Out Cornwall* was researched and revised by Andrzej Łukowski. Andrzej thanks the staff at Time Out London for their help, especially Ben Rowe and all contributors to previous editions of *Time Out Devon and Cornwall* whose work forms the basis of this guide.

Photography credits
Front cover Billy Stock/Shutterstock.com.

Back cover
Left: Boris Stroujko/Shutterstock.com;
Centre left: 10c_Photoclub/Shutterstock.com;
Centre right: Megs Pier/Shutterstock.com;
Right: Angie Latham Photography/Shutterstock.com.

Interior Photography credits, *see p187*.

Publishing information
Time Out Cornwall 3rd edition
© TIME OUT ENGLAND LIMITED 2021
June 2021

ISBN 978 1 914515 02 6
CIP DATA: A catalogue record for this book is available from the British Library

Published by Heartwood Publishing
www.heartwoodpublishing.co.uk on behalf of Time Out England.

Distributed by Grantham Book Services
Distributed in the US and Canada by Publishers Group West (1-510-809-3700)

Printed by Ashford Colour Press, Gosport, UK.